EDITED BY **STUART LOCK**
SERIES EDITOR **TOM BENNETT**

THE research ED GUIDE TO

LEADERSHIP

....

AN EVIDENCE-INFORMED
GUIDE FOR TEACHERS

First Published 2020

by John Catt Educational Ltd,
15 Riduna Park, Station Road,
Melton, Woodbridge IP12 1QT

Tel: +44 (0) 1394 389850
Email: enquiries@johncatt.com
Website: www.johncatt.com

© 2020 John Catt Educational

ISBN: 978 1 912906 41 3

Set and designed by John Catt Educational Limited

WHAT IS researchED?

researchED is an international, grassroots education-improvement movement that was founded in 2013 by Tom Bennett, a London-based high school teacher and author. researchED is a truly unique, teacher-led phenomenon, bringing people from all areas of education together onto a level playing field. Speakers include teachers, principals, professors, researchers and policy makers.

Since our first sell-out event, researchED has spread all across the UK, into the Netherlands, Norway, Sweden, Australia, the USA, with events planned in Spain, Japan, South Africa and more. We hold general days as well as themed events, such as researchED Maths & Science, or researchED Tech.

WHO ARE WE?

Since 2013, researchED has grown from a tweet to an international conference movement that so far has spanned six continents and thirteen countries. We have simple aims: to help teaching become more evidence-facing; to raise the research literacy in teaching; to improve education research standards; and to bring research users and research creators closer together. To do this, we hold unique one-day conferences that bring together teachers, researchers, academics and anyone touched by research. We believe in teacher voice, and short-circuiting the top-down approach to education that benefits no one.

HOW DOES IT WORK?

The gathering of mainly teachers, researchers, school leaders, policy makers and edu-bloggers creates a unique dynamic. Teachers and researchers can attend the sessions all day and engage with each other to exchange ideas. The vast majority of speakers stay for the duration of the conference, visit each other's sessions, work on the expansion of their knowledge and gain a deeper understanding of the work of their peers. Teachers can take note of recent developments in educational research, but are also given the opportunity to provide feedback on the applicability of research or practical obstacles.

CONTENTS

FOREWORD
BY TOM BENNETT

Leadership, like many parts of the education jigsaw, is one of those things we desperately need to be good, but frequently find that its discussion is deeply entangled in a combination of aspirational candy-floss and homoeopathic pseudo-science.

It's 2003. The Space Shuttle Columbia disintegrates on re-entry; Estonia joins the European Union; Concorde makes its last scheduled flight; and the last known speaker of the Akkala Sámi language dies, rendering it extinct. And in London, I'm being enrolled in a now-defunct 'leaders into teaching' conversion course called Fasttrack. The tagline was 'Be the inspiration – from the staffroom to the classroom', which gives you a sense of how inevitably hated the programme's graduates became. Its ambition was to attract the school leaders of tomorrow by casting nets in recruitment demographics that may not have considered teaching: professionals from other walks of life. School leaders, it was feared, would soon become an endangered species because nobody wanted to do it anymore. It faced the same malaise faced by the Catholic Church recruiting priests in secular countries: the downsides didn't look like they outweighed the perks anymore.

Looking back, it was almost a pastiche of every bad leader trope you can imagine. We were sent to a remote mansion in Wales for a week to be inducted into the secrets of bullshit-fu. Here we were brainwashed and groomed into every groovy millennial edu-cliché: Brain Gym, NLP, learning styles, multiple intelligences, and so on. We spent whole days unlocking the secrets of the ancients and attempting mind control on one another, as valiantly, earnestly and fruitlessly as children trying to move pebbles with their minds. We practised lie detection by observing minute, meaningless eye movements. We attempted instantaneous mindset resets by picturing imaginary circles of inspiration and then physically stepping into them. 'Did you feel anything?' we asked each other breathlessly, and we all confirmed that we did. Like dollar-store Scientologists, we audited one another and Hare-Rama'd our way towards the state of Clear, tiny finger cymbals tinkling as we did so.

It was all complete junk, of course. In a more sane, civilised world, such pursuits would have been confined to the minds and means of people who walk along Oxford Street wearing Eschatological placards and shouting into megaphones. But no, because education will buy anything shiny. We are capricious, jaded magpies with attention deficit. If it's shiny and cool, it's in a school.

Apart from the cargo cult homoeopathy I described, there was also a less outlandish but no more evidenced programme of learning that focused on second-tier mumbo-jumbo: the Myers Briggs catechisms, the dubious categorisation of people into simple character types and roles. Are you a radiator or a drain? Are you a planner, an architect, a monk or a follower? Can you believe this rubbish? The Sorting Hat from Harry Potter was a better and more scientific judge of character. And yet, this was sold to us as fact – at great expense, I should add. This was the era when education was awash with money and God forbid any of it should be carefully targeted at what was evidenced in some way. No, the strategy was to load all the money into an enormous blunderbuss and fire it in the air and hope some of it stuck.

And here is the horror at the heart of this darkness: none of this was unusual in leadership training, in lots of different sectors. This was all regarded as being frightfully cutting edge. At another course, also residential, in a huge mansion somewhere (I forget where) hundreds of us were treated to a session on leadership run by actors, who proceeded to enact key scenes from Henry V. From this pantomime we were encouraged to glean some kind of enlightenment about the nature of leadership. I made myself as popular as gas in a lift by asking what on earth this had to do with learning about how to lead a school, given that Henry V didn't run one, his depiction was entirely fictional, and Shakespeare didn't run one either. I'm not even saying that it couldn't provide an artistic device to reflect upon leadership issues – art has that capacity – but that it seemed such a remote and unlikely device to use to teach a room full of novice leaders, many of whom were unlikely to need to disguise themselves as soldiers to speak to the little people on the eve of the Battle of Agincourt.

I was shushed for my cynicism. I reattached myself into the clown-car Matrix of leadership training, closed my eyes, and let the Kool-Aid chug into my veins. We left our training year as ready to lead in schools as we were to perform open-heart surgery on the wing of a 747. But the catering was great and we all got a laptop so no one went home empty-handed. Apart from the children we would be teaching, of course, and the colleagues we would be expected to lead into the breach for Harry, England and St George, but would instead (unless we were protected from our naivety) frogmarch into Russian cannons at Balaclava. It was all junk. It was soothsaying, and runes, and astrology, and voodoo. But it was sold to us by serious people that we trusted to know better.

In many ways I should be grateful. I escaped the cult, and by doing so was inspired to start researchED, whose latest fruit you hold in your hand. And it tackles, head-on, the quackery and prestidigitation I was immersed in, and so many leaders in education find themselves. It is high time we started to take the investigation and discussion of leadership in education seriously because it is a serious subject. Get it right, and all things are possible; get it wrong and suddenly nothing is. Stuart Lock has done an admirable job assembling so many informed voices in this field to discuss (in the true scientific spirit) what we might be able to say with varying levels of probability about leadership strategy. I applaud his approach, which is not to seek eternal truths and foolish certainties but to embrace caution and philosophical scepticism about the limits as well as the possibilities of what we might be able to say.

I commit this book to you with my recommendation. Use it, as with any evidence base, as a springboard for further sincere, authentic reflection. At the very least, I hope it can be as useful as the well-thumbed copy of *Make it So: Leadership Lessons from Star Trek: the Next Generation* that sits on my bookshelf. The bar is high.

INTRODUCTION
BY STUART LOCK

This is a book about **school leadership**.

School leaders are surrounded by literature and advice on leadership. There is a plentiful supply of books, consultants and organisations, all willing to offer their guidance on how to be a better leader. But this is not a book about leadership; this is a book about **school leadership**. For this book takes the position that a conception of leadership separated from *what is being led* can be abstract and overly-generic, and in turn hard to define, unfocused and unhelpful. This book takes the position that for a discussion about leadership to be useful to practising leaders, it must be located in the field, subject or domain that is being led.

Generic leadership

One of the first leadership books I read was *The Seven Habits of Highly Effective People* by Stephen Covey. Other leadership books that have influenced me include *Legacy: What the All Blacks Can Teach Us About the Business of Life* by James Kerr, *The Power Paradox* by Dacher Keltner, *The New Leaders* by Daniel Goleman and *Leading* by Alex Ferguson. These are books that largely aim to talk about leadership separately from the specific domain or the specific people that are being led. While they can use examples from the particular domains or spheres that their authors or subjects inhabit – in particular the books that focus on sport – the assumption is that this is transferable to many different contexts and, more controversially in my view, other domains. I contend that it is difficult to talk about 'power' and 'influence' without reference to the domain within which that influence is gathered, exerted and the knowledge and experience necessary to do so.

This book takes the view that we have overestimated the usefulness of generic leadership competencies in improving schools.

The leadership industry

Over the last 30 years, an industry has formed around leadership development worth billions of pounds. This industry trades on books, keynotes, personality tests and development programmes, usually centred around improving the individual leader with the assumption that by improving the human condition of this individual, they will become a better 'leader' and consequently lead better teams, organisations or schools.

The leadership industry – largely centred on business – has correctly come under pressure many times. For example, in a polemic against this industry, Pfeffer points out that there are 'no "barriers to entry"… no credentials, rigorous research, knowledge of the relevant scientific evidence, or anything else required to pass oneself off as a leadership expert' (Pfeffer, 2015, p. 24). This, I contend, is equally true in a world where anyone can set themselves up as a leadership consultant or coach, regardless of their own success as a school leader or indeed, whether they have ever run a school at all. Pfeffer also highlights some of the problems with the adjectives that describe successful leaders. He continues quoting a study by Daan van Knippenberg and Sam Sitkin:

> "the study of charismatic leadership lacks a precise definition of the term and also an understanding of the psychological and behavioural mechanisms that presumably produce results from charisma… there is a great deal of invalid measurement of the concept of charismatic leadership. One cannot build a science this way, and, more important, it is impossible to develop valid recommendations that leaders can implement given the sloppy thinking about leadership that is so much in vogue." (Pfeffer, 2015, p. 26)

This book suggests that school leadership is a unique activity and that insight from the leadership of other fields may be of limited use.

The 'hero' model of the school leader

School leaders are often expected to be a number of things simultaneously. Job advertisements for leaders typically invite applications from (for example) passionate, driven, inspirational, optimistic, moral, creative, resilient, determined, astute, positive, courageous, communicative and strategic leaders. I have omitted a plethora of other adjectives that are often used that might describe someone superhuman. One might refer to this as the 'hero' model of school leadership.

This 'hero' orthodoxy of school leadership, and hence the vast majority of the literature on the subject, often subscribe to the perspective that great school leaders have a set of values and a vision that is remarkable, and that it is this vision and these values that in some manner drive their schools forward to exponential improvement. It is, of course, important to instil a sense of purpose and direction. However, these values, the vision and the qualities that make up a good school leader too often remain nebulous – again hard to define and too often separated from the institution or the specific area that is being led – and indeed aren't subject to scrutiny or sufficient exploration of their component parts. As a result, it is not uncommon to hear leaders retreat into educational jargon made up of acronyms, generic phrases and vague assertions about generic leadership. When we as leaders develop those pithy 'vision' statements and talk of 'values', we could be accused of using these phrases as a substitute for the complex, messy substance and detail of leading a school. This book believes that the 'hero' paradigm of school leadership demands the impossible and that this overwhelming focus on the individual and their personal qualities is misplaced.

How the 'hero' model has become the orthodox model

The rise of generic approaches to leadership within our education system has become institutionalised through common frameworks and approaches to school inspection and training within a performative system with high-stakes accountability. As Jen Barker and Tom Rees outline early in this volume, an example of this is the framework for the National Professional Qualification for Headship, which has the expectation that participants 'learn how to be an inspiring leader in a range of different situations', and can 'communicate and negotiate with a range of different people... to make progress' (Department for Education, 2019, p. 28). These generic nebulous competencies have to be 'evidenced' within headteacher training and are mirrored in much of the leadership training at all levels of school leadership.

Ofsted too, in reaching judgements of the quality of school leadership, often describe the individual characteristics or personal qualities of the leaders themselves. Indeed, in my own experience, Ofsted reports have described me as 'uncompromising' and 'tenacious' when praising my school after inspectors have visited for just two days. Others have been described as 'inspirational', 'passionate' and 'transformative'. These are nice to read, but I think more accurate would have been 'quite good, most of the time'. I don't think that Ofsted would write this because the prevailing view is that a 'Good' or 'Outstanding' school must have a 'hero' leader. It is clear that institutions within the education system have played their part in embedding the hero orthodoxy of school leadership through a manifestation of a generic orthodoxy of leadership.

This book believes that the hero paradigm of school leadership is a manifestation of generic leadership that has been institutionalised within the school system. Vague notions of generic leadership are unhelpful when it comes to leading schools.

Generic leadership in education

There are many examples of where generic approaches to leadership are embedded more widely across the education sector. Generic approaches to leadership are well established in our school system through training and resources. Even influential *educational* leadership resources, such as the *Leadership Matters* website run by Andy Buck – previously an experienced headteacher, National Leader of Education, and Director at the National College for School Leadership – identify a similar generic approach to leadership. The overview of the *Leadership Matters* model focuses on Steve Radcliffe's FED model – specifically the three areas of: future (set the strategic direction), engage (build and sustain relationships) and deliver (deliver results and get things done). In common with the books above, the working assumption is that the approach can be applied to any institution – there is very little that applies specifically to schools or even to education – it could be talking of leadership of a bank, hospital, or political party. In his book of the same name, Buck says 'whether you are running a group of schools or have just taken on your first middle leadership role, the job is basically the same' (Buck, 2018, p. 17).

More recently Buck has acknowledged that as 'teachers take on more formal leadership responsibilities, there is a cumulative requirement for additional expert knowledge and skills to carry out each role effectively' (Buck, 2020b, p. 57). In other words, he is arguing that both generic skills and domain-specific knowledge matter. At first sight, this seems a useful compromise, but I contend it creates a dichotomy by separating the apparent composite 'skills' that leaders have from the components of those skills. A significant proportion of the components that make up these skills, I contend, are the domain knowledge and experience and it is these that may appear like generic skills to an inexperienced observer.

Recently, there has been a move to describe good school leadership as being necessarily 'ethical'. Who wouldn't want leaders to be ethical? In the framework published by the Association of School and College Leaders (ASCL, 2019) this means the following guiding principles: selflessness, integrity, objectivity, accountability, openness, honesty and leadership. This goes on to say that leaders should show the following personal characteristics or virtues: trust, wisdom, kindness, justice, service, courage and optimism. I don't particularly object to any of these (though I might question whether being accurate might sometimes compromise being kind and whether optimism is always the right approach). I do, however, think that these generic competencies, characteristics and virtues, while desirable, are a version of the 'hero' model. These are all desirable, but why are they the most important? To take the first as an example, I would like to work for a selfless boss, but I do not believe that I am alone in desiring competence above selflessness. While generic, the ASCL framework explores this further and I perceive it is in part a reaction to recent high-profile excesses (e.g. in pay, or use of power) in the school sector, so I do not want to dismiss it completely. Rather, I use it as an example of how the 'hero' model is developed and reinforced.

School leadership is, consequently, something that is commonly seen as a generic activity and leaders have generic qualities that they apply to schools. The leadership industry, rooted in business, has moved organically into schools, and the impact on workload as a result of the investment in approaches that appear to be true – regardless of whether they are actually true – is significant.

The most common view of good school leadership is a generic view of leadership.

The merits of the generic view of leadership

The generic approach to school leadership has taken us this far. It has squeezed out other approaches and is a part of the hegemony of the orthodox 'hero' paradigm. It is vague, encourages performativity and the pursuit of the proxies of good leadership rather than the substance. It is tremendously inefficient. This critique means that I think we need to cast aside some of the old assumptions related to the orthodox approach to leadership. A vague vision, generic competencies and a plethora of adjectives do not cut it when it comes to running great schools. This does not mean that there is nothing at all that might be generic about school leadership. The generic approach described above may have some merit.

One can, then, take inspiration from generic approaches, and there are plenty of successful school leaders who have done so. My contention, however, is that we should note that it is well over 30 years since Stephen Covey and the associated generic approach was first widespread, and this approach has since had plenty of time to influence leaders, particularly through the work of the National College of School Leadership and the various generic leadership qualifications that have flowed from there. I certainly do not want school leaders to throw the baby out with the bathwater. By being overly dichotomous we may find that our insights in a book about research into leadership are compromised by leaving behind aspects that have some merit. While this book focuses on a different view of school leadership and suggests that the orthodoxy is limited, to embrace the perspective it takes and the research that is cited is not necessarily to the dismiss all of the insights of the last 30 years and far longer.

And so, while generic leadership books have been useful to me, they have left huge gaps in my knowledge and perspective on what good school leadership is because the books have in common that they assume, to one extent or another, that leadership expertise is easily transferable between domains. We can develop school leadership more effectively if we turn to thoroughly exploring what it means to be a **school** leader rather than just a leader.

Specific, relevant knowledge looks like generic competence

This book does challenge the generic perspective. Knowledge and experience of the domain of school leadership is a necessary ingredient of being an effective school leader, and it is probably a bigger ingredient than the orthodoxy has considered. When we try to copy what an effective school leader exhibits during their leadership, we copy the performance at the expense of the substance. Unpicking that substance is a significant part of this book, and is a difficult challenge.

As a young senior leader, one of the best headteachers I ever worked for was a fantastic communicator. She could stand and speak to audiences of staff or parents at a moment's notice. She was credible, never used notes, concentrated on eye contact and controlled her arms, thus appearing very natural. I concluded that to be a successful leader, amongst other things, I needed to be great at speaking in public, and so I enrolled on a public speaking course. The course was helpful and I am a better speaker as a result of going on the course. During that course I received a lot of advice. Amongst the things that I learned, the key bit of advice I received was to 'speak about something you know'. The best speech I delivered during the course was about Weston-super-Mare football club, mainly because, as a long-standing supporter of Weston, so much of the material I knew inside out. It was firmly ingrained in my long-term memory. It is, of course, true that one can become a better public speaker by practising public speaking, and indeed by preparing speeches and learning them so that one doesn't need to refer to notes. But the most significant improvement for most people, I contend, comes from knowing one's subject very well. On reflection, in the case of the headteacher I refer to above, her knowledge of education was broad and deep, and her knowledge of her school was close to total. This knowledge allowed the performance of public speaking to appear effortless. Consequently, I know, even now, that when speaking the performance or 'skill' of public speaking depends on several factors, but one of the most important is knowing what I want to say and talking about a subject that I know well. It is the knowledge of the subject that enables better communication, and this is particularly obvious with public speaking.

I contend further that most of the 'features' of school leadership which people look up to are similarly so dependent on knowledge – either tacit or formal (as explored further in Chapter 2) – to be effective. We miss something fundamental about leadership if we just urge leaders to copy the features displayed by successful school leaders. One of the weaknesses of poor school leaders is that, in attempting to copy the features of successful school leadership, we overlook and miss the substance that has enabled that leader to be successful. This can be exacerbated when the expert school leader suffers from the 'curse of expertise' – that experts in a domain know the domain so effortlessly they take it for granted, and so are unable to unpick the knowledge that makes up that expertise so that the novice can assimilate it. Consequently, those who teach, coach or mentor school leaders can reinforce the impression that the skills on display are innate, nebulous and generic.

You may gather by now that in my view too much school leadership development is about replicating the features of successful school leadership rather than the substance. To paraphrase an anecdote Dylan Wiliam is fond of using: to tell a headteacher to be a better public speaker is as helpful as to tell a comedian to be funnier. It might be accurate, but it is so vague as to be unhelpful. And if this is the case for public speaking, I contend that it may be true for resilience, determination, and being astute; in short, for all the adjectives that make up the 'hero' model of school leadership.

What looks like generic leadership competence is likely to be made up of specific educational knowledge and experience.

Which research should we use?

One would expect a book under the researchEd banner to sift the available research and present it to school leaders to be far better informed. This would enable insights for school leaders to use day-to-day. However, the whole field of school leadership is poorly defined and the insights so patchy that this is not possible to do to my satisfaction.

Over a year ago, I was persuaded to look at leadership from the different perspective that this book now takes. This position is that leading schools is a unique, complex activity and that 'uniqueness' means that knowledge of schools and education is a – and maybe *the* – crucial ingredient in school leadership. This alternative perspective of this book might appear new but, as Barker and Rees outline in Chapter 2, such an approach has an interesting history and I think that it is a strong bet for improving the quality of school leadership. As an explanation, I use the language of **bets** because I think that it is hard for us as school leaders to know for sure that we are always making the right decision. We cannot be sure of the impact of our decisions or the best ways to implement our decisions and solutions but if we are better informed then we are more likely to make the best possible choices based on our knowledge, i.e. the best bets.

School leadership research is of patchy quality – we have a lot to do as school leaders and we need to sift through a lot of research to make our best bets.

Persistent problems or challenges

Schools are, then, complex places to work and in which to lead. As a result, the work of school leaders is incredibly complex and can appear infinitely so. We should be cautious of simplifying this in the manner that a number of 'models' of school leadership can do. A great school leader has a combination of knowledge about their school or domain and education more widely, and knows what to do with that knowledge – this can be described as their 'mental model'. They are unlikely to transfer this to be able to lead well in a different context (such as a hospital or a retail business) because this mental model is domain-specific.

I have come to believe that we need first to understand the common challenges that school leaders strive to confront, and then to elicit the knowledge required to address them as best possible. We can think of the work as a series of persistent problems, as defined by Kennedy (2016).

It is not possible to write about everything school leaders need to know. In Kennedy's paper, she references many failed attempts to write about everything that teachers need to know. Additionally, we are unable to cover every challenge that leaders may face. However, in this volume we cover a selection of persistent challenges and contributors write about them from their perspective as leaders. Consequently, the chapters are examples of challenges and problems that school leaders face, and the unpicking of the challenges, combined with the knowledge and application that contributors offer, allow us to demonstrate and provide an insight into the domain-specific approach that this book takes. Each chapter, therefore, exemplifies a persistent problem or challenge, an aspect or aspects of domain-knowledge or an expertise-based approach to address the challenge.

Great school leaders develop mental models to assist them in being able to address common challenges in their schools.

The chapters

This book hopes to identify some of the common challenges and problems school leaders strive to address and about which they have to make judgements. It then attempts to then scour some of the best research to assist school leaders to know what they need to know, and how they should use that knowledge. It enables leaders to, therefore, consider how they make the best bets to meet those challenges. The chapters, subsequently, take the form of expanded case studies used to exemplify how expert school leaders have approached or should approach each kind of challenge.

After beginning with an exploration of what leadership is and how we can develop it in Jen Barker and Tom Rees' chapters, Nicole Dempsey gives us a punchy exploration of SEN and inclusion, challenging us to run our schools well for everyone, rather than run different forms of schooling for different pupils. Summer Turner then explores the challenges leaders have in leading curriculum development across a number of subjects without sliding into genericism, or allowing subject-specialists to use their expertise without being hampered by leaders with insufficient understanding of the issues in their subject.

In Luke Sparkes and Jenny Thompson's chapter on culture, they explore some different bets that run throughout their organisation and combine their perspective with an ability to sift through research and sources of inspiration, being explicit about which of these is being drawn on in order to make their bets.

Sarah Barker explores the knowledge and mental models required by a subject leader, in this case in English, in her chapter. This is insightful, for it builds on the chapter on curricular leadership and culture to explore one perception of what senior leaders need to be aware of to allow expertise to flourish at middle leadership level. I don't believe leadership of the curriculum can be separated from assessment, which Matt Stanford tackles elegantly in his chapter. The Reading Ape and Danielle Dennis in their respective chapters give expert perspectives on the teaching of reading and writing – I read these increasingly cognisant of my lack of knowledge and becoming aware that a very good bet for school leaders is to develop expertise in these areas.

Dylan Wiliam explores some of the recent insights on memory and learning that leaders should know about. Of course, knowing this and ensuring that teachers know it and put it into practice are different problems to address. One of the most significant challenges I have faced in my career as a school leader is how to ensure that teachers in schools I lead continue to get better. I have long known that 'coaching' is generically a *good thing* that leaders can do, but discussion amongst school leaders about the difference between coaching and mentoring (or even the different types of coaching), and the assumption that one can be good at either of these things without being an expert in teaching (and I would go further, the teaching of a specific subject and phase) has always made me feel like it is too difficult to implement something effective given the opportunity cost – the time and effort required across a school. Jon Hutchinson's expert unpicking of how instructional coaching works at Reach Feltham, sharing a series of solid examples of how one might navigate these leadership challenges, builds so well on the previous chapters.

This book further attempts to use the structure of challenges and persistent problems – and the expertise required to address them – to illustrate the approach to leadership whereby leaders draw on research and knowledge to make decisions in a highly complex environment. There are persistent challenges that school leaders face that are not included here – the necessary choices of what has been looked at here is a combination of the best 'bets', the areas of particular expertise of the authors and my own interest. I urge the reader to look at the approach and to consider how the perspective of knowledge and experience of the domain of school leadership enables school leaders to embrace the complexity of a job that is, as a result, as satisfying as it is unpredictable. It is this complexity and the experience and perspective of the individual school leader that Matthew Evans draws together skilfully in his chapter.

This book explores some of the challenges school leaders might face to exemplify an approach to school leadership. It is not comprehensive.

Conclusion

Artz et al (2017) is used by Barker and Rees to illustrate that wellbeing is best served by leaders who can do the job of those they lead. This might be one of the most important insights that should stimulate school leaders to know more about what goes on in their institutions, more about the context of their institutions, and more about what good school leaders know and do. While it might not be helpful to demand that headteachers are able to do every job in their institution better than the person doing it, it does demand that all school leaders know as much as possible about their schools, and the specific insights, informed by research, that are necessary to be able to lead colleagues to continually improve the performance of the institution.

'School leadership entails making judgements under uncertainty. You will rarely know unequivocally that you've made the best decision and you will often make poor decisions.' (Didau, 2020)

I take full responsibility for omissions and inadequacies. This book is a contribution aimed at opening up the debate. It does not expect to be the final word, but it is an effort to nudge school leadership to be as evidence-informed as possible.

References

ASCL (2019) 'Framework for ethical leadership in education', ASCL [Online] Summer. Retrieved from: www.bit.ly/2GFwfDA

Artz, B., Goodall, A. and Oswald, A. (2017) 'Boss Competence and Worker Well-Being', *ILR Review* 70 (2) pp. 419–450. Los Angeles: SAGE Publications.

Buck, A. (2018) *Leadership Matters 3.0: How Leaders at All Levels Can Create Great Schools*. Woodbridge: John Catt Educational.

Buck, A. (2020a) 'Introduction to the Leadership Matters Model', *Leadership Matters* [Online]. Retrieved from: www.bit.ly/32e5PBl

Buck, A. (2020b) 'School Leadership in Perspective', *Impact* [Online] May. Retrieved from: www.bit.ly/3jWWQdQ

Covey, S. R. (1989) *The Seven Habits of Highly Effective People: Restoring the Character Ethic*. New York: Simon and Schuster.

Department for Education (2019) 'National Professional Qualification (NPQ) Content and Assessment Framework'. Retrieved from: www.bit.ly/3jWXJDc

Didau, D. (2020) 'Five things new school leaders need to know', *Learning Spy* [Blog] 22 June. Retrieved from: www.bit.ly/2FsKhaY

Evans, M. (2019): *Leaders with Substance: An Antidote to Leadership Genericism in Schools.* Woodbridge: John Catt Educational.

Ferguson, A. (2015) *Leading.* London: Hodder and Stoughton.

Gilbride, N. (2018) 'The Relevance of Domain-General and Domain-Specific Skills for Educational Leadership'. Unpublished paper.

Hawkins, M. and James, C. (2018) 'Developing a perspective on schools as complex, evolving, loosely linking systems', *Educational Management Administration & Leadership* 46 (5) pp. 729–748.

Keltner, D. (2017) *The Power Paradox: How We Gain and Lose Influence.* New York: Penguin Random House.

Kennedy, M. (2016) 'Parsing the Practice of Teaching', *Journal of Teacher Education* 67 (1) pp. 6–17.

Kerr, J. (2013) *Legacy: What the All Black can teach us about the business of life.* London: Constable.

Pfeffer, J. (2015) *Leadership BS – Fixing Workplaces and Careers One Truth at a Time.* New York: HarperCollins.

WHAT IS SCHOOL LEADERSHIP?

BY JEN BARKER AND TOM REES

Jen Barker and Tom Rees were the people who, by challenging my view of school leadership, encouraged me to look at leadership from the view that it is a manifestation of expertise. Since then, I've admired how they confront difficult conversations, challenge the literature and reshape their position. They are credible because, in exchange for their challenge of the orthodox position, they are willing to confront their own position with the most robust of challenges and actively embrace and answer these. It reflects the high quality of thinking that Ambition Institute, where they work, bring to the debate.

The orthodox view of school leadership has rarely had challenge the like of which they bring. I've been personally privileged to have been able to be exposed to a fraction of their thinking – anything written on school leadership is kindly considered while putting forward a positive alternative and accepting critique. This is an act of bravery in a field this crowded with numerous vested interests. That Jen and Tom do this allows our collective understanding to be furthered.

I'm delighted and feel privileged that they present their position on school leadership below. It is one that aligns with my own views. The humility that Jen and Tom demonstrate as they accept that our understanding will develop further is one that I hope comes across throughout the book – that we know that we don't have the final word, but believe we have something to say.

This thoroughly referenced chapter is a real insight into how this perspective can shape our understanding of school leadership.

Schools are fascinating and complex places. Every single day, a billion young people across the world spend their day in a school of some description (UNICEF, 2019). Although schools have been in existence in some form since the early civilisations, mass formal education is a recent development. In

England, for example, it is only in the last century that we have been addressing the complex challenge of educating every child in the country (Gillard, 2018).

Society asks a lot of schools, expecting them to ensure that pupils succeed personally and academically, as well as tackling wider challenges such as social disadvantage and public health. These demands, alongside pressures from regulatory bodies and public accountability, lead to a huge amount of responsibility resting on the shoulders of those who work in our schools. Central to this story are those who hold responsibility for running schools; the decision-makers with titles such as headteacher, head of department, SENCos or key stage coordinator. Over the years, this group of people has been referred to using different terminology: administrators, coordinators and managers. More recently, we have come to know them as 'school leaders'.

School leadership

Today, approximately 200,000 people are working in leadership positions in England's schools (DfE, 2018). The work that these school leaders do is broad and varied. Although the discourse about school leaders often focuses on headteachers or CEOs of school trusts, the large majority of school leaders are 'middle leaders' – classroom teachers with additional responsibilities for subjects, phases or other aspects of school life such as behaviour or special educational needs (Busher, 2005). This variation of role and remit is increased further as a result of the many different contexts in which school leaders work and means knowing how best to support school leaders is not always clear.

In recent years, alongside concerns regarding recruitment and retention to the wider teaching profession, a significant and growing shortage of school leaders has developed. It has been estimated that this deficit could reach 19,000 by 2022, affecting almost one in four schools in England (Future Leaders, 2016). Ensuring that we have enough people who are prepared, confident and hold the relevant expertise to assume leadership responsibility is a significant challenge.

In the last ten years, we have seen insights from research flowing more widely into professional discourse and practice; the researchEd community has been significant in stimulating this and bringing the relationship between evidence and practice closer together. An increasingly evidence-informed and intellectually-curious profession is reading, talking and debating more critically about concepts such as assessment, cognitive science and curricular thinking. However, while myths about learning have been exposed and dubious theories and classroom practices are being avoided, we have more to do in understanding how school leaders use the findings from research to improve schools. Less progress has been made in using research to better understand the work of school leaders. We think that this book presents a timely and important opportunity to put school leadership under the spotlight, to explore what leaders do and why, and to explore how we might develop their expertise further.

Our contribution to this book is in the form of two chapters. In this chapter, we examine part of the research base to try and understand more about what school leadership is, and indeed what it isn't. In the second chapter, we propose a different perspective on school leadership – specifically, what is expertise in school leadership and how we might develop it.

What *is* school leadership?

'It is important to be clear from the outset that what has been learned about leadership in schools over the century has not depended on any clear, agreed-upon definition of the concept, as essential as this would seem at first glance' (Leithwood and Duke, 1999, p. 45).

This is inconvenient for those of us trying to understand how we can help school leaders to keep getting better. Many researchers have developed definitions of leadership: for example considering leadership as behaviours (Hallinger et al, 1983), as personality traits (Colbert et al, 2012), as influence (Connolly et al, 2017) or – instead of being linked to an individual – as something which resides within the systems, roles and networks of an organisation (Ogawa and Bossert, 1995). The variation in perspectives on what school leadership actually is appears to be significant, so much so that we might question whether school leadership is even a thing at all.

It is also worth noting that labelling senior staff in schools as 'leaders' is relatively recent. The term has been introduced within the span of our teaching careers. When Tom first took on responsibility outside of the classroom in 2001, he was given the title of 'key stage coordinator' and paid an allowance, known then as a management point. By the time Jen took on management responsibility in 2006, she was given the grander title of 'phase leader' as a Key Stage 1 leader and paid a TLR ('Teaching and Learning Responsibility' payment).

There are multiple reasons for the growth in the number of roles as a leader and the associated practice of leadership. Leaders and leadership have been positioned as integral to school reform (Gronn, 2003) and the school improvement movement (Bush, 2008). Education has been subject to the influences of other sectors, notably business, industry and commerce (Bell, 1991), and political or policy decisions, such as the influence of the Teacher Training Agency's creation of National Professional Qualification for Headship (NPQH). The National College for School Leadership (NCSL) undoubtedly played a significant role between 2000 and 2013 in advancing the concept of school leadership and its existence was predicated on the idea that leadership is important in securing improved school and pupil outcomes (Bush, 2008).

In responding to the question, 'What is school leadership?', a reasonable answer might be, 'it's complicated' but this would make for a short and unsatisfactory book and so, in an attempt to do better, we have broken this question down into six more manageable questions.

1. What can literature tell us about school leadership?
2. Why is school leadership so complex?
3. What is the purpose of school leaders' work?
4. To what extent is school leadership generic or domain-specific?
5. What impact can school leaders have?
6. How is school leadership defined?

1. What can literature tell us about school leadership?

Key idea: There are many different competing theoretical perspectives of school leadership.

A systematic review of studies into educational leadership models from 1980 to 2014 by Gumus et al (2018) reveals how models of leadership have developed in the last 30 years by tracking the use of different leadership-related terms during this period. The adjacent table shows that almost a thousand papers were written about 14 different school leadership models between 1980 and 2014.

Table 4. Number of papers on different leadership models.

Models	Total	80-84	85-89	90-94	95-99	00-04	05-09	10-14
Distributed/Collaborative Leadership	205	2	2	4	3	15	61	118
Instructional Leadership	181	11	9	18	8	15	35	85
Teacher Leadership	151	1	5	9	13	13	47	63
Transformational Leadership	147	-	4	13	7	16	32	75
Curriculum Leadership	49	-	2	2	1	8	16	20
Technology Leadership	46	-	-	2	1	5	13	25
Transactional Leadership	40	-	-	5	-	-	8	27
Ethical/Moral Leadership	38	1	-	1	5	8	8	15
Charismatic Leadership	27	-	1	4	-	5	6	11
Administrative/Managerial Leadership	21	1	1	2	7	2	3	5
Strategic Leadership	20	-	-	-	-	2	6	12
Authentic Leadership	18	-	-	-	1	-	8	9
Visionary Leadership	18	-	-	-	4	1	6	7
Servant Leadership	16	-	-	-	1	1	7	7

Note. Some papers focus on more than one leadership model, so they were included in two or more categories.

The authors report that distributed leadership, instructional leadership, teacher leadership and transformational leadership are – and continue to be – the most studied models. We consider three of these on the following pages.

Transformational leadership focuses on how leaders influence people through their use of 'inspiration, vision and the ability to motivate followers to transcend their self-interests for a collective purpose' (Warrick, 2011). Ken Leithwood, in Canada in the '80s, adapted the construct of transformational leadership in business and applied this to schools. Transformational leadership seeks to generate 'second-order' effects, i.e. transformational school leaders aim to increase the capacity of others in order to create first-order effects on pupil learning. As such, it has been credited with supporting teacher autonomy and professionalism (Hendricks and Scheerens, 2013). The extent to which transformational leadership results in direct engagement with teaching and learning is not always clear. Some of the literature suggests that effective transformational leaders still emphasise the importance and use of instructional (or pedagogical) leadership as being important for pupil outcomes (Day and Sammons, 2016). The transformational leader has been associated with a 'hero paradigm' (Gronn, 2003, p. 25) which has arguably been damaging in a multitude of ways for our education system, increasing performance expectations beyond what can be considered realistic. Transformational leadership is often recognised as the 'accepted orthodoxy' in school leadership (Gunter, 2016) with concepts such as vision, change and inspiration featuring prominently in the discourse.

Instructional leadership (sometimes called pedagogical leadership) is based on the idea that leaders should seek 'to influence conditions that directly impact the quality of curriculum and instruction delivered to students in classrooms' (Hallinger, 2003, p. 338). Broadly, the actions an instructional leader might take include defining the school mission, managing the instructional programme (teaching and learning) and developing a positive school learning climate (Hallinger and Murphy, 1985). At its core, it seeks to understand the link between school leadership and pupil learning and it has 'demonstrated the strongest empirically-verified impact on student learning outcomes' (Hallinger and Wang, 2015, p. 2). Robinson et al (2009) found that, when it comes to pupil outcomes, the impact of instructional (pedagogical) leadership was three to four times that of transformational leadership. Instructional leadership is not without criticism and has, for example, been described as being 'paternalistic and dependent on docile followers' (Marks and Printy, 2003, p. 373).

Distributed leadership was first posed by C. A. Gibb in *The Handbook of Social Psychology* (Gibb, 1954) and is used to describe leadership 'as something that takes place at different points within an organisation' (MacBeath, 2003, p. 3), often including the extension of 'leadership' responsibilities beyond a senior leadership team and to include classroom teachers. Tian et al (2015) report that there is no universal definition of distributed leadership and, despite being written about so prolifically, the idea is both poorly conceptualised and, hence, inconsistently implemented. A key argument within the concept is whether leadership can be actively distributed or whether its distribution occurs naturally according to 'attributed influence' (Gronn, 2002) that can be directed at any individual or group, not just those with a leadership title.

There are several criticisms of the theory, including a lack of clarity as to who leadership is distributed to, and not acknowledging adequately those to whom leadership is not distributed (Lumby, 2016). It has also been criticised for its lack of empirical evidence as to its impact in schools, both concerning instructional improvement and pupil achievement (Spillane, 2005). This is interesting when one considers that distributed leadership is the most written about leadership model.

These models are of interest in better understanding what school leadership is. However, the research also highlights the lack of conceptual clarity that exists around different models. Day and Sammons (2016) argue that instructional and transformational leadership are not mutually exclusive and that there may be benefits to school leaders in utilising aspects of both. A useful example of this can be found in Brown and Zhang (2017) who argue that to most effectively embed a research-informed approach to schools, leaders should start by employing transformational leadership, and then move to an instructional approach. Moreover, as schools' needs change over time, a neat model or set of approaches will likely be insufficient to address what is required. As Hallinger (2003) states, 'The type of leadership that is suitable to a certain stage of the journey may well become a limiting or even counter-productive force as the school develops' (p. 345-346).

The number of different leadership theories demonstrates a 'need to be sceptical about the leadership by adjective literature' (Leithwood et al, 2004, p. 8) – something that has become common in education. The pursuit of attempting to conceptualise school leadership has led us to what John Macbeath describes as the 'Alphabet Soup of Leadership'. Macbeath argues leadership is 'a term full of ambiguity and a range of interpretations' and goes on to call it a 'Humpty Dumpty' word that can mean 'just what we want it to mean' (Macbeath, 2003, p. 1). The challenge of conceptualising school leadership may be, in part, explained by understanding the complexity of schools and the work that school leaders do.

2. Why is school leadership so complex?

Key idea: Schools are complex places where links between inputs and outputs are often messy and inconclusive.

School leaders are responsible for the work of teachers who, in their classrooms, are attempting to simultaneously ensure that many individuals are learning, i.e. teachers are trying to affect about 30 brains at one time. These brains belong to immature humans with varying levels of motivation who are often distracted by a plethora of other things. It is difficult to know, therefore, whether these efforts in the classroom are successful. Although we have proxies such as assessments and qualifications, these are only proxy indicators as to whether the teaching is leading to the desired outputs of learning and beyond to better outcomes in life. Considering the work of school leaders through this lens, where their responsibility extends to multiple classrooms or schools, the relationship between decisions, actions and their impact is often messy and inconclusive. For example, May et al (2012) found that principals who spent more time on finance and personnel issues tended to work in schools with higher pupil test scores and that principals who spent more time on planning, setting goals and instructional leadership tended to work in schools with lower scores. However, the author's conclusion is that this is likely to be because the context drives the work, so leaders in higher-performing schools are likely to have more time to devote to matters of finance, and leaders in lower-performing schools are likely to have to respond to issues of poorer staff performance. So, what on paper could be interpreted as a causal relationship between effective leader performance and time spent on finance (instead of time spent supporting teaching and learning) is actually only a correlation between context and the activities that leaders undertake.

Hawkins and James (2018) argue that schools are complex – as opposed to chaotic, complicated or stable – places. That is, the 'interactions among its [the school's] constituent parts are such that it cannot be fully understood simply by describing its components' and that 'the components interact and are changed by those interactions' (Hawkins and James, 2018, p. 730). Unlike an engine or a production line where a component can be replaced or altered with a predictable outcome, this complexity means that it is not possible to define set ways in which leaders should operate, because various possible consequences are arising from one action or set of actions. We can, therefore, think of school leadership as a low-validity domain – it is difficult to make predictions or ascertain causality within the environment (Kahneman and Klein, 2009).

In practice then, leaders need to be aware of how complexity can manifest itself. All leaders have, no doubt, experienced the unexpected or unintended consequences of their actions over a particular aspect of their work. As Matthew Evans argues in his chapter, 'by simplifying, stabilising, ordering and structuring, leaders can work to mitigate the challenges that arise as a result of leading in a complex environment.' So far, we have considered what literature can tell us about school leadership, and why school leadership is a complex endeavour and can be considered as a low-validity domain. Next, we take a closer look at what the work of school leaders actually is.

3. What is the purpose of school leaders' work?

Key idea: School leadership can be viewed through the lens of addressing problems.

In identifying the purpose of the work that school leaders carry out, we can view school leadership as a role that addresses problems and challenges. This is not a new concept and researchers have used different definitions of 'problems' in the literature such as Wright (2010) who draws upon Rittel and Weber's (1973) description of 'wicked' and 'tame' problems. Wright maintains that because schools are Complex Adaptive Systems (defined by Plsek and Greenhalgh, 2001) as a 'collection of individual agents with freedom to act in ways that are not always totally predictable, and whose actions are interconnected so that one agent's actions change the context for other agents') the problems faced in schools are more likely to be 'wicked'. Pupil underachievement is a 'wicked' problem, for example, because it is arguably something all schools are trying to address in some way, it is difficult to consistently define, there is no consensus as to its cause, and there is no immediate or agreed-upon 'right' way to completely solve it. These criteria enable this problem to be described as 'wicked' (Gilbride, 2018).

Leithwood et al (1994) constructed a different model of leadership as a process of addressing problems, distinguishing between what they term 'high-ground' (routine) and 'swampy' (non-routine) problems. They argue that where a problem's 'givens, goals and obstacles' are less clear for school leaders, the problems become 'increasingly swampy' (p. 42). Leithwood et al (1994) maintain that how a problem is defined may be different for different people, and one leader's swampy problem maybe 'another's dancefloor' (p. 44), but ultimately those swampy problems – like wicked ones – are difficult to solve, time-consuming and expensive to address. The book *Developing Expert Leadership for Future Schools* identifies an important reason why a focus on problems is productive. Looking at school leadership in this way competes with other, more superficial conceptions of leadership including the conceptions centred around processes, personality, persuasion, power and influence.

In describing and defining the work of school leaders as work to address problems, a common concern can be with the word 'problem' itself, which has negative connotations and may suggest an approach that treats leadership as a deficit model. To counter this view, it's helpful to define the term 'problem' in a way similar to Thomas Nickles (1981): 'the demand that a goal be achieved, plus constraints on how it is achieved' (p. 111). A focus on problems might also lead one to think *generic* problem-solving skills should be prioritised to improve leadership. However, researchers find that to understand and solve problems, large amounts of knowledge of the *specific* domain in which you work is required (Willingham, 2008).

This leads us to consider the difference between generic and domain-specific approaches to school leadership.

4. To what extent is school leadership generic or domain-specific?

Key idea: Effective school leaders require deep educational (domain-specific) knowledge, yet approaches to educational leadership training and qualifications have been dominated by generic approaches to leadership.

The question of whether leadership of a school is dependent on domain-specific knowledge and domain-specific skills or whether these skills are transferable to and from other sectors can be explored by considering the following definitions:

Generic leadership	Skills, knowledge and attributes linked to the field of leadership as opposed to a specific domain. This could include individual traits and characteristics or leadership type practices, like setting a vision, implementing change or communication. The transferable nature of traits, characteristics and leadership type practices means that they can be developed without necessarily being connected to a specific domain and could, therefore, be relevant in any organisation.
Domain-specific expertise	Knowledge and skills with a specific field, area (domain) or type of organisation/team. The focus here is on deep knowledge and understanding of the domain in which a leader has responsibility of. In school leadership, this includes subjects or specialist domains such as behaviour, special educational needs, teacher development or school finance. It could also relate to an age range or type of school, organisation.

The personal traits or characteristics of leaders have played a prominent part in the discourse around school leadership as well as in leadership training and development programmes. Throughout the last decade, for example, it has become commonplace for leadership programmes to include personality tests, designed to help leaders learn about themselves and to consider how they might work with others. Reasons for the influence of 'trait-based' leadership are complex. One seminal paper written in 2008 contributed to this perspective. It claimed that 'a small handful of personal traits explains a high proportion of the variation in leadership effectiveness' (Leithwood et al, 2008). However, last year the same researchers revisited this claim and concluded that there was insufficient evidence to support this claim, writing that 'the claim that personal leadership traits, by themselves, explain a high proportion of variation in school leadership effectiveness cannot be justified' (Leithwood et al, 2019).

We think it is important to shift the conception of school leadership away from the traits, behaviours or personality of the individual and, to support us with this, Professor Viviane Robinson's work is significant and useful. In her 2006 paper 'Putting the Educational back in Educational Leadership', she argues for a shift in emphasis in research into school leadership that she says has been dominated for 15 years by 'generic leadership'. She acknowledges that research into generic approaches has been important but that a fresh focus on the leadership of teaching and learning has the potential to 'ground leadership in the core business of teaching and learning' (Robinson, 2006, p. 64). She suggests two ways that further research into the leadership of teaching and learning can be useful:

1. It tells us about what school leaders need to know and understand if they are to lead the improvement of teaching and learning.
2. It identifies some of the features of school and teacher culture which support principals or their designees in the leadership of teaching and learning.

(Robinson, 2006)

More recently, Robinson reiterates her argument that leaders 'need to be increasingly knowledgeable about the core business of teaching, learning, assessment and curriculum' and that 'they need to be able to use that knowledge to make good decisions' (Robinson, 2017).

In a paper considering the debate between generic and domain-specific approaches to school leadership, Neil Gilbride (2018, p. 1) writes:

'There is tension between research and policy for whether school leaders need a specific set of knowledge and skills. Within academic educational leadership research, tensions exist between those that promote transformational approaches (e.g. Leithwood et al 2006) and instructional approaches which imply the need for subject-specific knowledge (Robinson, Lloyd and Rowe, 2008; Hallinger and Heck, 1998) with emerging consensus on the need for both skills. However, policy direction over the last 20 years has granted the impression that there is far less priority for the specific knowledge and experience of schools. Successive marketing has advertised how teachers can be senior leaders within schools in a short time scale, for example the "Fast Track" scheme (DfES 2005). In 2010, the UK government introduced the "Tomorrow's Heads" programme, which allowed individuals without teaching experience to train as a headteacher (NSCL 2010).'

England's National Professional Qualifications (NPQs) for school leadership themselves are another example of how the generic leadership approach is embedded into our school system. Qualifications for middle, senior, executive leaders and headship are organised into the following six content areas which, with the exception of 'teaching and curriculum excellence', could apply to managerial posts in many other sectors or industries (DfE, 2019):

- Strategy and improvement
- Teaching and curriculum excellence
- Leading with impact
- Working in partnership
- Managing resources and risks
- Increasing capability

Within these content areas, we can see embedded further examples of generic knowledge and skills. For example, teachers undertaking an NPQ in Middle Leadership (NPQML) are required to 'anticipate other peoples' views or feelings and moderate [their] approach accordingly' and 'adopt different leadership styles to ensure the team meets its objectives'. Trainee headteachers, through the National Professional Qualification for Headship, are required to learn how to 'lead a successful whole-school change programme', 'distribute responsibility and accountability throughout the school to improve performance' and 'be an inspiring leader in a range of different situations'. Each of these statements can be applied as easily to other sectors as they can to schools and education which can be seen to imply that leadership is something that can be learned as a generic skill, rather than specific to a domain. Another, more recent development is that of the apprenticeship levy to fund leadership training for school leaders within which the apprenticeship framework rests on a general leadership and management qualification. School leaders undertaking leadership training for example linked to the team leader/supervisor standard will be taught content including 'operational management', 'understanding learning styles' and 'project management' (Institute for Apprenticeships, 2019).

It is argued that such policy developments have been shaped by the dominance of private-sector goods and services over public. Courtney et al (2018) suggest that the period starting in the mid-1980s has been characterised by an increase in private sector involvement in what were once public services. Apple (2005) argues that education has been shaped by the importing of business models which has happened because public goods and services have been devalued. Critique of the current approach to school leadership training and qualifications in England lays some of the problems in our school system at the door of leadership genericism and the absence of domain-specific expertise amongst school leaders. Christine Counsell (2018), for example, argues eloquently for greater curricular knowledge, writing that: 'the absence of an adequate model of *senior* curriculum leadership seems to me to deepen fundamental and long-standing problems in schools with which we have all wrestled, from weak assessment systems to problems with generation and interpretation of data, from problematical judgements about teaching and learning, to attraction and retention of fine teachers, from teacher development to the effectiveness of CPD.'

In headteacher Matthew Evans' recent book *Leaders with Substance: An Antidote to Genericism in Schools*, he argues that leaders should not rely on a toolkit of generic skills, but on 'our schema of knowledge'. He suggests that the best leaders don't study the field of 'leadership' but build relevant knowledge which helps them to solve the educational problems they face in their school (Evans, 2019, p. 43). A relevant model when considering the domain-specific knowledge of school leaders is 'expert leadership', defined by Amanda Goodall (2016). She calls it a 'theory of expert leadership' (TEL). The theory is based on evidence from psychiatry, higher education and sports and Goodall's research demonstrates 'a strong relationship between a leader's knowledge and expertise in the organization's core business activity, and future performance' (Goodall, 2016, p. 232). In the TEL model, the influence of expertise is thought to operate along two channels. First, through the decisions and actions expert leaders take – including, for example, around goal setting, work evaluation and staff development – and second, through the way they signal their expertise to internal and external stakeholders in relation to, for example, strategic priorities or working conditions. As we'll see in the next chapter, there are close connections between these ideas and the way knowledge is held and utilised by experts in their work.

In summary, we are persuaded by the evidence that successful school leadership requires domain-specific expertise related to teaching and learning and that there should be a greater emphasis on this both within training, professional qualifications and the leadership narrative more broadly. Next, we consider next the impact school leadership can have and what might cause this impact.

5. What impact can school leaders have?
Key idea: Effective school leadership can have a positive impact on a range of measures affecting pupils, staff and school performance.

In accepting that school leadership can have a significant impact on various outcomes, we adopt a normative view of school leadership: that it is a thing we can define, observe and measure the impact of. But the precise way in which school leadership impacts upon different outcomes in schools is not straightforward (Helal and Coelli, 2016). Moreover, the literature questions whether it is even possible to identify the impact that leadership can have. Specifically, the research questions the extent to which the effects of leadership can be separated out from other factors (Witziers et al, 2003). However, there exists a significant body of research that details the impact of school leadership on pupil outcomes (Branch et al, 2013; Leithwood, 2008; Marzano et al, 2005). School leadership has also been reported to have a positive impact on other measures, including teacher absence (Böhlmark et al, 2015), teacher satisfaction (Sims, 2017) and teacher turnover (interestingly, not just in the retention of good teachers – Hanushek et al [2013] report that the least effective teachers are most likely to leave schools with the most effective principals).

This impact can be examined in 'reverse', that is by looking at what happens when school leadership is inconsistent. For example, research suggests that unstable leadership can have difficult consequences for a school. Fink and Brayman (2006) cite practice in Ontario – where school boards rotate principals – as leading to a situation where teachers 'quickly learn how to resist and ignore their leader's efforts' and 'school's efforts to sustain "deep learning" experiences for all its students are severely limited' (p. 63). The impact of this on schools – as opposed to the system – is an important point to consider as it may be that one school's loss (of an effective leader) is another school's gain. As we report in the next chapter, a core element of expertise is the knowledge of the setting a leader works in. A lack of this contextual knowledge can be reasoned to be a factor in weaker leadership. The impact of a lack of effective leadership has similarly been reported with regard to pupil attainment – Hanuskek et al (2013) have estimated that ineffective leadership leads to lower achievement by between two and seven months a year, and also leads to an impact on the retention rates of teachers – Fuller et al (2007) identified an association between less experienced principals and higher teacher-turnover.

There are various mechanisms by which effective leaders have an impact on school quality. Research suggests the impact of leadership can vary according to the expertise of the leader in question. Artz et al (2017) have explored the impact of what they term 'boss competence'.[1] They report two interesting

---

1.   'Boss competence' is defined as:
       1) whether the supervisor worked his or her way up inside the company;
       2) whether the supervisor could, in an emergency, do the employee's job;
       3) the supervisor's assessed level of competence.

findings: first, that boss competence 'is the single strongest predictor of a worker's job satisfaction' and second, 'that even if a worker stays in the same job and workplace, a rise in the competence of a supervisor is associated with an improvement in the worker's well-being' (p. 419). They go on to cite a growing body of literature which links the level of happiness of workers to productivity, findings supported by Banerjee (2017) who reports that higher job satisfaction in teachers has been linked to higher pupil achievement in reading. These findings have been further corroborated by Hitt and Tucker (2016) who reason the underlying mechanism of such findings, that 'teachers may open themselves to accepting leadership and influence from those they perceive to be at once credible in terms of curriculum, instruction, and assessment and also empathic and supportive of their realities' (Hitt and Tucker, 2016, p. 556).

6. How might we define school leadership?

Key idea: The concept of school leadership is hard to define. Instead, we place our attention on the work that school leaders do and how they do it.

Like many before us, we struggle to construct a straightforward definition of the term 'school leadership' but draw on the work of others in an attempt to better understand it. Connolly et al (2017) argue that leadership is different to management. Management, they maintain involves 'carrying the responsibility for the proper functioning of a system which others participate in' (p. 1). This is a description they argue doesn't *necessarily* require action, although it frequently does. Leadership, they write, 'is the act of influencing others in educational settings to achieve goals and thus necessitates actions.' Within the literature, it is well established that leadership and management activity is intertwined and both are vital components of how school leaders carry out their work effectively (Gilbride, 2018).

We draw also from the work of Viviane Robinson, who argues that 'three capabilities are central to achieving the role-related purpose (of leadership); **using educational knowledge** to **solve complex problems** while **building trust** with those involved' (p. 75). Finally, we consider the language used by The Confederation of Schools Trusts in their recent publication which makes clear how important it is that leaders and the practice of leadership can transform outcomes for their pupils. Doing so requires leaders to exercise agency to both act in – and act on – the system (CST, 2019).

We have established that the concept of school leadership is hard to define and so, rather than attempting to create another definition of the concept, we shift our focus to the work that school leaders do and how they do it. We draw upon the above ideas to propose the following description of the work school leaders do. We can think of the work of school leaders as the use of educational knowledge to address complex school-based problems in ways that build trust and enable leaders to act within and upon the school system.

Summary – what is school leadership?

In this chapter, we have reviewed what literature can tell us about what leadership is – and isn't. We have considered the idea that leaders – doing the work of leadership – are enacting policy, reform and an improvement agenda. We have also suggested that current approaches to training school leaders are rooted in generic ideas with a focus on traits and personality and influenced heavily by transformational leadership theory and that this emphasis has lacked sufficient focus on domain-specific expertise.

1. There are many different theoretical perspectives of school leadership yet the concept is hard to define.
2. Schools are complex places where the links between input and output are often messy and inconclusive.
3. School leadership can be viewed through the lens of addressing problems.
4. Effective school leaders require deep educational (domain-specific) knowledge, yet approaches to educational leadership training and qualifications have been dominated by generic approaches to leadership.
5. The concept of school leadership is hard to define. Instead, we place our attention on the work that school leaders do and how they do it.
6. We can think of the work of school leaders as the use of educational knowledge to address complex problems in ways that build trust and enable leaders to act within and upon the school system.

In the next chapter we build on this way of thinking about school leadership and the use of domain-specific knowledge to address problems to explore a conception of expert school leadership, asking what it is and how might we develop it?

References

Apple, M. W. (2005) 'Education, markets, and an audit culture', *Critical Quarterly* 47 (1-2), pp. 11-29.

Artz, B., Goodall, A. and Oswald, A. (2017) 'Boss Competence and Worker Well-Being', *ILR Review* 70 (2) pp. 419-450.

Banerjee, N., Stearns, E., Moller, S. and Mickelson, R. (2017) 'Teacher Job Satisfaction and Student Achievement: The Roles of Teacher Professional Community and Teacher Collaboration in Schools', *American Journal of Education* 123 (2) pp. 203-241.

Bell, L. (1991) 'Educational Management: An Agenda for the 1990s', *Educational Management and Administration* 19 (3) pp. 136-140.

Böhlmark, A., Grönqvist, E. and Vlachos, J. (2016) 'The Headmaster Ritual: The Importance of Management for School Outcomes', *Scandinavian Journal of Economics* 118 (4) pp. 912-940.

Branch, G., Hanushek, E. and Rivkin, S. (2013) 'School Leaders Matter', *Education Next* 13 (1) pp. 62-69.

Brown, C. and Zhang, D. (2017) 'How can school leaders establish evidence-informed Schools: An analysis of the effectiveness of potential school policy levers', *Educational Management Administration & Leadership* 45 (3) pp. 382-401.

Bush, T. (2008) 'From Management to Leadership: Semantic or Meaningful Change?', *Educational Management Administration & Leadership* 36 (2) pp. 271-288.

Busher, H. (2005) 'Being a middle leader: Exploring professional identities', *School Leadership and Management* 25 (2) pp. 137-153.

Colbert, A., Judge, T., Choi, D. and Wang, G. (2012) 'Assessing the trait theory of leadership using self and observer ratings of personality: The mediating role of contributions to group success', *Leadership Quarterly* 23 (4) pp. 670-685.

Connolly, M., James, C. and Fertig, M. (2019) 'The difference between educational management and educational leadership and the importance of educational responsibility', *Educational Management Administration & Leadership* 47 (4) pp. 504-519.

Counsell, C. M. (2018) 'In search of senior curriculum leadership: Introduction – dangerous absence', *The Dignity of the Thing* [Blog] 27 March. Retrieved from: www.bit.ly/33wfd2z

Courtney, S. J., McGinity, R and Gunter, H. (2018) *Educational leadership : theorising professional practice in neoliberal times*. London: Routledge.

Cruddas, L. (2020) *Systems of Meaning: three nested leadership narratives for school trusts*. Confederation of School Trusts. Retrieved from: www.bit.ly/3mp9HYg

Day, C. and Sammons, P. (2016) *Successful School Leadership*, Education Development Trust [Online]. Available from: www.bit.ly/3kwKMjV

Department for Education (2018) *School leadership in England 2010 to 2016: characteristics and trends*. London: The Stationery Office.

Department for Education (2019) *National Professional Qualification (NPQ) Content and Assessment Framework*. London: The Stationery Office.

Evans, M. (2019) *Leaders with Substance: An Antidote to Leadership Genericism in Schools*. Woodbridge: John Catt Educational.

Fink, D. and Brayman, C. (2006) 'School leadership succession and the challenges of change', *Educational Administration Quarterly* 42 (1) pp. 62-89

Fuller, E. J., Baker, B. and Young, M. D. (2007) 'Examining the relationship between principal attributes and school-level teacher quality in Texas'. [Presented at the annual meeting of the American Educational Research Association]. Chicago, IL.

Future Leaders, (2016) The school leadership challenge: 2022

Gibb, C. A. (1954) 'Leadership' in Lindzey, G. (ed) *Handbook of social psychology* (Vol. 2). Reading, MA: Addison-Wesley, pp. 877-917.

Gilbride, N. (2018) 'The Relevance of Domain-General and Domain-Specific Skills for Educational Leadership'. [Unpublished Paper].

Gillard, D. (2018) 'Education in England: a history', *Education in England* [Online] May. Retrieved from: www.bit.ly/33t4VQM

Goodall, A. (2016) 'A theory of expert leadership (TEL) in psychiatry', *Australasian Psychiatry* 24 (3) pp. 231-234.

Gronn, P. (2002) 'Distributed leadership as a unit of analysis', *The Leadership Quarterly* 13 (4) pp. 423-451.

Gronn, P. (2003) *The new work of educational leaders: changing leadership practice in an era of school reform.* London: P. Chapman Pub.

Gumus, S., Bellibas, M., Esen, M. and Gumus, E., (2018) 'A Systematic Review of Studies on Leadership Models in Educational Research from 1980 to 2014', *Educational Management Administration & Leadership* 46 (1) pp. 25-48.

Gunter, H., (2016) An Intellectual History of School Leadership Practice and Research, Bloomsbury Publishing Plc.

Hallinger, P. (2003) 'Leading Educational Change: reflections on the practice of instructional and transformational leadership', *Cambridge Journal of Education* 33 (3) pp. 329-352.

Hallinger, P., Murphy, J., Well, M., Mesa, R. P. and Mitman, A. (1983) 'Identifying the Specific Practices, Behaviors For Principals', *NASSP Bulletin* 67 (463) pp. 83-91.

Hallinger, P. and Murphy, J. (1985) 'Assessing the Instructional Management Behavior of Principals', *The Elementary School Journal* 86 (2) pp. 217-247.

Hallinger, P. and Wang, W. (2015) *Assessing instructional leadership with the Principal Instructional Management Rating Scale.* Dordrecht: Springer.

Hanushek, E., Branch, G. and Rivkin, S., (2013) 'School Leaders Matter', *Education Next* 13 (1) pp. 62-69.

Hawkins, M. and James, C. (2018) 'Developing a perspective on schools as complex, evolving, loosely linking systems', *Educational Management Administration & Leadership* 46 (5) pp. 729-748.

Helal, M. and Coelli, M. B. (2016) 'How Principals Affect Schools', *Melbourne Institute Working Paper Series.* Retrieved from: www.bit.ly/3mozgIT

Hendricks, M. and Scheerens, J. (2013) 'School leadership effects revisited: a review of empirical studies guided by indirect-effect models', *School Leadership and Management* 33 (4) pp. 373-394.

Hitt, D. and Tucker, P. (2016) 'Systematic Review of Key Leader Practices Found to Influence Student Achievement: A Unified Framework', *Review of Educational Research* 86 (2) pp. 531-569.

Kahneman, D., Klein, G. and Kahneman, D. (2009) 'Conditions for intuitive expertise: a failure to disagree', *The American Psychologist* 64 (6) pp. 515-526.

Leithwood, K., Begley, P. and Cousins, J. (1994) *Developing expert leadership for future schools*. London: Falmer Press.

Leithwood, K., Seashore Louis, K., Anderson, S. and Wahlstrom, K. (2004) *How Leadership Affects Student Learning*. University of Minnesota and University of Toronto.

Leithwood, K. and Duke, D. L. (1999) 'A century's quest to understand school leadership' in Louis, K. S. and Murphy, J. (eds) *Handbook of research on educational administration* (2nd ed.). San Francisco: Jossey-Bass, pp. 45-72.

Leithwood, K., Harris, A., and Hopkins, D. (2008) 'Seven strong claims about successful school leadership.' *School Leadership & Management* 28 (1) pp. 27-42.

Lumby, J. (2016) 'Distributed leadership as fashion or fad', *Management in Education* 30 (4) pp. 161-167.

Leithwood, K., Harris, A. and Hopkins, D. (2020) 'Seven strong claims about successful school leadership revisited'. *School Leadership & Management* 40 (1) pp. 5-22.

Macbeath, J. (2003) *The Alphabet Soup of Leadership* (no. 2). The Cambridge Network: Leadership for Learning.

Marks, H. and Printy, S. (2003) 'Principal Leadership and School Performance: An Integration of Transformational and Instructional Leadership', *Educational Administration Quarterly* 39 (3) pp. 370-397.

Marzano, R., Waters, T. and McNulty, B. (2005) *School Leadership That Works: From Research to Results*. Virginia: ASCD.

May, H., Huff, J. and Goldring, E., (2012) 'A longitudinal study of principals' activities and student performance', *School Effectiveness and School Improvement* 23 (4) pp. 417-439.

Nickles, T (1981) 'What is a problem that we might solve it?', *Synthese* 47 (I) pp. 85-118.

Ogawa, R. and Bossert, S. (1995) 'Leadership as an Organizational Quality', *Educational Administration Quarterly* 31 (2) pp. 224-243.

Plsek P. and Greenhalgh T. (2001) 'The challenge of complexity in health care', *British Medical Journal* 323, pp. 625-628.

Rittel, H. and Webber, M. (1973) 'Dilemmas in a general theory of planning', *Policy Sciences* 4 (2) pp. 155-169.

Robinson, V. (2006) 'Putting the Education back into Educational Leadership', *Leading & Managing* 12 pp. 62-75.

Robinson, V., Lloyd, C. and Rowe, K. (2009) 'The impact of leadership on student outcomes: An analysis of the differential effects of leadership types', *Educational Administration Quarterly* 44 (5) pp. 635-674

Sims, S. (2017) *TALIS 2013: working conditions, Teacher Job Satisfaction and Retention*. Department for Education. London: The Stationery Office.

Spillane, J. (2005) 'Distributed Leadership', *The Educational Forum* 69 (2) pp. 143-150.

Tian, M., Risku, M. and Collin, K. (2016) 'A meta-analysis of distributed leadership from 2002 to 2013: Theory development, empirical evidence and future research focus', *Educational Management Administration & Leadership* 44 (1) pp. 146-164.

UNICEF (2020) 'UNESCO Institute for Statistics'. Retrieved from: www.data. uis.unesco.org/

Warrick, D. D. (2011) 'The urgent need for skilled transformational leaders: Integrating transformational leadership and organization development', *Journal of Leadership, Accountability and Ethics* 8 (5) pp. 11-26.

Willingham, D. T. (2008) 'Critical Thinking: Why Is It So Hard to Teach?', *Arts Education Policy Review* 109 (4) pp. 21-32.

Witziers, B., Bosker, R. J. and Krüger, M. L. (2003) 'Educational Leadership and Student Achievement: The Elusive Search for an Association', *Educational Administration Quarterly* 39 (3) pp. 398-425.

Wright, N. (2011) 'Between "bastard" and "wicked" leadership? School leadership and the emerging policies of the UK Coalition Government', *Journal of Educational Administration and History* 43 (4) pp. 345-362.

DEVELOPING SCHOOL LEADERSHIP
BY JEN BARKER AND TOM REES

In our previous chapter, we considered what the literature tells us about school leadership. We found that establishing causal links between leaders' actions and their impact is difficult and that we can consider it as a low-validity domain. However, evidence suggests there is a correlation between successful leadership and improved pupil outcomes and teaching performance, satisfaction and retention. We explored the concept of understanding school leadership as a process of addressing problems and established the importance of domain-knowledge as a basis for effective decision-making and influence. We also considered what a definition of school leadership might be, suggesting it can be seen as the use of knowledge to solve complex school-based problems in ways that build trust, and enable leaders to act within and upon the school system.

Building on this definition, it is important to understand – both for leaders themselves and the schools they work in – how school leaders can become more 'expert' in their roles.

This second chapter is organised into the following two parts: **Part 1 – Expert school leadership: what is it?** and **Part 2 – Expert school leadership: how might we develop it?**

Part 1 – Expert school leadership: what is it?
We explore a model of expert school leadership by exploring the following concepts:

1. Expertise
2. Mental models
3. Persistent problems
4. Knowledge

1. Expertise

Key idea: In viewing school leadership as expertise, we consider the mechanisms that underpin school leaders' successful behaviours and actions. We find that expert school leaders are 'made, not born'.

Most of us will be able to recognise a school leader we've worked with who consistently performs at a high level. Think of the colleague who commands control of any classroom or corridor, appearing to have eyes in the back of her head, or the head of department who deals with complex staffing challenges serenely, or the headteacher who knows what to do in the most challenging of circumstances. Like experts in other fields, these 'expert leaders' can respond to the challenges of their role in 'fast, fluid and flexible' ways, using less 'conscious effort' than their novice counterparts (Berliner, 1988). Although we use the term 'expert' to describe the best performers in a field, it can also be helpful to think of expertise as a spectrum, ranging from novices – those with little or no expertise in a domain – through to expert – those who are able to consistently perform at a very high level. Expertise is helpful in understanding high performance as it focuses on the mechanisms underlying superior achievement (Ericsson, 2000) whereas analysis of high performers often focuses on observable behaviours. Focusing on the observable characteristics of experts risks imitation of only a small part of what experts do. Observable behaviours are often arbitrary, they do not necessarily reflect what it means to be an expert and attending to only them misses the complex holistic nature of true expert performance.

It is common to hear people talk about 'natural' or 'born' teachers and school leaders, however research across a wide number of fields consistently finds that expert performance has little to do with innate talents or traits (Bloom, 1985). Researchers claim that experts are 'made and not born' (Ericsson et al, 2007) because expertise is 'effortfully acquired', something that 'carries us beyond what nature has specifically prepared us to do' (Bereitner and Scardamalia, 1993, p. 3). These insights into expertise and the development of high performance are applicable to the expertise of leaders and managers as well as other domains such as music, sport or medicine: 'If you want to achieve top performance as a manager and a leader, you've got to forget the folklore about genius that makes many people think they cannot take a scientific approach to developing expertise' (Ericsson et al, 2007).

Having established expertise as a lens through which we can understand the high performance of school leaders, we now turn to the question of what it is that underpins expert performance. We consider the literature in this area that suggests it is primarily knowledge – organised to guide action – that is responsible for this, which can be described as an expert mental model.

2. Mental models

Key idea: School leadership expertise relies on expert mental models: the knowledge held by an individual and how this knowledge is organised to guide action.

Mental models are representations people hold about the enormous range of things they do. They are underpinned by knowledge and developed through instruction, experience and significant amounts of practise and feedback (Ericsson and Pool, 2016; Bereiter and Scardamalia, 1993). Once acquired, they result in some benefits:

- intuition, being able to solve problems in less time or with less effort (Simon, 1992);
- and, improved pattern recognition, i.e. being able to spot where a problem is similar to one that has been dealt with previously or to recognise where a situation poses a novel challenge (Kahneman and Klein, 2009).

The term 'mental model' is thought to have been most significantly developed by Kenneth Craik (1943) in his book *The Nature of Explanation*. In it, he writes 'If the organism carries a "small-scale model" of external reality and of its own possible actions within its head, it is able to try out various alternatives, conclude which is the best of them, react to future situations before they arise, utilise the knowledge of past events in dealing with the present and the future, and in every way to react in a much fuller, safer, and more competent manner to the emergencies which face it' (p. 61). Craik's ideas developed into what we now understand by the term mental models.

Mental models can be described as **the knowledge held by an individual and the way it is organised to guide action**. This is an important definition as simply acquiring formal or academic knowledge about a subject does not in itself lead to expert performance. We can, therefore, think of expertise in school leadership as having an iteratively better understanding of persistent problems, progressive developments in knowledge and the resulting change in behaviour.

3. Persistent problems

Key idea: Understanding the persistent problems school leaders face can help us to have a better understanding of the purpose of their work.

We borrow the term 'persistent problems' from Mary Kennedy (2016) who has defined teaching – and associated professional development – in relation to such problems. She describes five persistent problems that teachers face: containing pupil behaviour, exposing pupils' thinking, portraying the curriculum, enlisting pupil participation and accommodating personal needs. Kennedy argues it is important to look beyond the behaviours and actions that teachers take, to the purposes served by them.

'**We have misplaced our focus on the actions we see; when what is needed is a focus on the purposes those actions serve.' (Kennedy, 2016, p. 9)**

Based on our work with school leaders, and a review of a considerable research base, we have identified seven 'persistent problems' we think school leaders face. We think these persistent problems are universal and unavoidable: school leaders will face them irrespective of the context they work in and irrespective of how experienced or effective they are. We think they are controllable, and school leaders have a high degree of control over them. Finally, we think that they are causal: if tackled effectively, the outcome of the leader's work will be positive.

Seven persistent problems of school leadership

	Persistent problem
School culture	Establishing a professional and supportive school culture and enlisting staff contribution
Development	Ensuring effective approaches to professional learning and development
Curriculum	Organising and teaching the curriculum
Behaviour	Attending to pupil behaviour and wider circumstances
School improvement	Analysing and diagnosing problems; planning and implementing strategies for continuous educational improvement
Administration	Managing an efficient and effective organisation
Self	Developing personal expertise, self-efficacy and self-regulation?

We believe there are several benefits to organising through work of school leaders around these persistent problems.

- We remove the problem of 'grain size'. School leaders are responsible for hundreds of daily activities – an unwieldy, exhaustive list of behaviours and actions is unlikely to be useful (and at the very least unhelpfully daunting). By organising the work of leaders around these seven problems, we can then explore more of the many school-based problems at different levels, nested within these seven broad categories.
- School leaders have varied personalities and characteristics and they behave and fulfil their responsibilities in many different ways. It is not generally possible to explain why one way of working is so much more (or less) effective than another. By focusing on the problems that underpin leaders' work, rather than the behaviours, characteristics or traits of the individual we acknowledge that effective practice comes in many forms.
- We can avoid being swayed by fads, fashions and policy shifts by identifying the core work of school leaders and the knowledge needed to make this possible. Rather than starting with initiatives such as assessment for learning, lesson study or knowledge organisers, instead we begin by asking what problems need to be solved.
- A comprehensive understanding of the problems that leaders face and the knowledge needed to solve them means we can effectively structure and sequence the development of leaders. It focuses development on depictions of practice, not simply on developing formal knowledge. We think this can enable leaders to adapt their behaviour or approach to solve problems in a variety of ways and across different contexts.

Persistent problems in context

Having argued that these persistent problems are universal and unavoidable, we should quickly acknowledge that these problems manifest themselves in different ways depending on the context in which the school leader works. *Attending to pupil behaviour and wider circumstances*, whilst fundamentally the same challenge, will present differently for an early years coordinator planning for the transition of a new intake from nursery than the same problem for a Head of Year 9 or the principal of a school providing alternative provision. Likewise, the challenge of **managing an efficient and effective organisation** for a small village primary will have both similarities and differences to the headteacher of an urban 1400-place secondary school or a school trust chief executive running 20 schools. To understand more about the expert mental models required to respond to these fundamentally similar, but contextually different problems, we need to get an insight into the sophisticated knowledge that leaders will need.

4. Knowledge

Key idea: Expertise is predicated on knowledge. It is important to adopt a broad definition of knowledge including formal and procedural and to understand the 'hidden' knowledge of experts: informal, impressionistic and self-regulatory.

To define knowledge we draw heavily on categories defined by Bereiter and Scardamalia (1993). In their book, *Surpassing Ourselves*, the authors write that people don't want to believe that 'research shows expert performance is mainly a matter of knowledge' (p. 43) because they suspect that people 'have too limited a conception of knowledge' (p. 44). Stein and Nelson (2003) argue that it is educational (domain-specific) knowledge that enables effective leadership, writing that 'without knowledge that connects subject matter, learning, and teaching to acts of leadership, leadership floats disconnected from the very processes it is designed to govern' (Stein and Nelson, 2003, p. 446).

Further evidence that broad educational knowledge underpins the success of school leaders is found in the work of Helen Timperley who, in 2011, studied the practice of five elementary school principals in New Zealand whose pupils achieved three times the expected rate of progress. She found that these principals held a deep knowledge about teaching and learning, and were able to help teachers to translate this knowledge into practice (Timperley, 2011, p. 166):

'What was so evident in these highly effective principals' activities was their deep knowledge of teaching and learning. Their knowledge was both declarative, in that they actively sought to understand underpinning theories and could talk about important ideas with staff, and procedural, in the sense of helping their teachers enact appropriate strategies based on these theories within their classrooms. This knowledge base is very different from the management roles promoted over the last thirty years, as schools in many countries have been given greater autonomy to manage their buildings (e.g. Whitty, 1997). It is also very different from the strong relationship focus of transformational leadership that has formed the basis of many principals' training programs (Leithwood et al, 1996). Both of these approaches to leadership have required generic knowledge of management and relationships. The principals participating in this study demonstrated a deeply specialized knowledge of teaching and learning.'

Leadership content knowledge

When thinking about knowledge, it's common for people to think initially of 'formal' knowledge: the type of knowledge that can be codified in books, compared, contrasted and relatively easily taught. Formal knowledge enables those who hold it to 'give justifications and explanations that will withstand critical examination' (p. 64). As Dylan Wiliam outlines in his chapter, it acts as a foundation for learning because learning occurs when new knowledge is assimilated into existing knowledge. Formal knowledge is essential for school leaders, who must have a deep knowledge of a huge number of areas. So huge is the requisite knowledge of leaders, we feel it is an area that needs codifying, such that it can be more easily sequenced and developed. In the same way that the work of Lee Schulman led to the definition and understanding of the importance of pedagogical content knowledge for teachers, we support an equivalent for leaders. A starting point for this has been developed by Stein and Nelson (2003) who have defined 'leadership content knowledge' as the knowledge leaders need to have about the curriculum and how pupils learn. Of course, leaders need to know more than this, but it is an important starting point. To develop a taxonomy of leader knowledge is an enormous task, but one which we think may pay dividends, given the importance of educational knowledge that we have proposed within these first two chapters.

The hidden knowledge of experts

Beriter and Scardamalia argue that formal (declarative) knowledge and procedural knowledge represent two of five categories of knowledge that, in areas of expertise, are developed to a high degree. Declarative and procedural knowledge have been described, respectively, as 'knowing that' and 'knowing how' (Roediger et al, 1989). The following three categories of knowledge Bereiter and Scardamalia term the 'hidden knowledge of experts'.

1. **Informal knowledge** – Informal knowledge can be thought of as 'expert common sense' – the type of knowledge that those with high levels of expertise often take for granted and may find hard to identify or explain. To describe this type of knowledge, the authors use an example of predicting which cups – made of different materials – will smash if dropped on a hard floor. Even when guessing, they argue, most people would probably score well above chance and in the process would draw upon a whole range of knowledge about the cup's material, strength, how brittle each cup is likely to be and a range of other factors. Most people would lack formal knowledge related to this, and yet would be able to make good informed predictions. The practice

51

of school leadership, relies on a great deal of informal knowledge which requires practise and experience to acquire. Acquiring formal knowledge through, for example, listening to podcasts or reading books alone, is insufficient to become a more expert school leader. Informal knowledge is extremely difficult to codify, that is, to specify in words exactly what the knowledge is. Bereiter and Scardamalia describe informal knowledge as a form of expert common sense, but state that 'it is much more highly developed and usually heavily influenced by formal knowledge' (p. 54).

2. **Impressionistic knowledge** – Bereiter and Scardamalia describe impressionistic knowledge as the feelings associated with knowledge which allows us to form opinions/impressions of people and things. Impressionistic knowledge may not be always be relevant but in some situations will be essential. When a school leader decides, for example, about whether to allow a person to take a leave of absence, they draw upon knowledge of immediate circumstances, the person asking and the short and long-term consequences of saying yes or no. In such an example, leaders will be drawing on impressions of these things, understanding which is rooted in past experiences or impressionistic knowledge.

3. **Self-regulatory knowledge** – Bereiter and Scardamlia write that self-regulatory knowledge 'is not knowing how to do the job but knowing how to manage yourself to do the job that way' (p. 49). It is not necessarily knowledge of a domain (although it can be), but knowledge that is relevant to performance in the domain in question. Self-regulatory knowledge can 'be thought of as knowledge that controls the application of other knowledge' (p. 60), it is metacognitive in nature. High levels of self-regulatory knowledge are reliant on knowledge of the domain an individual works in; a school leader who is calm under pressure in school is not necessarily so in all environments if they lack the knowledge that guides their action. However, self-regulatory knowledge is the most generalised of all categories; habits like planning, practising and checking that are useful in any number of situations. Key to self-regulatory strategy is that it is applied at the right time, in the right way, and to do so requires knowledge of the domain.

We include a description of these categories of knowledge for two reasons. First, because it is important to recognise that expertise rests on knowledge of significant breadth (and importantly not just formal knowledge). Second, to dispel the myth that expert knowledge is some way mysterious or unobtainable.

Whilst it is true that non-experts also possess these kinds of knowledge the difference, the authors argue, 'is in how much they have, how well integrated it is, and how effectively it is geared to performance' (p. 74).

In practice, the knowledge held – and required – by individuals will vary according to factors like leader role, experience, seniority, remit and context but to develop expertise requires knowledge from the five categories outlined above. A significant amount of the knowledge experts hold will be formal: knowledge about curriculum, assessment or pedagogy. Some of it will be impressionistic: the knowledge leaders have about the people they work with, their development needs and what it might take to motivate them. Some of it will be self-regulatory: the work leaders do to continually improve their own knowledge and understanding. Collectively, knowledge from these four categories – and the way it is organised to guide action – enables experts to perceive and respond to situations in a different way to novices (Elio and Scharf, 1990). Experts are able to automate certain parts of their work and in doing so, free up cognitive bandwidth to invest in the most complex aspects.

Across the categories, some knowledge is more easily 'codified', and will be virtually the same across different school settings. Some of it will be less easily codified and completely unique to the school.

More easily codified: Exam administration. An important statutory duty of school leaders is to administer examinations in line with strict rules and regulations. This practice can be distilled and communicated clearly into guidance documentation which can then be replicated in schools across the world and monitored with reliability.

Less easily codified: Teacher development. Whilst there is significant research into effective teaching (although by no means conclusive) the methodology and extent to which it applies to teachers in any given school will vary considerably because of the variation to the developmental needs of teachers and the difference between the systems and process established in each school around teacher development. There is a lot that research can tell us, but knowing this does not mean it will be easily applied to the circumstances of the school.

Part 2: The expertise of school leaders – how might we develop it further?

In part 1 of this chapter, we considered what expert school leadership is. We have argued school leaders need to have a good understanding of the complex problems they face in their role and we suggested seven persistent problems that underpin their work. We have also established that leaders need significant amounts of knowledge about education and schools to address these problems well and that a broad conception of knowledge is required, as outlined by the five categories of knowledge described above. In offering this perspective of school leadership, we hope it will be useful in understanding more about how expert school leaders can be better developed in the future.

We know from our findings in the previous chapter that defining the expertise of school leaders in this way is counter-cultural; it is in contrast to many of the existing orthodoxies of school leadership discourse and training or development which are dominated by generic approaches to leadership and ideas from theories of transformational and distributed leadership. We think that through understanding more about how expertise develops we could learn more about how to improve the quality of school leadership development, leading to better outcomes for young people. We finish by making the following five recommendations as to how leaders, schools and the system might develop more expert school leaders in the future.

1. **Understand more about what the 'persistent problems' look like in different leadership roles.** There are so many things that we could do to help school leaders get better, and so little time to do it. Using 'persistent problems' as a starting point, it is possible to identify how these problems manifest in different school leadership roles. By eliciting the relevant knowledge that school leaders need to respond to these problems – the substance of school leadership – this can then form the basis of a curriculum for school leaders' development.
2. **Learn about school context more intentionally.** Although educators face universal persistent problems which require common bodies of knowledge, these problems manifest themselves in different ways depending on a school's context. Fundamentally similar challenges such as curriculum design, professional development or teacher recruitment all require nuanced responses tailored around the people and the place in question. It is in the local context where much of the 'hidden knowledge of experts' is

acquired, which is why experience is a necessary (if not sufficient) ingredient in the development of expertise.

3. **Sequence and structure school leaders' development carefully.** We know that developing expertise takes a long time and, for leaders to create meaningful shifts in knowledge and behaviour, they will need significant experience alongside a carefully sequenced curriculum. To build expert mental models, school leaders will need structured opportunities for instruction, coaching, practice and feedback. Creating the conditions in school for leaders to be able to make time for this development is important, as is working alongside expert leaders to better understand how their knowledge is utilised in practice.

4. **Respect domain-specific expertise; allowing colleagues to lead in areas they are expert in and prioritising their expertise around the highest impact activities.** Understanding where expertise is currently well-developed in a school is challenging, but important if leadership is to be distributed to those who can most effectively address problems. Knowing the school, the staff and the challenges that exist can enable leaders to deploy colleagues' expertise to the places it is most likely to lead to the greatest impact.

5. **Establish a structured body of educational knowledge required by expert school leaders.** Defining and codifying this relevant educational knowledge more explicitly would help establish a body of knowledge for school leaders to work from and root their methods in, as well as create a shared language for them to communicate with. Establishing this knowledge, for example, in professional standards and national professional qualification frameworks could be a powerful lever in ensuring school leaders across the country are equipped to better deal with the complex challenges that come with running a school. Such an approach has been called for as part of proposals for educational reform by the Confederation of Schools Trusts (CST) who articulate the need for a 'well established and agreed body of knowledge, standards and frameworks' and broad agreement about what school leaders should 'know and are able to do' in their 2019 paper, 'Systems of Meaning' (Cruddas, 2019).

In Robert MacFarlane's 2008 book *Mountain of the Minds*, he tells the story of cartography through the ages and describes how explorers were able to codify their growing knowledge of the world through the form of maps. These maps became increasingly accurate and sophisticated through the centuries, enabling others to understand new territories better and follow in the explorers' footsteps.

The remaining chapters of this book offer insight into how different experts think about some of the common and persistent problems in our schools and make explicit some of the knowledge that they draw upon to do so. As Stuart Lock says in the introduction, this isn't an exhaustive list and it is unlikely we will ever come close to defining the vast amount of knowledge that school leaders hold. Nevertheless, we think it is a worthy pursuit and we hope that others may use knowledge as the language to map the domain of school leadership in the future. The better we can codify and accurately chart this territory, the more sure-footed will be those who venture there in the future.

In summary

1. Through exploring expertise, we consider the mechanisms that underpin school leaders' successful behaviours and actions. We see that expert school leaders are 'made, not born'.
2. Expertise relies on expert mental models: knowledge held by an individual and how this knowledge is organised to guide action.
3. Understanding the persistent problems school leaders face can help us to have a better understanding of the purpose of their work.
4. By 'parsing the practice' of leaders, we can identify seven 'persistent problems' of school leadership that help us to organise the work leaders do.
5. Expertise is predicated on knowledge. It is important to adopt a broad definition of knowledge including formal and procedural but also to understand the 'hidden' knowledge of experts: informal, impressionistic and self-regulatory.
6. By establishing a structured body of professional knowledge (what school leaders need to know, and be able to do), we can better 'map the territory' of school leadership and improve how we develop more expert school leaders in the future.
7. Considering school leadership as expertise challenges us to think about how school leaders develop from novices to becoming more expert and how we might sequence and structure their development opportunities accordingly.

And...

Education, and particularly educational leadership, is a highly contested area and – because of what we know about leadership being a low-validity domain – we're a long way from having a final word in what is still both a relatively young and immature field. If we are to make progress in understanding how we can better equip school leaders to run schools successfully, we must be able to propose, contest and refine ideas in ways that bring together the work of researchers and school leaders in discussion and debate. We believe that it is possible to do that in respectful ways that critique ideas and theories rigorously, without resorting to criticism of individuals or organisations. If you like, it's possible to 'play the ball, not the player'.

We are grateful to everyone we've talked to about school leadership in the last year as we've written these chapters, to our colleagues at Ambition Institute who read, think and write with ferocious intelligence and commitment to improving how we can help improve educator development, and to the many people who have taken the time to comment and offer us feedback on our work. We're particularly grateful to those who have taken the time to disagree and argue with us, respectfully of course. We learn more with every conversation we have and paper or blog we read. We accept that there will be other models of school leadership that will be important and useful but, for now, remain convinced that it is through educational expertise, rather than the field of generic leadership, that we stand to learn the most.

References

Bereiter, C. and Scardamalia, M. (1993) *Surpassing ourselves: An inquiry into the nature and implications of expertise.* Chicago, IL: Open Court

Berliner, D. (1998) *The Development of Expertise in Pedagogy.* Washington, DC: American Association of Colleges for Teacher Education.

Bloom, B. S. (1985) 'Generalizations about talent development' in Bloom, B. S. (ed) *Developing talent in young people.* New York: Ballentine Books, pp. 507-549.

Craik, K. J. W. (1943) *The nature of explanation.* University Press, Macmillan.

Cruddas, L. (2019) *Future Shape of the Education System in England – a sector led white paper.* Confederation of School Trusts.

Elio, R. and Scharf, P. B. (1990) 'Modeling Novice-to-Expert Shifts in Problem-Solving Strategy and Knowledge Organization', *Cognitive Science* 14 (4) pp. 579-639.

Ericsson, K. A. (2000) 'How experts attain and maintain superior performance: Implications for the enhancement of skilled performance in older individuals', *Journal of Aging and Physical Activity* 8 pp. 346-352.

Ericsson, A., Prietula, M. and Cokely, E. (2007) 'The Making of an Expert', *Harvard Business Review* (July-August, 2007).

Ericsson, A. and Pool, R. (2016) *Peak: Secrets from the new science of expertise.* Boston, MA: Houghton Mifflin Harcourt.

Kahneman, D. and Klein, G. (2009) 'Conditions for intuitive expertise: a failure to disagree', *The American psychologist* 64 (6) pp. 515-526.

Kennedy, M. (2016) 'Parsing the Practice of Teaching', *Journal of Teacher Education* 67 (1) pp. 6-17.

Macfarlane, R. (2003) *Mountains of the Mind: A History of a Fascination.* London: Granta Books

Roediger, L. H., Weldon, M. S. and Challis, B. H. (1989) 'Explaining dissociations between implicit and explicit measure of retention: A processing account' in Roediger, L. H. and Craik, F. I. M. (eds) *Varieties of memory and consciousness: Essays in Honor of Endel Tulving.* Hillsdale, NJ: Erlbaum

Simon, H. A. (1992) 'What is an explanation of behavior?', *Psychological Science* 3 pp. 150-161.

Stein, M. K. and Nelson, B. S. (2003) 'Leadership Content Knowledge', *Educational Evaluation and Policy Analysis* 25 (4) pp.423-448.

Timperley, H. (2011) 'Knowledge and the Leadership of Learning', *Leadership and Policy in Schools* 10 (2) pp. 145-170.

Author bio-sketches:

Jen Barker is the Dean of Learning Design at Ambition Institute. Before this, she led the Teach First design team through the creation of the new Leadership Development Programme and spent seven years in senior leadership in schools. She is studying school leadership as part of a doctorate at Manchester University.

Tom Rees is the Executive Director of School Leadership at Ambition Institute and author of *Wholesome Leadership.* Prior to this, he was a headteacher for ten years and the education director of a multi-academy trust.

TRUE INCLUSION
BY NICOLE DEMPSEY

In my experience, there are few problems harder to address than catering for the most vulnerable, while not conferring labels to them. In labelling children as 'disadvantaged' or placing them on the SEN register, or even placing prior attainment grades next to them, school leaders risk inadvertently lowering expectations on exactly the groups of pupils we profess to care most about, and need to do the most for. This is not to categorise SEND as being analogous to 'vulnerable'. It is to say that SEND is one label that I have found a tremendously difficult problem to address while maintaining high expectations.

In 2017, my SENCO and Head of School at Bedford Free School, Jane Herron, asked where she could find the finest SENCO in the country 'with high expectations'. Without hesitation, I suggested Nicole Dempsey of Dixons Trinity Academy. Dixons Trinity is one of the best secondary schools I have visited, and the high expectations that are evident throughout the school are exemplified in the leadership of SEND.

Given the combination of how intractable and universal this problem is for school leaders and the very high expectations that Nicole exemplifies, she was also my first choice to write this chapter. Nicole takes on the orthodoxy and challenges us all to examine where we might be lowering expectations. Even those who are doing an exceptional job may find the robust outline of the challenges that Nicole presents difficult. She also illustrates the way that she addresses these problems, via a whole-school approach that is inspirational. Her passion and drive come through in this chapter which challenges my practice and challenges the orthodox approach to inclusion generally and SEND specifically.

Key questions for truly inclusive leadership in education:
If the objective of attending school is to access high-quality education that facilitates successful adulthood, with the assumption that **all** pupils are entitled to that,[1] what is your honest answer to the following questions?

- When pupils identified as SEND are *included* in your school, what specifically are they included in? Does this include **all** aspects of academic and school community life? For example, do these pupils go to **all** of their timetabled, qualified-teacher led lessons? Are they subject to the same expectations to be making progress? Are they proportionally included on trips and rewards events? Are they proportionally represented in sanctions?
- Are your pupils identified as SEND experiencing the same access to qualified and experienced teachers as their non-SEND peers? If not, what are they accessing instead and why?
- When a pupil identified as SEND cannot access the main offer at your school, whether that is a lesson or non-lesson time such as lunchtime or a school trip, are you placing the deficit – the 'problem' – within them as an individual and providing them with an alternative or are you recognising the deficit within your building, routines or provision and removing that systemic barrier in order to facilitate their inclusion?
- When your pupils identified as SEND leave your school are they going on to the **best** next step that you could have prepared them for?
- What are your pupils not identified as SEND learning from your systems? What are they learning about diversity, community, social responsibility and social justice?

---

1.   The SEND Code of Practice 0-25 (DfE, 2015), section 1.26, states that, as part of its commitments under articles 7 and 24 of the United Nations Convention of the Rights of Persons with Disabilities, the UK government is committed to inclusive education of disabled children and young people and the progressive removal of barriers to learning and participation in mainstream education. The Children and Families Act 2014 secures the general presumption in law of mainstream education in relation to decisions about where children and young people with SEN should be educated and the Equality Act 2010 provides protection from discrimination for disabled people.

Special educational needs and disability (SEND)[2] will continue to be poorly considered in education as long as it continues to be discussed as something separate from the education provided for all pupils.

Leaders need to know that we are on a journey towards inclusion and we can no longer accept the current status quo as sufficient for some young people; being a great leader for SEND is simply being a great leader for all pupils. An exacerbating factor in the conversation about inclusion[3] is that there is no single definition of 'inclusion' in the education-specific sense of the word and, at best, it is an umbrella term covering multiple ways in which a pupil identified as having SEND can be included into a mainstream school setting. This can range from attending a specialist unit or base within the school building through to accessing all aspects of learning and community alongside their non-SEND peers.

Whatever 'inclusion' means in a particular setting, the problem that leaders need to solve is that children identified as SEND must achieve at least as well as their peers but, based on educational and adult outcomes, they do not. As I will explore, the evidence base suggests that education is not working for many of these pupils. They neither lead on to academic achievement or equitable life

---

2.   The legal definition(s) of SEND, taken from the SEND Code of Practice 0-25, are: 'A child or young person has SEN if they have a learning difficulty or disability which calls for special educational provision to be made for him or her.' 'A child of compulsory school age or a young person has a learning difficulty or disability if her or she: has a significantly greater difficulty in learning than the majority of others of the same age, or; has a disability which prevents or hinders him or her from making use of facilities of a kind generally provided for others of the same age in mainstream schools...' 'Many children and young people who have SEN may have a disability under the Equality Act 2010 – that is "... a physical or mental impairment which has a long-term and substantial adverse effect on their ability to carry out normal day-to-day activities".' (DfE, 2015) However, it should be noted that, although this is the legal definition, the wording is vague and widely contested. A vast range of needs and differences are summarised into this single statement, resulting in homogenisation and oversimplification, and potentially facilitating segregation and separation.

3.   UNESCO's Salamanca Statement on Special Needs Education (1994) states that '... those with special educational needs must have access to regular schools which should accommodate them within a child-centred pedagogy capable of meeting these needs' and '... regular schools with this inclusive orientation ... provide an effective education to the majority of children and improve the efficiency and ultimately the cost-effectiveness of the entire education system', although this definition is not without flaws.

chances, measured by being in employment, having financial independence, accessing their local communities, or health and life expectancy. And why would it? Schools and the education system were well-established long before the concept of integration or inclusion; they simply were not designed to accommodate the range of needs we now aim to address. The rhetoric around SEND has, arguably, led to the education profession – and society – possessing an entrenched belief that there are two types of children: those with SEND and those without. It is this narrative that results in leaders and practitioners treating pupils identified as SEND as though they need something different to succeed and as if it is *inclusion* and not a *high-quality education* that is the goal.

The issue is not a simple one. Decisions are often made and support is implemented by people who themselves were educated in communities where the 'something different for those pupils' set of beliefs is entrenched. Hence, the disadvantage for people with additional needs and disabilities is self-perpetuating. Another exacerbating factor is that this SEND/non-SEND dichotomy is based in segregation and propagates a lack of experience and understanding that makes it even more difficult for the cycle to be broken. This 'othering' of additional needs and disability results in lack of input at Initial Teacher Training (ITT) and Continued Professional Development (CPD) and compounds the issue even further. The heavily bureaucratic systems in place to support SEND at the local authority and national levels can force management of SEND into a niche and specialised role, usually a special educational needs and disability coordinator (SENCO)[4] or private SEND consultants bought in to advise, and the message that SEND is something different and difficult to deal with is once again reinforced. Schools working to provide an education for all pupils that is not based on this false dichotomy could contribute to pupils identified as having SEND being able to thrive and also enhance the experience of pupils overall, and this could potentially drive positive change for people with disabilities at a societal level.

---

4.   A statutory obligation for every mainstream school, as set out by the Children and Families Act 2014, to have someone designated as having responsibility for coordinating the provision for pupils with special educational needs. The SENCO must be a qualified teacher and must achieve a recognised master's level qualification within three years of taking on the role. They may or may not be a member of SLT (DfE, 2015).

In schools, we have come to accept the artefacts of inclusion – the SENCO and their team of teaching assistants (TAs),[5] the SEND or inclusion base, area or corridor, the withdrawal for extra literacy and numeracy, the bending of rules and exemption from expectations, the tension between maintaining high expectations and the unhelpfully vague concept of 'reasonable adjustments' – as the norm, or even something to celebrate as a sign of our kindness and empathy. In reality, this is nothing less than a form of ableism,[6] as it is based in misguided – although well-intentioned – assumptions that children with SEND are different to other children and that a different approach is required. This is not to suggest that we should throw the baby out with the bathwater, but a properly researched, funded and visionary review of the education system, taking the wide range of needs it has to accommodate into account, does need to be undertaken.

There are two hard-to-swallow truths about inclusion that, to progress, all leaders in schools need to understand. Firstly, our enactment of inclusion is often not inclusive and, secondly, our enactment of inclusion is often not effective. Ultimately, being a great leader of SEND is simply being a great leader for all pupils. True equality and inclusion for pupils identified as having SEND needs to be more than just considering them in every decision you make about your pupils; it must be considering the needs of all pupils equally from the outset, so the need to consider SEND separately is eradicated. Leadership in education is about improving pupils' outcomes (Day et al, 2016; Rayner, 2007; Bartram, 2019) and being committed to creating the culture and conditions to achieve this (Dyson and Millward, 2000; Booth and Ainscow, 2002; Ekins, 2010; Garner, 2016); great leadership for SEND is simply applying this to all pupils.

As the biggest attainment gap at age 16 nationally is between SEND and non-SEND learners (EEF, 2017), and changes that affect in-school variation have a much greater impact on national averages than changes that aim to influence

---

5. Teaching assistants (also known as TAs or classroom support assistants) are adults who support teachers in the classroom. TAs duties can vary widely from school to school (EEF, 2018). It is my observation that many schools are now employing adults without qualified teacher status under a number of other names, for example learning fellows, and I would include these in my own use of the term teaching assistant.

6. On their website, the disability charity Scope defines ableism as 'discrimination in favour of non-disabled people' (bit.ly/3jLLXvN). In a blog post on the BBC's 'Ouch' disability awareness website, posted in 2014, they go further describing ableism as incorporating a range of issues from lack of access, misguided but well intentioned assumptions, and active abuse of disabled people (bbc.in/2FeyJZi).

between-school variation (OECD, 2004), the issues of improved outcomes in general and improved outcomes for pupils identified as SEND are inexorably linked. Pupils identified as SEND have, on average, consistently made less progress than other pupils with the same starting points (NAO, 2019) and, although it would be easy to pass this discrepancy off as a product of their additional needs or disabilities, we routinely adjust our expected outcomes of pupils based on their starting points and then work on quality of input and environment in order to ensure they achieve. I contend that it is discrimination to exempt a child from this process based on our own rudimentary understanding of disability. What gives us the right to lower expectations for any pupil? Maybe it is the neglected progress of our pupils identified as SEND that can have the greatest impact on the overall outcomes of our schools.

There is no escaping the minefield that is the history and political context for SEND and inclusion. It is not that long since the Education Acts of 1972 and 1981 abolished the concept of the ineducable child and inclusion, known then as integration, was born (Clough, 2000; Warnock, 2005). Enacted in the wake of the original Warnock Report, setting out the right to education for every child and a system to achieve this, these new acts of law were nothing short of revolutionary in establishing the entitlement of children with more complex needs to be educated (Warnock, 1978; Clough, 2000). The Education Act of 1981 came about against a backdrop of financial cutbacks in education and, indeed, no additional funds were allocated for integration (Warnock, 2005); perhaps it was doomed to fail long before the Great Educational Reform Act of 1988 introduced league tables and the conflict of interests that would negatively impact inclusion thereafter (Warnock, 2005), with this dissonance being recognised from the very outset (Weddell, 1988; Norwich, 2010). In reality, the reforms of the 1970s and 1980s were never going to be the long-term solution to the issue of inclusion. Schools and systems already existed before the concept of inclusion came into being and it is difficult to turn a moving ship; the thing we call inclusion is actually a series of add-ons, afterthoughts, annexes and exceptions designed to fit a wide diversity of children into a system that simply was not intended for them. Those artefacts of inclusion all take the pupil identified as SEND away from the things that we have deemed to be right for the education of children. Whatever one thinks of the state of education as a whole, the reality is that the system in place represents our best endeavours for our learners. So why would – why should – any of our pupils sit outside of that system?

It may be considered that integration and then inclusion in its present form are steps on a journey to true equality, but they alone are not equality. Simply being present in the building is not necessarily inclusion. True inclusion would be systems designed from the ground up to accommodate the full range of needs that society has. It would be a monumental task and would need to incorporate a level of flexibility to meet even the most complex needs. True inclusion is intrinsic, seamless and equitable. Take, as an example, the paradigm of the accessible building. We have, as a society, come to accept and even celebrate the sight of segregated and second-rate provision as the norm for some people. It is not uncommon for the steps to the door of a public building to be accompanied by a 'wheelchair access at rear' sign or 'ring bell for assistance' notice but the truly inclusive building does not need such signage or segregation. A level access door or ramp access alongside the steps is sufficient to serve this purpose. People who need to use a ramp – many more people that just those with physical disabilities – do not need a sign to tell them which route to use. I digress, but there is a point here; the school with the biggest SEND department, inclusion area, or the most TAs, may not be the most inclusive. The school where all those same pupils are achieving without the need for such segregation could be. This is not to say that additional and different provision should not be there for those who need it. It is to say that the additional and different provision should be of equitable quality, based on needs and not labels, and without the stigma of being presented as either benevolence or an inconvenience.

Our current context, though, is set by the 2014 reforms and their aftermath. Some 20 years after the original, Warnock issued another report raising concerns about ideas it contained and how they had been implemented (Warnock, 2005). Instigated with the best of intentions, the resultant system had become characterised by a dissonant desire to both acknowledge and meet need whilst also not labelling or using negative language to describe pupils, as well as a focus on 'under one roof' inclusion at the expense of providing specialist settings for those who need it (ibid), and was not fit for purpose. This, and a number of subsequent government and government-related reports (Lamb, 2009; DCSF, 2010; DfE, 2011; Ekins, 2012), then recognised that the systems in place for pupils with SEND were based on outdated models (Ofsted, 2010; Ekins, 2012). The findings of these reports resulted in the Children and Families Act 2014 and the new Special Educational Needs and Disabilities Code of Practice 0-25 (DfE, 2015), introducing EHCPs,[7] increased parent and child/young person participation, decreased bureaucracy, greater collaboration

---

7.   Education, Health and Care Plans, or EHCPs, outline the special educational provision needed to meet the special educational needs of a child or young person in order to secure the best possible outcomes for them across education, health and social care and, as they get older, to prepare them for adulthood (DfE, 2015).

between the education, health and care sectors, and confirming every teacher as a teacher of SEND.

At the time of writing, a number of reports have been released or are pending, detailing piecemeal implementation and nominal accountability of the 2014 reforms (ESC, 2019; Keer, 2019; Moore, 2019; NAO, 2019) and, once again, the government has set out its intention to review the system (DfE, 2019a). Although, of course, it differs from area to area, in my experience all of my pupils who had Statements of Special Educational Needs under the old systems have had these converted to the Education Health and Care Plan (EHCP) format, but none of these EHCPs have been updated in the four years that I have known my current pupils, despite the statutory annual review process being followed. Nationally, 60% of new EHCPs are being issued within the statutory timeframes (DfE, 2019b), but there seems to be minimal accountability or reprisal trickling down to an individual school level, despite a recent increase in the proportion of published Ofsted reports that explicitly reference SEND.

When it comes to quality of education, including both curriculum design and quality of teaching and learning, there is one key question that leaders should be asking themselves – if what we are offering does not work for some learners, why not? Taking the pupil out of the school's systems, however well-intentioned, places the difference – or problem – within the pupil and is an outdated 'medical model' of inclusion (Bartram, 2018; Clough, 2000). Indeed, it has been suggested that narrow curricula and our tendency to provide lower quality inputs for some children may exacerbate, even create, some 'additional needs' (Clough, 2000; Dyson, 2000). Creating broad, diverse and flexible curricula to enable the learning of more pupils has been discussed concerning comprehensive and inclusive education and education as a facilitator for social mobility for decades (Corbett, 2000; Clough, 2000). Perhaps achieving this in 'under one roof' provisions is unrealistic, but as leaders, seeing and taking ownership of the limitations within our systems instead of what I describe as within our young people is a good start, and local authority teams and multi-academy trusts may offer the ideal vehicle for spreading this good practice. By removing systemic barriers, not pupils, from the curriculum we could facilitate greater progress, both academic and personal, and greater inclusion overall.

In short, the systems that are in place to support our pupils with SEND are fragile and unstable and adherence to them, although statutory, is not going to provide the answer to the issues around inclusion. If it is true equality and equity in education that we want as leaders then we are going to have to own it, deliver it, and be accountable for it ourselves.

The projected adult outcomes for pupils identified as SEND are horrifying. There are inevitable disparities between cohorts identified as having special educational needs whilst they are compulsory school age and definitions of learning disability in adults, but even so, some careful comparisons can be made. At 7.3%, disabled people are more than twice as likely to be unemployed as non-disabled people, for whom the unemployment rate is 3.4% (House of Commons Library, 2019), sometimes referred to as the disability employment gap, and only 6% of adults with a learning disability are in paid work (NHS Digital, 2018). People with a learning disability die, on average, 15 years younger than their peers without a learning disability (Glover and Ayub, 2010; O'Brien, 2016) and four million disabled adults are considered to be living below the breadline, accounting for over a third of all adults in poverty in the UK (DWP, 2019; Ryan, 2019). In some cases, it may be true that a person's disability and related circumstance is such that they are unable to work at all or that their additional need directly contributes to them having a shortened lifespan, though I would contend that this is a very small minority.

I have never worked with a child with learning disabilities in a mainstream setting that I did not think was capable of paid employment of some kind. Further to this, the statistic cited here regarding life expectancy is referring to those with learning, not physical or medical disabilities; why would this result in a shortened lifespan? The picture while our children identified as having SEND are still at school is no better. Primary-age pupils identified as SEND are twice as likely to experience bullying as their non-SEND peers (Chatzitheochari et al, 2014; O'Brien, 2016) and 44.9% of permanent exclusions in 2017/18 involved children with SEND (NAO, 2019). Perhaps more concerning, that last statistic does not include any illegal informal exclusions[8] that may be occurring and, although evidence for this remains largely anecdotal, it is thought that pupils with SEND are more likely to be victims of this, off-rolling and other 'gaming' activity (O'Brien, 2016; NAO, 2019). If we assume – and there is no choice at present but to work on assumptions[9] – that most schools are implementing the

---

8. Informal exclusion, or off-rolling, is described in the Timpson Report into School Exclusion (Timpson, 2019) as the practice of pupils being told leave the school, either for a fixed period or permanently, without the right processes being followed.

9. The recent releases by both NAO and ESC have been clear in asserting that both monitoring of the 2014 reforms and capturing outcomes has been severely lacking.

accepted systems, ticking the boxes and trying to do the right thing for their learners with SEND, the outcomes from both education and adulthood cannot, in my opinion, be considered to be indicative of this system being successful.

For me, adult outcomes are hardly surprising. At school, our children learn more than the curriculum and specification. They also learn how to function as part of a community and their place in society, and this 'hidden curriculum' can only really be assessed through observation of individual adult outcomes. What does the current orthodoxy of inclusion teach our pupils identified as SEND about themselves and their relationship with the community and its systems? Just as importantly, what does it teach our pupils who are not identified as SEND about difference and diversity and how we interact with it? The children in our schools are the employees and employers of the future; what we teach them about society in school is what they will go on to recreate as adults. In their report on the disability perception gap (2018), the disability equality charity Scope found that, when speaking to people who have stated that they know a person with a disability in some capacity, the percentage of them who think of disabled people as 'getting in the way' either some or most of the time ranged from 2 to 5% but, when speaking to people who stated that they did not know anyone with a disability, this rose to 10%. Similarly, when surveying people who stated that they were close or fairly close to someone with a disability, between 30 and 37% felt that there was a lot of prejudice against disabled people. This dropped to just 17% when asked of people who stated that they did not know anyone with a disability. Although the figure is not broken down by proximity to people with disabilities, the report also found that around 32% of people surveyed felt that disabled people were not as productive as non-disabled people at least some or most of the time and this may be a factor in explaining the persistent nature of the aforementioned disability employment gap. In a previous report, they had found that 48% of disabled people worried about discussing their disability with employers because they felt it may damage their employment prospects (Scope, 2017; 2018).

It is clear that proximity and interaction between disabled and non-disabled people in society is closely linked with disabled people's prospects of gaining employment and, therefore, independence and quality of life. Where, other than in our schools, are we going to address that? Like much of the thinking around inclusive education, recognising the link it has with societal change and social justice is not new. Writing in 2010, Angharad E. Beckett acknowledged that inclusion was becoming about more than simply 'mainstreaming' but also creating inclusive environments with associated values and ethos (Sapon-

Shevin, 2005; Armstong and Barton, 2007; Beckett, 2010). Addressing disabling attitudes is an important part of achieving this and '...if we are concerned about the life-chances of our disabled pupils, then we will want to do our best to foster an inclusive and enabling society' (Beckett, 2010, p. 126). The 2018 statistics from Scope show that we still have a long way to go.

What can leaders do, then, to ensure that children identified as SEND can achieve at least as well as their peers? The challenge is achieving this goal in conditions that are not currently conducive to it. Recognising that whole-school culture and school leadership's role in creating and maintaining that culture, is crucial in driving forward change and improvement is hardly revolutionary and nor is the direct link with leadership for SEND and inclusion (Dyson and Millward, 2000; Booth and Ainscow, 2002; Day et al, 2006; Rayner, 2007; Ekins, 2010; 2012; Garner, 2016; Bartram, 2019). Despite this well-established accord, how pupils identified as having SEND are supported has changed very little since the inception of inclusion, now nearly 40 years ago, and the outcomes for those pupils have remained dire. It would be easy to say that the reforms that were supposed to address this have not been properly implemented (ESC, 2019; Keer, 2019; Moore, 2019; NAO, 2019) but, in reality, the conversation about what inclusion actually is and how to implement it has been on a loop since long before 2014. The policy that originally underpinned it – its review, its subsequent reincarnations and their reviews including the one that is pending – are unlikely to answer the question of what a truly inclusive school culture is and how to achieve it. For this reason, the answer to the question is going to have to come from within our own schools; what is it that we want for our pupils identified as SEND and how are we going to get it for them?

It is not possible to discuss leadership of SEND without taking into consideration the role of the SENCO. Established in the original Special Educational Needs Code of Practices (1994; 2001), the creation of the role was seen as progressive and, at the time, conducive to the improvement of the experience of pupils identified as having SEND (Hallett and Hallett, 2010). It is the only statutory role aside from that of headteacher (DfE, 2015) and is the only role legislated to require qualification to master's degree level (Curran et al, 2018). The specific definition has changed over the years as the socio-political situation has shifted, bringing us to the current version established in 2014. Partly due to the increased prevalence of teaching assistants, the role underwent its first significant review in response to the Education Select Committee's 2006 report and the statutory expectation for all SENCOs to be qualified teachers and to undertake a specialist qualification, the National SENCO Award, was made law in 2008 (Tutt and Williams, 2015). Overall, the role has gained status over the years and it is notable that much of the research now predates more recent reforms and is itself in need of updating.

The statutory guidance set out has not resulted in uniformity or consistency in the role from school to school (Kearns, 2005; Layton 2005; McKenzie, 2007; Hallett and Hallett, 2010; Ekins, 2012; Curran et al, 2018) but strategic deployment of the SENCO is crucial to getting the culture of the school right for inclusion (Ekins, 2010; Bartram, 2019). Central to this lack of uniformity is the dissonance between the SENCO as a day-to-day practitioner – potentially in conflict with other policies, such as those that state that 'all teachers are teachers of SEND' – and their role as a strategic leader of SEND. The suggestion that the SENCO should be on the senior leadership team has been in every version of the code but, despite this, only 62% of primary and 22% of secondary SENCOs are on the senior teams as part of their SENCO role (Curran et al, 2018). This lack of clarity, and sometimes overt conflict, has led to implementation that, maybe rightly, is dependent on the individual school, but leaders in education need to be aware of how they use their SENCO and how this communicates their ethos on inclusion without them realising it. Undoubtedly, being on the senior team has the potential to give SENCOs greater influence at a strategic and school policy level as well as raising the status of SEND and inclusion. Hallett and Hallett (2010) identify the SENCO as a 'street-level bureaucrat' – powerless and needing to develop practice by interpreting policy – and that being on the senior team simply shifts that problem on to class teams instead (Lipsky, 1980; Layton, 2005; Hallett and Hallett, 2010). They advocate a distributed model of leadership as being most conducive for successful SEND and inclusion practice. This approach focuses on a move away from the hierarchies that are in danger of dividing practitioners into those focused on the product of learning, the day-to-day process of SEND coordination, and the non-experts who need telling what to do and have no autonomy in the delivery of inclusive practice (Lave and Wenger, 1991; Hallett and Hallett, 2010). This could be difficult for SENCOs who see themselves as 'rescuers' or 'auditors' as it reframes the peripheral and non-expert practitioners as valid contributors to the community of practice, instead of them requiring correction or redirection (Kearns, 2005; Hallett and Hallett, 2010). This is not to say that poor practice should be accepted, but it is to say that the moral imperative of all practitioners is superior to the non-expertise of some (Kearns, 2005; Hallett and Hallett, 2010). In another study, SENCOs identified not being on the Senior Leadership Team as a barrier to achieving their moral purpose to serve the best interests of all their pupils. Arguably, this is the moral purpose of all teaching staff and, therefore, not requisite of being on the senior team (Layton, 2005; Hallett and Hallett; 2010). Juggling the various responsibilities of the SENCO, plus the common requirement to pick up other vulnerable pupils or responsibilities with the role such as safeguarding and Looked After Children (Ekins, 2012), may have made the role unwieldy and impossible for a single individual. Indeed, it may be unlikely that any one person can encompass all the required qualities (Norwich, 2010; Ekins, 2012). Leaders must recognise this in developing the strategic role of the SENCO.

The tendency towards recognising a whole-school approach to SEN as best is clear and increasingly explicit (Ekins, 2010; 2012; Bartram, 2019), and there are models to facilitate it being suggested. Andy Buck (2012) and Pendleton (2012) that set out a structure that includes avoiding falling into the trap of being reactive and responsive to external demands, through having a strong, evidence-based vision, building the relationships to facilitate it, and then delivering on it persistently (Bartram, 2018; 2019). The first step of this could only be achieved if the leaders implementing it were able to develop their vision based on understanding the current situation with SEND, knowing what is working well for other practitioners, and knowing how to meet the statutory duties without falling victim to the many pitfalls. Another example is the 'saturation model' as set out by Morewood et al (2011). The model details practical strategies and suggestions for the true inclusion of pupils with autism but underpinned by a whole-school culture of the principles and practices of inclusion, as well as understanding and awareness of diversity, permeating – or saturating – every aspect of life in school, achieved in some part through having an appointed 'agent of change' and through a strong emphasis on professional learning (Morewood et al, 2011; Bartram, 2019). Models and examples are useful as inspiration and to generate ideas but are unlikely to be able to be transplanted to other settings. All of these models are similar in that there is a focus on taking the responsibility for SEND away from an individual or specialist and sharing it with all of the school community. This is the theme of the distributed model set out in 2010, before the 2014 reforms, and the models for leadership being suggested in 2019 and yet, it seems, the legislation and bigger picture continue to mitigate this.

The biggest danger of the SENCO role is that it communicates a belief, already being transmitted by a heavily bureaucratic system and a history of segregation, that pupils identified as SEND are something separate and must be dealt with by specialists. Classroom teachers often doubt their ability to meet the needs of pupils with SEND in their classrooms and senior leaders may lack the confidence to implement change for this significant minority (Thomas and

Loxley, 2007; Bartram, 2019) and thus the negative feedback loop is reinforced. There are examples of good practice out there, and people are writing about good ideas to support improvements for pupils identified as having SEND, but no single model is going to work for every school. Instead, leaders must reset their understanding of what SEND is. Whilst some pupils need more than others and some need individualised activities or resources, the expectation for all pupils must be the same thing – that they are known, they are safe, and they have access to high-quality learning opportunities through great qualified teachers and a great curriculum.

There is no silver bullet, but based on my own experience and what has worked well for us at Dixons Trinity Academy, I have identified three key principles that leaders can use to continue on the journey to true inclusion:

1. The quality of input, high expectations and staff accountability that we apply to our highest-attaining learners is the right of all learners.

The provision our learners identified as SEND need is not being made available to most of them due to barriers in our systems. The high-quality teaching, relentless focus on progress and expectation of staff to teach in a way that facilitates pupil learning (and accountability if they do not) is happening in schools already, it just needs to happen for pupils identified as SEND as well. The specific strategies and approaches we use may differ (and they should) to ensure pupils with SEND learn, but it should be delivered by qualified, accountable and experienced staff. In fact, for our most vulnerable learners, it should arguably be delivered by the most qualified, most accountable and most experienced staff if it is to be equitable and maximise their opportunity to make progress.

No single thing sums up our approach to inclusion, but not having teaching assistants seems to be the thing that gets people's attention. The decision was not to have no teaching assistants but to provide every learner with a qualified accountable teacher. Overall, the consensus is that teaching assistants can add value if deployed carefully and strategically, especially if they deliver targeted interventions for which they have been trained. The Education Endowment Foundation (EEF) does acknowledge, however, that low-attaining pupils on average make less progress in classes with a teaching assistant present (Blatchford et al, 2012; EEF, 2018). However, none of this is the reason we do not have any teaching assistants at Dixons Trinity. If any pupil, including those identified as having SEND, needs one-to-one or small group intervention or support with literacy, numeracy, or any subject, we ask ourselves who would be the right person to deliver it and, invariably, the answer has been qualified, experienced, subject-specialist teachers.

Purchased literacy and numeracy programmes and interventions are often rooted in the belief that pupils identified as SEND need something different to their peers, and are rarely evidence-based. The things that we know to be effective at supporting progress – high-quality teaching and personalised feedback, for example – are available to all in our schools. We, therefore, use additional curriculum time, especially in English and maths, and our 'double staffing' model (see page 76) to facilitate increased access to classroom learning and small group (even 1:1) work, with subject specialist teachers and in academic departments. Our pupils identified as SEND have achieved a 'progress 8' score of around +1 for the last three years of standardised outcomes.[10]

2. The individualisation, structure and nurture we apply to our lowest-attaining and most vulnerable learners is the right of all learners.

Instead of seeing a pupil who is unable to cope with an aspect of the school day as a pupil who requires individualised provision, consider if their need is simply highlighting a deficit in your universal provision and if addressing that deficit would benefit the majority of pupils. For example, one pupil needing 1:1 support to get from lesson to lesson may be an indication that they have a difference that is incompatible with the normal routines of the day or it could be an indication that something about the normal routine of the day can be improved. That one pupil may not be able to cope but many of their peers could be, undetected and unsupported, barely coping with that same issue. At Dixons Trinity, all transitions between lessons are either led by the teacher of their next lesson from a whole year group line-up or teachers supervise from their classroom doors as all pupils walk on the left, without talking.[11] This enables our most vulnerable pupils to transition alongside their peers and for everyone to be safe and on time.

Another fairly commonplace practice is having 'safe spaces' for vulnerable pupils to access at break and lunchtime. Some pupils needing this provision

---

10.   These scores have been +1.03 (2017), +1.35 (2018), +0.91 (2019). No standardised examinations were sat by any pupils in England in 2020.

11.   It is really difficult to describe in words exactly what happens, but visitors remark on this regularly. Classes are called from line-up in a communal space (e.g. the yard, or the heart space [main hall]) at the end of a break, or lunchtime, and then the teacher that is about to teach them leads them to their classroom, like a mother duck.

may not be indicative of a vulnerability unique to that child but a vulnerability in the school; the whole school needs to be a safe space for all of its pupils. At our school, creating an environment where pupils are well-supervised, supported to transition and take their breaks safely and in a calm and purposeful atmosphere, is not a provision just for those identified as having SEND – it is a provision available to all. At lunch, we have 'family dining', whereby everyone has an allocated seat, staff eat with the pupils, and everyone has a role to play (e.g. serving the main course or clearing the desserts). For those with cognition, communication, or social needs, they are learning and practising important skills, and so is everyone else. Everyone can thrive together.

Simply having the same expectations and accountability of teachers of the highest-attaining and lowest-attaining pupils is a great start, and actively quality assuring the experience of the lowest-attaining pupils, comparing it with the provision afforded to the highest-attaining is crucial to further this start (Bartram, 2018). Providing the same access to qualified specialist staff, curriculum hubs, sanctions and rewards for the highest-attaining and lowest-attaining pupils, and having the confidence, creativity and flexibility to make that happen, as well as providing high-quality CPD, support and information to all staff to upskill them and build their confidence to support a wider range of abilities in the classroom, should be as routine as lesson planning, curriculum design and staff timetabling.

3. The history, socio-political context, and current statutory frameworks are unhelpful and train us to celebrate segregation as inclusion; we have to actively combat this.

This chapter has not been a set of instructions or an example of how leaders in education can be more inclusive. Nor could it have been – too much depends on individual cohorts, contexts, where a school is on its journey and the expertise and experience of its staff. Instead, I aim to have addressed the issues that underlie the need for urgent, drastic and radical change in how we approach inclusion and support some of our most vulnerable and currently short-changed learners. The history of SEND education and inclusion is not a long one, but it is an important one. However, educators can, it seems, have short memories when it comes to making positive change for pupils with special educational needs and disabilities. There is a political framework in place to support these pupils but it is poorly funded and implemented, and lacks clarity and accountability. With (another) review on the horizon, it may be that things are about to change but, unfortunately, previous experience far from guarantees us that. These are the pupils we get away with not working for. They are the ones that get put on the back-burner time and time again. They are also the ones that may have the greatest potential to improve outcomes both as individuals, for their schools and for their communities and society at large. If we, as leaders in education, truly want that to happen, we have no option to but to take ownership of the issues, be research, history and politically informed, be flexible and open-minded, create a vision that is truly for all learners equally and then implement it ourselves.

The first and most crucial step and the bottom line in achieving this is something that sounds easy but is so difficult to do. It is to not see our SEND pupils as separate to all of our pupils. This forms the basis for every decision related to our environment, our routines and our curricula. We are the ones who know our context and our pupils and we are the ones that need to be motivated to make things right for them. We have the resources and nothing is stopping us as leaders from making those changes in any school immediately. This could be simple – for example making it a priority that all staff have in-depth knowledge of crucial aspects of SEND and then building confidence and ownership through staff induction and professional learning. It could be the process of analysing every 'intervention' and questioning whether it is better than those children learning with their subject teacher. It could be looking at the provision in place for one pupil identified as SEND and considering making that provision the norm for all pupils to enable pupils to be fully included, and maybe for all pupils to be safer, happier and more successful. Proper inclusion is a journey that we are still on and it is us, as leaders in education, that have the power and responsibility to drive it forward.

Features of provision at Dixons Trinity explained

Double staffing

Double staffing is the timetabling of two subject-specialist, qualified teachers to one typically sized class (i.e. around 30 pupils) to meet a wider range of needs with equitable expertise and accountability for all pupils. It is the main way we meet the academic needs of our pupils, including EHCP outcomes and professional report recommendations, and the management of it is the responsibility of the academic department heads and classroom teachers, with support and CPD from the SENCO, Mountain Rescue and other professionals.

We have identified six main ways in which double staffing can be used – hub, helicopter, split class, tutorial, co-teaching, and break out – and each has strengths and weaknesses, but it is down to the particular expertise, needs, and subject/topic/content being taught in each specific situation. Although predominantly based in classes with pupils who have EHCPs or are on a potential pathway to an EHCP being issued, the provision is not static and can move to support any class where pupils are not making expected progress, as long as SEND pupils' statutory entitlement to additional and different is being met. Subject specialist does not necessarily mean two maths teachers in a maths lesson, two English teachers in an English lesson and so on. Science lessons can benefit from the second teacher being a mathematician or geographer, for example, and there may also be primary or SEND specialist teachers depending on the pupils' needs.

The biggest challenge for double staffing is creating an infrastructure around it that supports teachers, especially as they were not likely to have been supported to work in this way by their own education, initial teacher training or previous experience, to meet a wider range of needs and have the knowledge and understanding of EHCP outcomes that will enable them to address pupils long term goals in the context of their subject, topic and lessons. Knowledge and strategies for supporting additional need in the classroom and around the academy are prominent in staff CPD and any staff training or new initiative has to work within the true inclusion ethos and framework that we have in place. Although we do not use the more commonplace Individual Education Plan (IEP) format, we do have a document with the purpose of sharing EHCP and professional report outcomes with teaching staff and its review is facilitated through dedicated staff briefings throughout the academic year.

Family dining

Every day, every pupil and staff member sit and eat their lunch together and share conversation and appreciation for the support they have received. There is a set meal (with dietary requirements catered for), a seating plan, and every pupil has a role (i.e. collecting the food, serving the sides, wiping the table). Although never intended to be a SEND provision per se, pupils are well supervised, we know every single pupil has eaten, they are developing social and communication skills, while strengthening relationships and the academy community. It supports a wider range of needs and common EHCP outcomes more naturally than setting up a lunch club or similar and protects pupils – often non-SEND children who might slip under the radar – from potential lunchtime issues such as not having someone to sit with, not getting through the lunch queue in time to eat, undetected eating disorders and so on.

Family dining is just one example of how we structure and consider our routines so that more pupils can succeed as part of the main offer. The level of structure and supervision we have in place can seem alien to people who have not spent time with us, but ultimately our pupils are children and deserve our care and attention. By having this approach, not only can pupils identified as SEND succeed as part of the main offer of the academy, but those who would be getting by just coping – perhaps with no one even knowing – in other schools can thrive.

Mountain Rescue

At Dixons Trinity, all pupils are climbing their personal mountain so that they can go on to have a great life. We refer back to this metaphor to support their learning and personal development every day and in everything we do, and having the right team of people around you and knowing when and how to ask for help is as much part of their journey as independence and resilience. Mountain Rescue is what we call our holistic approach to meeting our pupils' wider needs and is fundamental to our true inclusion ethos. It can be difficult to define, especially as it is still (and maybe will always be) evolving, as it is no one thing, no one space, and in some ways boundary-less in its scope. In essence, it is an acceptance that any pupil

The researchED guide to leadership

may need support at any time, for any length of time and any reason, and that is fine. On a practical level, Mountain Rescue incorporates many roles and individuals that are commonly found in secondary schools – year heads, SENCO, LAC coordinator, safeguarding, mentors, and so on – as well as many more specialist roles that we have prioritised for our own setting, including a school nurse, child psychotherapist, youth worker, and a safer schools police officer. As much as possible, staff in middle and senior leadership roles within Mountain Rescue share offices so that pupils' needs can be met and decisions can be made that consider the complexity and uniqueness of each pupil's situation – there is significant overlap between SEND, LAC, and safeguarding, for example. Any pupil can access Mountain Rescue for any reason. Whether you have forgotten your pen, got into trouble in a lesson, feel ill, feel down in the dumps, or need to talk about a serious incident, Mountain Rescue has got your back. Of course, some pupils access Mountain Rescue's provisions more than others but, because it is not segregated by space or pupil group, it is not a stigma to do so. 'Going to Mountain Rescue' could mean so many different things. We do not have a SEND or inclusion department or area or safe space for vulnerable pupils. Mountain Rescue works alongside having a highly structured, supervised, safe and purposeful environment, and alongside double staffing, to meet as many children's needs as part of the main and any additional and different as part of the norm.

References

Armstrong, F. and Barton, L. (2007) 'Policy, experience and change and the challenge of inclusion' in Barton, L. and Armstrong, F. (eds) *Policy, Experience and Change: Cross-Cultural Reflections on Inclusive Education*. Dordrecht: Springer.

Bartram, D. (2018) *Great Expectations: Leading an effective SEND strategy in schools*. Woodbridge: John Catt Educational.

Bartram, D. (2019) 'Leading Great SEND Provision in Schools', *Chatter Pack* [Online] 14 September. Available at: www.bit.ly/2RNB3ZZ

Beckett, A. E. (2009) 'Challenging disabling attitudes, building an inclusive society: considering the role of education in encouraging non-disabled children to develop positive attitudes towards disabled people', *British Journal of Sociology of Education* 30 (3) pp. 317-29.

Beckett, A. E. (2010) 'Challenging disabling attitudes and stereotypes' in Hallett, F. and Hallett, G. (eds) *Transforming the Role of SENCO: Achieving the National Award for SEN coordination.* Maidenhead: Open University Press.

Blatchford, P., Russell, A. and Webster, R. (2012) *Reassessing the Impact of Teaching Assistants: How research challenges practice and policy.* London: Routledge.

Booth, T. and Ainscow, M. (2002) *Index for Inclusion: Developing Learning and Participation in Schools.* Bristol: CSIE.

Chatzitheochari, S., Parsons, S. and Platt, L. (2014) *Bullying experiences among disabled children and young people in England: Evidence from two longitudinal studies.* London: University of London, Department of Quantitative Social Science. Working paper no. 14-11. Available at: www.bit. ly/2RQemEq

Clough, P. (2000) 'Routes to Inclusion' in Clough, P. and Corbett, J. (eds) *Theories of Inclusive Education: A students' guide.* London: Sage.

Corbett, J. (2000) 'Linking Theory with Practice' in Clough, P. and Corbett, J. (eds) *Theories of Inclusive Education: A students' guide.* London: Sage.

Curran, H., Moloney, H., Heavey, A. and Boddison, A. (2018) *It's about time: The impact of SENCO workload on the professional and the school.* Available at: www.bit.ly/300Zrfb

Day, C., Gu, Q. and Sammons, P. (2016) 'The Impact of Leadership on Student Outcomes: How successful school leaders use transformational and instructional strategies to make a difference', *Educational Administration Quarterly* 52 (2) pp. 221-258.

Department of Children and Family Services (2010) *Breaking the link between special educational needs and low attainment: Everyone's business.* London: The Stationery Office.

Department for Education (1994) *Code of Practice on the Identification and Assessment of Special Educational Needs.* London: The Stationery Office.

Department for Education (2011) *Support and Aspiration: A new approach to special educational needs and disability: A consultation.* London: The Stationery Office.

Department for Education (2015) *Special Educational Needs and Disability Code of Practice: 0-25 Years.* London: Department for Education.

Department for Education (2019a) *Major review into support for children with special educational needs.* Available at: www.bit.ly/32PzBMZ

Department for Education (2019b) *Statements of SEN and EHC Plans: England, 2019.* Available at: www.bit.ly/3cke4iC

Department for Education and Skills (2001) *SEN Code of Practice.* London: The Stationery Office.

Department for Work and Pensions (2019) *Households below average income: An analysis of the UK income distribution: 1994/95-2017/18.* Available at: www. bit.ly/2RMrBWD

Dyson, A. and Millward, A. (eds) (2000) *Schools and special needs: issues of innovation and inclusion.* London: Paul Chapman.

Dyson, A. (2000) 'Journeys in Inclusive Education: Profiles and Reflections' in Clough, P. and Corbett, J. (eds) *Theories of Inclusive Education: A students' guide.* London: Sage.

Education Endowment Foundation (2017) *The Attainment Gap.* Available at: www.bit.ly/3cnmFBc

Education Endowment Foundation (2018) *Teaching and Learning Toolkit.* Available at: www.bit.ly/30g85qv

Education and Skills Committee (2006) *House of Commons Education and Skills Select Committee report on SEN.* London: The Stationery Office.

Education and Skills Committee (2019) *School and college funding inquiry.* London: The Stationery Office.

Ekins, A. (2010) 'Developing a joined-up approach to strategic whole school processes' in Hallett, F. and Hallett, G. (eds) *Transforming the Role of SENCO: Achieving the National Award for SEN coordination.* Maidenhead: Open University Press.

Ekins, A. (2012) *The Changing Face of Special Educational Needs: Impact and implications for SENCOs and their schools.* Abingdon: Routledge.

Garner, P. (2016) Final Evaluation Report Send Review: London Leadership Strategy. London: London Leadership Strategy.

Glover, G. and Ayub, M. (2010) *How People With Learning Disabilities Die.* Available at: www.bit.ly/33P1Xq7

Hallett, F. and Hallett, G. (2010) 'Leading Learning: the role of the SENCO' in Hallett, F. and Hallett, G. (eds) *Transforming the Role of SENCO: Achieving the National Award for SEN coordination.* Maidenhead: Open University Press.

Powell, A. (2020) 'People with disabilities in employment', *House of Commons Library* [Online] 13 August. Available at: www.bit.ly/2RPKiZC

Kearns, H. (2005) 'Exploring the experiential learning of special educational needs coordinators', *Journal of In-service Education* 31 (1) pp. 131-50.

Keer, M. (2019) 'SEND funding "completely inadequate," says Education Select Committee report', *Special Needs Jungle* [Online] 19 July. Available at: www.bit.ly/3kwuTKa

Lamb, B. (2009) *SEN and Parental Confidence.* London: Crown Copyright.

Lave, J. and Wenger, E. (1991) *Situated Learning: Legitimate Peripheral Participation.* Cambridge: Cambridge University Press.

Layton, L. (2005) 'Special educational needs coordinators and leadership: a role too far?' *Support for Learning* 20 (2) pp. 53-60.

Lipsky, M. (1980) *Street-level Bureaucracy: Dilemmas of the Individual in Public Services.* New York: Russell Sage Foundation.

McKenzie, S. (2007) 'A review of recent developments in the role of the SENCO in the UK', *Support for Learning* 34 (4) pp. 212-18.

Moore, C. (2019) 'SEND Review: a game-changer or playing politics with vulnerable children', Special Needs Jungle [Online] 9 September. Available at: www.bit.ly/34BYLhG

Morewood, G. D., Humphrey, N. and Symes, W. (2011) 'Mainstreaming autism: making it work', *Good Autism Practice Journal* 12 (2) pp. 62-68

National Audit Office (2019) *Support for pupils with special educational needs and disabilities, National Audit Office* [Online] 11 September. Available at: www.bit.ly/3mKtd1l

NHS Digital (2018) 'Measures from the Adult Social Care Outcomes Framework: England 2017-18, Final Release', *NHS Digital* [Online] 23 October. Available at: www.bit.ly/2FHdjV9

Norwich, B. (2010) 'What implications do changing practices and concepts have for the role of SEN Coordinator?' in Hallett, F. and Hallett, G. (eds) *Transforming the Role of SENCO: Achieving the National Award for SEN coordination.* Maidenhead: Open University Press.

O'Brien, J. (2016) *Don't Send Him in Tomorrow: Shining a light on the marginalised, disenfranchised and forgotten children of today's schools.* Carmarthen: Independent Thinking Press.

OECD (2004) 'How student performance varies between schools and the role that socio-economic background plays in this' in *Learning for Tomorrow's World – First Results from PISA 2003.* Available at: www.bit.ly/30lHPzP

Ofsted (2010) *The special educational needs and disability review: A statement is not enough.* London: The Stationery Office.

Ofsted (2019) 'The education inspection framework'. Available at: www.bit.ly/33P0WhI

Pendleton, D. and Furnham, A. (2012) *Leadership: all you need to know.* London: Palgrave Macmillan.

Radcliffe, S. (2012) *Leadership: plain and simple.* (2nd ed) Edinburgh: Pearson.

Rayner, S. (2007) *Managing Special and Inclusive Education.* London: Sage Publishing.

Rowland, M. (ed) (2017) *Learning without Labels.* Woodbridge: John Catt Educational.

Ryan, F. (2019) *Crippled: Austerity and the demonization of disabled people.* London: Verso.

Sapon-Shevin, M. (2005) 'Ability differences in the classroom: teaching and learning in inclusive classrooms' in Byrnes, D. and Kyger, G. (eds) *Common Bonds: anti-bias teaching in a diverse society* (3rd ed). Olney, MD: ACEI.

Scope (2017) 'Let's Talk: improving conversations about disability at work', [Online] Scope. Available at: www.bit.ly/2Eotupv

Smith, C., Dixon, S. and Touchet, A. (2018) The disability perception gap: Policy report', *Scope* [Report] May.

Thomas, G. and Loxley, A. (2007) Deconstructing special education and constructing inclusion (2nd ed). Maidenhead: Open University Press.

Timpson, E. (2019) 'The Timpson Review into School Exclusion'. Available at: www.bit.ly/301fIkf

Tutt, R. and Williams, P. (2015) *The SEND Code of Practice 0-25 Years: Policy, Provision and Practice.* London: Sage.

UNESCO (1994) 'The Salamanca Statement and Framework for Action on Special Needs Education', adopted by the World Conference on Special Needs Education: Access and Quality, 7-10 June. Available at: www.bit.ly/2RQWWaY

Warnock, M. (1978) *Warnock Report: Special Educational Needs, Report of the Committee of Enquiry into the education of handicapped children and young people.* London: The Stationery Office.

Warnock, M. (2005) *Special Educational Needs: a new look.* Salisbury: Philosophy of Education Society of Great Britain.

Weddell, K. (1988) Special educational needs and the Educational Reform Act, *Forum* 31 (1) pp. 19-21.

Author bio-sketch:

Nicole Dempsey is a SENCO and safeguarding lead at Dixons Trinity Academy in Bradford. She writes about SEND, inclusion, the role of SENCO, and disability equality, mainly on her blog inco14.wordpress.com, but will share her views with anyone who will listen. On Twitter she tweets as @NDempseyDTA.

CURRICULUM

BY SUMMER TURNER

Prior to it being the zeitgeist as a result of the Ofsted framework, I could count on two hands the number of people I knew in the UK taking curriculum leadership in schools seriously. Those who are working in schools and have written clearly and concisely on the subject are even rarer. Summer Turner is one of those people.

I have been privileged to attend Summer's training on senior curricular leadership. My schools are better schools as a result of her input, and in that session three hours felt like mere minutes as she skilfully weaved a narrative of curricular leadership, subject-specificity and school leadership. I left knowing I needed to know more. As someone who leads curriculum-focused schools, this was challenging and welcome.

It is my belief that – as Christine Counsell is fond of saying – the distinctiveness of subjects is the beating heart of a school. One of the most difficult challenges is addressing the complicated balance of enshrining subject-specificity in a school while a senior leader is leading on the curriculum, which includes a majority of subjects outside of the leader's specialism and leads to a push towards genericism. Summer's ability to navigate this challenge with clarity is her real skill.

Part one: the curriculum leadership conundrum

'The test of the curriculum is what our children become, not only in the workplace but in being able to think about themselves and their society imaginatively and constructively, able to use the resources provided by the past in order to envisage and implement new possibilities' (Macintyre, 2002).

The curriculum is the heart of a school; it is the substance of pupils' experiences in education and sets out the aspirations and ultimate goals of school education. The centrality of the curriculum and curricular thought to the quality of a school also means it is one of the most complex areas to lead and the dominance of curriculum within the fabric of school life means that it is the responsibility of every member of staff. To lead on curriculum at a senior level is as much about knowing where you lack expertise as it is about building expertise; it requires humility and bravery in equal measure.

The initial complication of curriculum leadership is that we tend to use the word 'curriculum' to describe a multitude of school experiences. In the most general sense, it can describe all of the activities which happen within a school from assemblies, to lessons, to carol concerts, to sports fixtures. Historically, the term 'curriculum' has been used to simply describe the timetable and has often, bizarrely, been seen as something distinct from 'teaching and learning'. In this chapter, I will focus on the curriculum as a term which represents the subjects that pupils study, and which can be broken down into different categories that require different knowledge bases and approaches. In particular, it is worth highlighting the 'intended' curriculum which is the specified topics, ideas and content that pupils should learn and the 'implemented' curricula which represent the schemes of work and lesson plans (Wiliam, 2013). The 'enacted' curriculum or the 'curriculum portrayal' (Kennedy, 2016) is how the curriculum is translated into learning in the classroom, including the classroom interaction, where each teacher therefore becomes a curriculum thinker through the choices they make about what content they emphasise and what content they leave out, how they order this content and how they draw out links between chosen content.

Each of these different categories presents challenges for senior leaders. No senior leader can be an expert in every subject and, indeed, some senior leaders may completely lack subject expertise. Therefore, leadership of the curriculum at a senior level has often taken two approaches. In the first approach, leaders leave subject leads and teachers to develop the curriculum themselves and do not get involved in curriculum discussions other than during Year 6 and Years 10 and 11. In the second approach, senior leaders heavily prescribe and control the curriculum by using whole-school approaches to curriculum, often shaped by exam specifications such as lessons dominated by ticking off assessment objectives or schemes of work which focus on 'practising' for national exam years ahead. In the first scenario, schools are completely at the mercy of the strength of their middle leaders and there are no appropriate checks to ensure that the curriculum is coherent. Yet in the second, generic structures straitjacket the curriculum or the curriculum is replaced by proxies, like knowledge organisers or assessments based on examination specifications – themselves supposed to be a sample of the subject. Either way, the dominating force of curriculum intent becomes assessment and this negatively influences the implemented and enacted curriculum (referred to as 'curriculum portrayal' by Kennedy, 2016).

Leaders of curriculum must, therefore, develop a body of knowledge about curriculum which sets out rules and principles, informed by what we know about how pupils learn, as well as a body of knowledge about the rules and principles which are specific to subjects. To avoid this ushering in a return to 'genericism', senior leaders need a set of questions and a shared language that enable them to converse with subject leaders about how these rules and principles play out in each subject's curriculum.

Part two: the knowledge we need about curriculum

If we understand that the purpose of education is 'the development of a rational mind' (Hirst, 1969), or to put it another way '[to develop] an educated public [...] constituted by educated generalists people who can situate themselves in relation to society and to nature, because they know enough astronomy, enough geology, enough history, enough economics, and enough philosophy and theology to do so' (Macintyre, 2002) then we are left with two main areas of consideration: (a) what can fields such as sociology, philosophy, psychology and cognitive science tell us about the way we learn, the type of content to prioritise and how to sequence this content effectively and (b) what do the subject disciplines tell us about the subject-specific rules and boundaries which shape the way this content should be chosen and sequenced?

By beginning with (a) we can start to build a shared language that will help us when we come into contact with the variances expressed within (b). As soon as we begin to delve into the world of sociology or philosophy of education, we come across political and ideological stances which shape the curriculum and curriculum thinking, however we must wade through these waters and try to avoid being caught in ideological traps if we are to find the 'best bets' for the curriculum. We need to make a distinction between curriculum content which was 'largely driven by tradition [...] and, therefore, often reflected the power structures of those making such decisions' and content which 'might be viable and valid in some way that went beyond the social circumstance of its creation' (Blake, 2019).

For Young et al this is the distinction between 'knowledge of the powerful' and 'powerful knowledge', which they propose as a curriculum principle for their model of a 'Future 3 curriculum'. This curriculum model comes as a reaction against the traditional curriculum (Future 1) and the progressive curriculum (Future 2). Young et al argue that in a Future 1 curriculum, knowledge is seen as fixed and is dominated by looking backwards to learn from the past, and elitist because this curriculum was often reserved only for pupils in grammar and public schools. However, a Future 2 curriculum in trying to overcome this elitism, made the mistake of taking the approach 'that there is no "best knowledge" or that the criteria for "best knowledge" are highly variable and context-dependent, and so the curriculum should be defined by pupils' interests or situation, or by relevance to future employment' (Walker, 2019).

A Future 3 curriculum model proposes that there is 'best knowledge' which is 'fallible and always open to change through the debates and research of the particular specialist community' (Young, 2014). Within a Future 3 curriculum, we must look to this 'specialist' (subject) community because this is the most reliable means for determining the most important knowledge we need to teach our pupils. Unlike Future 1, where knowledge is fixed and intends to preserve a tradition, in Future 3 'powerful knowledge' is dynamic and is driven by an explicit agenda of developing an 'emancipatory' curriculum because of the way it allows pupils to connect with theoretical concepts which take them beyond their own experience and empowers them to become creators of new knowledge by joining the subject community. This model sits comfortably with the educational goals outlined at the start of the chapter: the development of a rational mind and the creation of an educated public. Both Young and Macintyre are keen to note that this model of liberal education is about 'powerful knowledge for all' or 'an education for the many and not just for the few. A society in which fishing crews and farmers and auto mechanics and construction workers were able to think about their lives critically and constructively in the light afforded by this kind of education.'

The idea that knowledge can be emancipatory and is the guiding principle of the curriculum is echoed in research from cognitive scientists such as Daniel Willingham and educators such as E. D. Hirsch and Daisy Christodoulou. In particular, these academics have been keen to note that 'trying to teach students skills such as analysis or synthesis in the absence of factual knowledge is impossible... Factual knowledge must precede skill' (Willingham, 2010). In her book *The Knowledge Gap*, Natalie Wexler argues that this perception of knowledge preceding skill is the correct reading of the infamous Bloom's taxonomy (a taxonomy used by progressive educators to articulate the importance of skills such as analysis and evaluation over knowledge) because the placing of knowledge and comprehension at the bottom of the pyramid indicates they 'are *prerequisites* for higher-order thinking, and teachers should never ask students to start analyzing or evaluating a topic until first ensuring they have a solid understanding of it' (Wexler, 2019). This cuts through the historic argument about whether schools should teach skills or knowledge to note that we need to think of knowledge as foundational and skills as domain-specific applications of knowledge. A common thread running through this is that in order for pupils to grasp a subject, they need to have schemata (mental models of interlinked components of knowledge stored in long-term memory) which allow them to make generalisations, apply knowledge to complex tasks such as writing, reading or problem-solving and make links between concepts. These schemata are built by focusing on securing components of knowledge within long-term memory and developing strong links between these components.

In a Future 3 curriculum model, this idea of schemata is handled in the discussion of subject concepts, with Young et al arguing that each subject's curriculum must be based on concepts and the 'systematic interrelatedness' of these concepts. Advocates of this approach take issue with what they see as a 'laundry list' curriculum proposed by Hirsch and other followers of the 'core knowledge curriculum' in America, arguing that the curriculum is not a simple relaying of facts but should make room for teachers and pupils 'to negotiate the conceptual links that animate the curriculum matter and make the content listing meaningful' (Muller and Young, 2019). Although Hirsch has come to regret the use of 'the list' which was simply an appendix to his book 'Cultural Literacy' in which he too 'advocated for a curriculum that would *introduce* the words and concepts in their broader context' (Wexler, 2019).

Simply put, every subject and, therefore, its curriculum has key concepts at the heart and to grasp these concepts we need to build strong schemata in our long-term memory. We know that our working memory is limited and that our long-term memory is (as good as) infinite but that the transfer of knowledge between working memory and long-term memory is really difficult, as is retrieval of knowledge from long-term memory (Willingham, 2010). We can transfer knowledge more easily if it is chunked together with other components of knowledge linked to our prior knowledge in organised structures (schemata). New knowledge links together with prior knowledge within a subject because, for example, if we know what a cell is then we can more easily grasp the process of mitosis but also knowledge links together around concepts in our long-term memory, so for instance when we read a newspaper article about climate change we can more easily assimilate the new information within the article because of existing structures (schemata) of background knowledge such as vocabulary about the climate which may have come from geography, science or pieces of literature.

Consequently, senior curriculum leaders must prioritise how we determine the prior knowledge needed for pupils to access new curriculum content, and how we organise that new content over time so that it can be chunked meaningfully and also retrieved more easily. To achieve this aim, senior leaders have to know enough about the science of how we learn (see Dylan Wiliam's chapter for more on this) to grasp that these are key priorities and know enough about the subjects they manage to be able to ensure subject leaders are able to make judicious decisions for their curriculum. We cannot avoid that a non-specialist leader to be a great curriculum leader must immerse themselves, to the greatest extent possible, in the detail of the subjects which they lead or line manage. Knowledge within a curriculum can be a useful springboard for conversations between middle and senior leaders: what relationship does the specified content have with the subject's underlying concepts? What proportion of the specified content needs to be committed to long-term memory by all pupils and why?

Senior leaders need to be careful not to confuse proxies such as knowledge organisers or factual quizzes with the curriculum. These types of proxies help to isolate the component factual knowledge, but divorced from a wider subject narrative, do not illustrate the conceptual links. Instead, a senior leader would be well advised to explore subject leads' understanding of what they view to be the key concepts in their subject and how the curriculum will enable pupils to build schemata around these concepts and to make links between these concepts. This is where we begin to delve into the subject-specific nature of curriculum content and structure, and how knowledge manifests in each subject. We also enter dangerous territory when we assume that subject leaders and teachers have the knowledge to answer these questions, and this has to be confronted through a radical transformation of schools' approach to professional development which includes an expectation that senior leaders take scholarship and engagement with subject communities as seriously as they do, for example, timetabling. Before we make the leap into these areas it is important to recognise that there are some more general points that we can make about curriculum which are useful for senior leaders. To summarise up to this point:

- The school curriculum can be divided into different categories: intended, implemented and enacted.
- The school curriculum is driven by its educational purpose, and the curriculum is a journey towards this purpose while assessments are

the checkpoints along the way.
- Knowledge is a crucial foundation for a school curriculum as complex skills rely on a body of domain-specific 'background knowledge'.
- Pupils learn by developing schemata in their long-term memory, which allow them to have a firm grasp of concepts and the links between concepts which bring a subject to life.
- A subject's curriculum has its own distinct rules and boundaries but these are centred on key concepts and how these concepts interrelate; this is powerful knowledge.

The structure of the curriculum is both an area for subject-specialism and an area where we can apply more general principles. Two distinct curriculum structures are the spiral and the strand curriculum. The first exposes pupils to several different topics at a pace and comes back to these at a later point in the pupil's journey through school. The second includes 'fewer units of work which are covered in more depth until mastery is reached' (Turner, 2019) and includes strands of content woven together over time. Whilst there is ongoing disagreement about these two types of curriculum structure and whether the approach depends on the nature of what is being taught, there has been some consensus that 'curricular materials in high-performing nations focus on fewer topics, but also communicate the expectation that those topics will be taught in a deeper, more profound way' (Schmidt et al, 2006). Depth communicates a connection to 'mastery' and the proposition that 'learning is a change in long-term memory' (Kirschner, Sweller and Clark, 2006), which brings us back to the organisation of knowledge in the long-term memory. A curriculum must have a coherent structure in that it pays attention to the knowledge which precedes and follows it and ensures that this allows pupils to organise and group knowledge meaningfully and that this enables the construction of schemata in long-term memory.

For senior curriculum leaders, there should be an expectation that they could ask the question 'why this and why now?' to their subject leaders and teachers, and be assured that, if a piece of content is not being mastered at this point in the curriculum, there is a firm subject-specific reason for this decision – such as being one example of a concept which they will build upon and it is not simply because there is an overload of topics in the curriculum design. This relies on at least a basic knowledge of the content and structures of each subject so that senior leaders know whether they can be confident in the analysis provided by subject leaders who may themselves be inexperienced in substantial curriculum thinking.

We cannot avoid the problem at the centre of curriculum leadership which is that all of these general principles are intangible without concrete examples from subjects and that the way that these principles are applied varies from subject to subject. Take the concept of 'creation' in religion: pupils need to build up multiple examples of relevant stories across multiple religions over many years of study to have a full, rich schemata around the religious concept of 'creation' as opposed to the everyday concept of 'creation' as the act of producing something. However, to take another example, if we want pupils to be secure in the mathematical concept of multiplication we want to design a curriculum which breaks this concept down to its simplest components (the multiplication of one-digit numbers) and ensures pupils master these by learning these by heart before moving on to the next layer of complexity (for example, multiplying multi-digit numbers, accepting there is a debate I am sidestepping for this purpose about the extent to which pupils need to *understand* about multiplication at each stage). The differences here arise because the structure of the subject 'religious education' is more cumulative (we build knowledge of concepts from repeated exposure to a number of different examples in different contexts) whereas the structure of school 'mathematics' is more hierarchical (we build knowledge of concepts from mastering components step-by-step). Imagine the trouble when a senior curriculum leader decides that the general research on curriculum suggests it is important for pupils to achieve mastery so they demand that Year 5 pupils should all have mastered the concept of 'creation' because they have *mastered* multiplication.

As well as considering the types of concepts in each subject and the different ways in which this conceptual knowledge manifests, we also need to consider the different forms of knowledge within a subject: the substantive knowledge (accepted facts, ideas and concepts) and disciplinary knowledge (the modes and means of inquiry and debate which are distinct within each discipline) (Counsell, 2018). These are particularly important when it comes to considering how the curriculum is portrayed within the classroom; we want to avoid knowledge being handled generically in the guise of 'teaching and learning' as plays out in the following scenario.

Cara, a business studies leader at a large secondary school, has recently been promoted to the senior leadership team and is responsible for teaching and learning across the school. After achieving an excellent set of results for the Business Studies GCSE and A Level cohorts, she has also been given the role of line managing English and mathematics in order to improve outcomes in these subjects. Cara's experience suggests that the best strategies for improving results is to give pupils frequent feedback and her research on the curriculum tells her that pupils improve through regular retrieval practice and lots of practice so she creates a whole-school policy which dictates that every lesson must contain a quiz and that every three weeks pupils will practise an extended question from a GCSE style paper. The quiz scores are to be recorded and checked by heads of department who will create interventions for those children falling behind, and the extended questions will be deep-marked.

Dave, the head of English, and Louisa, the head of mathematics, are aghast; they have spent their summer holidays planning out new approaches to the Key Stage 3 curriculum to tackle some of the problems arising in Year 11. Dave has identified that pupils are struggling to comprehend and analyse poetry because they are focusing too much on technique rather than making room for discussion of meaning and tone; he has worked to develop a new approach where they will recap knowledge orally through choral response and cold call questions to make more space for whole-class reading and discussion of poetry. Meanwhile, Louisa has been trying to help her team understand the purpose of mastering the hierarchical content of the curriculum bit by bit before applying to extended problems: this model will stop teachers being able to identify and correct misconceptions before they sink in and will ask pupils to answer questions on knowledge they have not yet encountered. Cara is confronted by both heads of department who explain that this doesn't work for their subjects and will create unnecessary workload. However, Cara has already had the backing of the rest of SLT and has been warned about poor performance in these departments so decides she will carry on with this policy as she fears that the departments might be resisting because they are work-shy. After a year of this policy in place, the departments are both unstable as several members of staff are leaving or threatening to leave and there has been no improvement in pupil attainment.

Experienced and effective subject specialists in English and mathematics can see why Cara's whole-school policy would prove problematic because they can see that learning how to discuss a poem in English is key disciplinary knowledge, which, alongside the substantive knowledge of the poem(s) prepares pupils for analysing poetry within a GCSE question (and beyond exams – for the joy of it) and that this can't necessarily be captured within a quiz or retrieval practice. In mathematics however, the substantive content is at the fore and it is only once pupils have mastered this content and that misconceptions have been corrected in the moment (so that they will never get this content wrong) that they can start to move towards problem-solving tasks and extended questions.

Whilst senior curriculum leaders cannot expect to have this knowledge at their fingertips, they can avoid imposing generic and reductive strategies by accepting that they are in servitude to subjects and must ask questions such as:

- What are the key concepts of this subject?
- How does knowledge build in this subject: is it hierarchical or cumulative?
- What is the substantive knowledge of the subject and what is the disciplinary knowledge?
- What is core (the facts and conceptual knowledge to be remembered) and what is hinterland (the examples and narratives used to animate the core and ensure it is remembered)?
- What forms of assessment will allow us to be sure that pupils are secure in the components and composites (precise units of knowledge and applied knowledge) of the subject?

These questions are not exhaustive (see Counsell's nine areas for questions in her 2018 blog post 'In search of senior curriculum leadership: Introduction – a dangerous absence') but they are a useful start and answers can be derived either from subject leads or through conversation with subject communities and engagement with subject scholarship. Senior curriculum leaders must count development of subject leadership and fostering of subject communities (within and across schools and with universities to link the school subject with the academic subject) as a critical component of their leadership.

Part three: what are our 'best bets' for curriculum leadership?

Senior curriculum leadership requires a firm grasp of the general principles of curriculum design, a keen awareness of the importance of preserving disciplinarity and a clear strategy for leading others which can be categorised as management, culture development and embodiment. One way to make this bet in terms of our leadership is to determine how to structure an approach to curriculum design when handling several subjects. I have outlined the knowledge needed to navigate general curriculum principles and subject-specificity but have found that senior leaders are still in need of a framework (see figure 1; Turner, 2016) for thinking about curriculum design across a school or a network of schools. These 'key considerations' or guiding areas offer some structure to the complex web that is curriculum design.

A senior leader can begin with the overarching purpose – what does your 'educated' pupil look like and how will you build towards this goal in your curriculum? This can be addressed across a school, in collaboration with subject leaders, or used to direct conversations about an individual subject's purpose and how this does or does not align with the school's educational goals. This purpose can be broken down into specific principles which will shape curriculum design; whether these are school-wide principles such as introducing children to a range of tier 2 and tier 3 vocabulary (Beck et al, 2013) which immediately gives a starting point for content choice, or subject-specific principles such as all pupils have an entitlement to learn about impressionism in art.

After this, senior leaders could consider the expectations and ambitions of the curriculum. These expectations may also be guided by a vision of the most powerful knowledge qualified in Future 3, remembering again the purpose: is this about simply pushing pupils over the exam line or ensuring they have the substantive and the disciplinary knowledge that will prove to be emancipatory? With these broad foundations in place, leaders should ensure consideration of the big ideas of a subject curriculum, the over-arching concepts which pupils need to grasp. If we take English as an example, metaphor is a crucial concept which every child should thoroughly understand before they leave school. This is not simply content, metaphor cannot be taught by learning the definition, it is through bumping into this concept in multiple ways across the curriculum journey and seeing specific high-quality examples that it becomes a secure concept. These ideas and an understanding of how knowledge manifests in each subject drive the content and sequencing choices that subject-leaders must make. We can consider the big ideas or concepts as the skeleton of the curriculum but the specific examples, the content, is 'the flesh and muscle' (Turner, 2016). The curriculum mapping which happens at this stage when you consider how knowledge builds over time is an essential and thrilling undertaking. Every curriculum lead should be able to answer with relish the questions 'why that?' and 'why then?' This curriculum design process must also build in opportunities for review. A thought-through curriculum shouldn't see drastic changes every year but there must always be tweaks and development if we are to ensure it maintains its dynamic power and that we mitigate the danger of becoming complacent in our thinking.

If we are to develop strong models of curriculum leadership, we must concentrate on the three interrelated strands of management, culture development and embodiment. Much of this comes from getting a clear grasp of opportunity cost: if we are to spend more time on curriculum, then leaders will need to decide what to stop doing. Firstly, we must acknowledge that how we manage our teams directly influences their ability to become great curriculum thinkers;

if we want to make radical change we must ensure that our systems allow for this change. A management phrase coined by Steven Kerr is 'the folly of rewarding A, while hoping for B' (1995) and this has been a common model in too many schools. If we continue to reward the short-term: valuing last-minute, exam-centred intervention work and examination outcomes at the expense of substance, then we cannot expect our staff to take curriculum development seriously. If we want teachers and leaders to focus on developing a sustainable long-term curriculum model but at the same time the financial and performance incentives are centred entirely around short-term results and impact, then we are unlikely to see the shift of behaviours which will mean teachers and leaders focus on the curriculum. Equally, if we are trying to cultivate a culture of conversation, continuous professional development and subject communities but after-school meeting time is dedicated to whole-school training on generic policies or endless data meetings, then we are not truly allowing this culture to flourish.

Our best bets must also include an acknowledgement that to lead effectively on curriculum, we must develop a culture of curriculum thinking within our schools. One of the dangers of the recent, partly Ofsted-driven, increased interest in the curriculum is that it becomes confused with an 'education fad' as something which requires box-ticking until it fades away again. This would be a travesty for our schools, and we will only preserve the investment in curriculum if every teacher and leader is given the time and resources to build curriculum and subject knowledge. Schools and leaders are beginning to be more innovative with the time they have available for professional development by setting up staff book groups, arranging meetings between subject specialists from across different schools to share expertise and funding subject-specific research and access to scholarship. This approach to culture requires an SLT who think carefully about the curriculum needed for their staff, choosing and sequencing content with the same attention to domain-specificity and coherence as is needed in the curriculum for their pupils.

Finally, senior leaders must be prepared to walk the walk. Leading on curriculum means being willing to make the room for the amount of reading, thinking and subject engagement which you expect of your staff. You have to be an embodiment of curriculum knowledge and thought. As the leader of behaviour walks the corridor, so the leader of curriculum must make the intellectual strides alongside their colleagues, setting out together on the journey towards new possibilities.

Key considerations

- **Purpose** – does the curriculum drive towards achieving your school's purpose? Is this true across the curriculum?
- **Principles** – does your curriculum match your school's vision and principle? Can you draw direct lines between the two? If not, why?
- **Expectations** – are pupils being significantly challenged by the content of the curriculum and does the curriculum build sufficient background knowledge to allow all pupils to access the challenge?
- **Big ideas** – does each subject have a clear picture of the big ideas and can they explain this to other staff, pupils and parents?
- **Content** – look at examples from other schools and compare them with your curriculum: is there anything essential missing?
- **Sequencing** – do pupils remember what they have been taught? Why/ why not? Is there a sense of building knowledge and understanding of the subject? Does the curriculum link together effectively through use of chronology, threshold concepts, interleaving or another focus?

Figure 1

References

Beck, I., McKeown, M. and Kucan, L. (2013) *Bringing Words to Life, Second Edition: Robust Vocabulary Instruction*. New York: The Guilford Press.

Blake, J. (2019) 'All children can be taught' in Boxer, A. (ed) *The researchED guide to Explicit & Direct Instruction*. Woodbridge: John Catt Educational.

Blake, J. (2019) 'Future 1 versus Future 3: are all curricular traditionalisms created equal?', *researchEd* [Online] September. Available at: www.bit. ly/3jdANzx

Counsell, C. (2018) 'In search of senior curriculum leadership: Introduction – a dangerous absence', *The Dignity of the Thing* [Online] 27 March. Available at: www.bit.ly/33wfd2z

Hirst, P. H. and Peters, R. S. (1969) *The logic of education*. London: Routledge and Kegan Paul.

Kennedy, M. (2016) 'Parsing the Practice of Teaching', *Journal of Teacher Education* 67 (1) pp. 6-17.

Kerr, S. (1995) 'On the Folly of Rewarding A, While Hoping for B', *The Academy of Management Executive* 9 (1) pp. 7-14.

Kirschner, P. A., Sweller, J. and Clark, R. E. (2006) 'Why Minimal Guidance During Instruction Does Not Work: An Analysis of the Failure of Constructivist, Discovery, Problem-Based, Experiential, and Inquiry-Based Teaching', *Educational Psychologist* 41 (2) pp. 75-86.

MacIntyre, A. and Dunne, J. (2002) 'Alasdair MacIntyre on Education: In Dialogue with Joseph Dunne', *Journal of Philosophy of Education* 36 (1)

Muller, J. and Young, M. (2019) 'Knowledge, power and powerful knowledge re-visited', *The Curriculum Journal* 30 (2) pp. 196-214

Schmidt, W. H. and Prawat, R. S. (2006) 'Curriculum coherence and national education: issue or non-issue?' *Journal of Curriculum Studies* 38 (6) pp. 641-658.

Turner, S. (2016) *Bloomsbury CPD Library: Secondary Curriculum and Assessment Design*. London: Bloomsbury

Turner, S. (2019) 'Spirals, strands and revisiting: importance of review and making links in curricular design' in Boxer, A. (ed) *The researchED guide to Explicit & Direct Instruction*. Woodbridge: John Catt Educational.

Walker, R. (2019) 'Powerful Knowledge: What it is, why it's important, and how to make it happen in your school', *The Fruits Are Sweet* [Online] 18 October. Available at: www.bit.ly/3mXxYVs

Wexler, N. (2019) *The Knowledge Gap: The Hidden Cause of America's Broken Education System And How To Fix It*. New York: Penguin Random House.

Wiliam, D. (2013) *Principled Curriculum Design*. London: SSAT

Willingham, D. (2010) *Why Don't Students Like School?: A Cognitive Scientist Answers Questions About How the Mind Works and What It Means for the Classroom*. San Francisco: Jossey-Bass.

Young, M., Lambert, D., Roberts, C. and Roberts, M. (2014) *Knowledge and the future school: curriculum and social justice*. London: Bloomsbury

Author bio-sketch:

Summer Turner is Director of Curriculum at the Inspiration Trust and a subject specialist leader for English. She has spent the last 11 years teaching in state comprehensive schools and academies in London and Norfolk, leading on English, teaching and learning and curriculum. Summer is the author of the book *Bloomsbury CPD Library: Secondary Curriculum and Assessment Design* and is on Twitter as @ragazza_inglese.

SCHOOL CULTURE

BY LUKE SPARKES AND JENNY THOMPSON

As I wrote at the beginning of Nicole Dempsey's article, Dixons Trinity Academy is amongst the most impressive of schools in the country. The approach that they take to their culture is one of the most obvious 'bets' I've ever witnessed in education.

Jenny Thompson is Principal of Dixons Trinity and an Executive Principal of Dixons Academies Trust; Luke Sparkes was the founding Principal of Dixons Trinity and is now an Executive Director of Dixons Academies Trust. Their leadership has influenced me significantly, raising my expectations of what schools can do.

I make no apology for offering a second chapter in this book from leaders at Dixons Trinity, and Jenny and Luke have taken the opportunity to write a manifesto for how they promote such positivity at the school. They have unpicked their assumptions and their bets here, and given references to their sources of inspiration. School culture is both hard to define and exceptionally hard to find robust research on. In this chapter, the authors use some of the research that exists, and where there is an absence of extensive evidence and the resultant temptation to be tentative, Luke and Jenny have been anything but. This means that the chapter conveys very high expectations. It exudes an expectation of maximising performance, conduct and culture. This mirrors what I have felt every time I have visited Dixons Trinity Academy.

One of the great injustices of the British education system is that pupils from low-income backgrounds are less likely to make good progress at school compared to pupils from more privileged families. Indeed, in some cases, schools may be actively (though unintentionally) perpetuating the injustices that they hope to challenge (Shaw et al, 2017). An even greater wrong must be that this has been known for some time and yet it persists. An industry of oftentimes evidence-informed intervention, training and consultancy has coalesced around challenging this; however, without a strong culture, irrespective of how successful strategy appears in design or evidence, it will be squandered. Put simply, if you are a leader(ship) who no one listens to, then you can design any system or purchase the best interventions and they will not happen. Put simply, if you are a leader(ship) who does not provide classrooms where pupils can learn, then the very best teachers will not be heard.

Budgets will be washed away, it will look like interventions are not working – the evidence base becomes muddy – teachers will be left to think they are ineffective and it may all have a single root because leaders are responsible for creating a culture that means teachers can teach and pupils can learn. And then… we have to sustain it. Every day.

Sometimes, this can be the problem. Leaders are often prideful of their intelligence, and sustaining culture is not an intellectually sophisticated daily endeavour. Instead, it is about being willing to do the mundane tasks, finding the energy to maintain expectations every day, and caring unconditionally. It is Sisyphean and often deeply unglamorous. And it is about so much more than behaviour. It is a pleasure to indulge in the endless deployment of metaphor to express culture's elemental scope of influence and then there are those too clever, or wry, even to try. Culture is a notoriously difficult term to define (Lebron, 2013). All schools have cultures, the question is whether it is the one you want. It is bigger than compliance, it is the intentional behaviours and mindsets that shape the thinking, the communication, the values and mission, which is why – in all its ill-defined, holding-water-in-your-hands inelegance – there is so little good educational research on it. It's big and awkward and probably the most important thing that it is easy for leaders to talk about without acting.

There is a difference between being research-informed and being held in stasis by a research gap. Sometimes common sense is a fair place to start.

Nothing here is new. This is about taking what will already exist between four walls and making it all our choice: a maximally effective culture is the origin of, and amplifier for, all else. What emerging research there is makes links – an intentional positive school culture draws in great staff and keeps them, it enables strong relationships between home, staff and pupils, and, importantly, it delivers most clearly for disadvantaged pupils – and this includes their outcomes. It deals with the meta-question perhaps because the scale and scope match: as a bet, the odds are strong.

At our school, we hire on fit – we seek pre-dispositional alignment. This is tough. Recruitment is difficult everywhere and we have been faced with the decision to leave a post unfilled rather than bring someone into our organisation where doing so would effectively be hardwiring misalignment into our school. Around 20% of our timetable is now delivered through large-group teaching (a solution born of necessity that has grown to be a gift). Ultimately, we believe that teaching is teachable – the lesson that we ask candidates to teach during an interview is only to facilitate the practice session that follows. We participate in instructional coaching (see Jon Hutchinson's chapter for more detail of how they develop this in a different school), we role-play the practice, and we judge not the quality of the teaching but the ability to act on feedback given. For us, this has become the strongest marker of our recruitment process because it speaks so much of our culture: it strips away ego and surfaces pre-dispositional mission alignment.

It is impossible to deliver our mission as an individual. We all have moments of vulnerability because we are real people: we get sick, we are tired, we have families of our own; this is why communication matters. The clarity with which expectations are shared will decide the proportion that is daily-dependent on you as a leader. Clarity creates an aligned team and an aligned team sustains culture.

If you have to give the instruction every day to have a chance of it being followed, then the system is dangerously weak; you may choose to give the instruction every day to create clarity so that, when the instruction disappears, the action remains. And sometimes, in golden moments, the action becomes the instruction. Put simply, all schools have cultures – where they are not intentional, the systems can get lost and communication becomes about compliance. Where they are intentional, saying the same things over and over again is reinforcing and supportive. Eventually, the saying can become a different kind of communication – more about shared language and sentiment (but always there, just the same, in case anything or anyone needs to hear it).

As a worked example of this, at our school, we raise our hands for silence. This is not novel, nor our idea (like lots of things in our school). In the morning, the whole school mills around our noisy Heart Space (where we eat, where lockers are, where we sit together for morning meeting). Hands go up at 8:03 in readiness for an 8:05 start. The pedantic timings prevent a drift – they are intentional. Every teaching day of the year, we put our hands up at 8:03 and the wall of noise falls to silence. It is a piece of theatre. A culture writ large. On brilliant days, the silence washes across the huge space and seats are scurried to – we staff, scattered across the room, look at the oversized lit-up clock. Our heads flick in Busby Berkeley synchronicity to see it read 8:02 and everyone smiles as the noise quietly rises again waiting for 8:03. You know those will be great days.

Our culture is embedded in a commitment to developing intrinsic motivation through the drivers of mastery, autonomy and purpose (Pink, 2009). This accepts the attainment gap injustice acknowledging that compliance is not enough – our relentless dedication to the drivers is because we want to develop true motivation and engagement that lasts. We talk about mastery, autonomy and purpose positively every day using them to shape our feedback to pupils. They form a shared language about our expectations which means, as a staff, we all positively support each other but also that, as a team, we can set highly specific shared understandings around them. Our pupils have had such varied experiences at primary school that we have lots of different meanings attached to the routine language of education. So, we rename things to facilitate redefinition and then we use the drivers to talk about them. A lot. Our assemblies are not called 'assembly', they are 'morning meeting' because in one feeder primary maybe 'assembly' meant singing, in another visitors, in another once a week or once a month or once a year. Morning meetings happen every day at 8:03. Again, our timings are pedantic because we are intentional. Then the drivers shape the process, in morning meeting, for example, we show autonomy by starting the session with completely independent revision from our '100% Sheets' (not named 'knowledge organisers' – they are fact sheets that act in service to knowledge). As such, our culture is both an infrastructure of mechanisms that support (preventatively and reactively) the minutiae of daily decisions, choices and needs that ensure making progress is as free of blockers as possible and the mindset that predicates them. Our culture is both our why and our how.

We work hard to ensure that theorising language is not distancing. Real schools need real decisions being driven by real people who all agree on what the words they use mean. In reality. Every day.

While the pupils are in morning meeting, staff are in morning practice – because our culture is strong, there are only a couple of staff leading all of the children. Everyone else is working on our routines framed through role-play – this is designed to build consistency, but it is so much more than that: it facilitates cohesion through trust, vulnerability and, critically, humour. We can strip away everything else and call it what it is: fun. It is a great way to become better but also to develop the relationships that are a foundational prerequisite to constructive conflict (Lencioni, 2002). If we can laugh together as a team, we can challenge each other because everyone has played the fool at some point (happily without a child in sight).

In a strong culture with high expectations, pupils work hard, they know how to work towards achieving their aspirations (by focusing on attainment) and they enjoy being challenged; they are intrinsically motivated. This requires a shift on the assumptions around aspiration – the Millennium Cohort Study (MCS) shows that, at their child's birth, 97% of new mothers hope that their baby will grow up to go to university. Yet, when it comes to confidence about actually achieving this aspiration, by the time their children are 14, only 53% of the poorest parents think their children will make it (Menzies, 2013). We must focus on raising attainment not aspirations: be concrete and draw the aspiration into reality. As school leaders, our role is to make real the assumption that university will be a choice; we must be the amplifiers of those families' aspirations by delivering on attainment. We must make it feel present and credible every day. Just as the effective mechanics of a school culture mitigate for the daily blockers to progress, so too should the mindset challenge institutionalised assumptions about entitlement and access. What if instead of taking a select group of pupils to visit a university, you take everyone? What if, before taking the children, you offer to take the families? What if, when someone is critical of university as an aspiration, you ask if they went or if they expect their own children will go?

And we know our team need to feel this too – so much in education is crafted carefully to meet the needs of pupils sometimes despite (or at least irrespective of) the potential impact on staff. At our school we consider the motivational culture of our team: teachers have the autonomy to teach how they (as subject experts) judge best; they can choose and shape their personal growth plans and own their appraisal (far away from pupil outcome data). With true motivation the role of the leader transitions from managing (in)efficacy to channelling skills and often getting out of the way. Educational research into culture (e.g. Berkowitz et al, 2017; Berkowitz et al, 2016; Allen and Sims, 2018) shows a correlation between positive school culture and positive outcomes, but the evidence base falls short of determining causation. However, outside education, the scale of research permits more adamance. Culture has a causal priority over outcomes and there is no evidence for a reciprocal performance-to-culture feedback loop (Boyce et al, 2015).

Put simply, a positive culture generates improved outcomes; improved outcomes are not a prerequisite to creating a positive culture.

This should be hugely important (and encouraging) in challenging the great injustices because it provides the starting point. It is also not very surprising; it feels like no more than common sense. Culture is bigger than organisational structure and it has the depth and scope necessary to close the attainment gap. In great schools that are already doing this, culture is everything. These schools share three important characteristics:

> **Aspiration:** great schools focus on keeping pupils' – and their families' – aspirations on track; pupils know what they need to do to achieve their aspirations and their attainment increases.

> **Social norms:** great schools have strong and clear norms for how people are expected to act and behave in school; what exactly people believe and how they act depends on the messages (both direct and indirect) that the leaders and others send (Shafer, 2018).

> **Motivation:** great schools develop intrinsic motivation for learning; pupils engage not for external reward but because they find the activity of learning itself interesting and gratifying (Usable Knowledge, 2016).

Put simply, complete alignment between high aspirations, high expectations and high achievement is the most important predictor of future educational behaviour amongst pupils (Khattab, 2015). As a leader, accepting the complexity of creating strong and clear norms (the great public edifice of culture) is an important place to start. At our school, we explicitly teach and practise our expectations using the same methods as any learning process. We understand the need to learn not just the expectations but also how to meet them. Behaviour expectations and support opportunities need to be taught as explicitly as knowledge. We daily generate opportunities to share how to meet our expectations: we narrate the positive in every lesson, every day. As staff, we do not grow tired of saying the same things in our shared language. Our culture is grounded in the knowledge that it is up to the leaders to ensure children behave and that opportunities for staff to develop behaviour management confidence must be abundant.

Through role-play in morning practice, we explicitly practise how to support the learning habits in our school. As often as possible, we make our mistakes away from the children. We plan and practise our approaches together – just as we do our curriculum. All staff participate in 1:2:1 instructional coaching every week; as such, professional development can be completely bespoke. At our school, we all have agency: teachers can teach and pupils learn. We build the mechanics of culture to facilitate the individual personalities and skilful preferences of our staff. Routines make safe our differences and coaching brings out personal strengths rather than developing automatons. There is huge variation in delivery but not quality. We have no hard evidence to prove this, but common sense would suggest this is why we can work really hard without being exhausted: we are not performing in the classroom. We are not taking on a persona or trying to force a methodological agenda. We are learning to be the most skilfully developed authentic versions of ourselves and it is so much less diminishing.

For our culture, as with our curriculum, we start from the needs of our most vulnerable: our high expectations shape our learning habits and, crucially, our pastoral offer. We do not lower our expectations for pupils, but we will absolutely enhance the support they receive to be successful. Doing this in collaboration with families is critical. We have a dual expectation, that support will be put in place preventatively for pupils who need it but also that, if difficulties arise, sanctions are accompanied by helpful action. Any pupil may need support at any point. Sometimes, this can be as small as a conversation. What we have learnt is that it is the little things that matter.

In our school, we are unafraid to talk about the love we share as a community and that shapes our communication with children: the method is the message. We know that learning to follow our drivers is a journey as high in expectations as our curriculum and we do not make limiting presumptions based on our pupils' data-based characteristics. Instead, we focus on developing our pupils' intrinsic motivation: wanting to develop the learning habits so you can work really hard and make lots of progress needs to be a deeply held desire because it asks so much. We overrationalise so that the pupils always know why: we tell the pupils that we can't do it for them but we will do it *with* them. Being clear with the children and making sure they always know the purpose that sits behind our decisions or expectations means they can move beyond compliance. Just as clarity is needed for staff, the same applies for pupils: the team net widens.

For example, at Dixons Trinity, a pupil will receive a 30 minute, centrally-held, same-day, after-school sanction if they do not have the correct equipment. That is a pretty high expectation. As such, we have to make sure it is purposeful and supported. This means that our equipment list is comprised only of items that pupils will definitely need every day and that, without which, their learning would be hampered. It is all purposeful. We communicate the list with families when we first meet them and every time after that. Alongside this, every morning, before the day starts, when we meet together in our daily morning meeting, every pupil makes a little pile of their equipment on their desk (exactly what this pile is comprised of is displayed on the screen every day even though the pupils and staff know it inside out). The pupil's advisor checks the pile while completing the register and replaces any missing equipment. This is a daily commitment that takes just moments longer than the completion of a register; it has been practised over and over again in staff role-play. Every day, the pupil will also have had the opportunity to go to our pastoral support and independently replace any missing items before this process even begins. This means the pupil is facilitated to have a successful day. If the pupil has not independently replaced anything missing, then yes, the pupil will receive a 30 minute, centrally-held, same-day correction, during which their advisor will meet with them to identify both the issue and supportive intervention – but they will also be given the equipment they need. Often, this meeting doesn't take the full 30 minutes and it can be completed at another time during the day by the advisor if that is more convenient (if this is the case, the after school time is spent working on a reflection document and supporting revision). As all educators know, serious underlying needs can often be identified from the most innocuous of starting points when time is committed to listening. At Dixons Trinity, knowing our pupils as individuals is so important – relationships come first. The mechanics of our culture – the pedantic routines – surface problems, highlight changes in behaviour and make need explicit.

For more serious, or repeated, behaviours we call these 'red lines'. Every red line is also accompanied by a meeting with family before the pupil returns to any lesson. Sometimes, this can be tricky as some families are hard to reach but we are tenacious and thoughtful in equal measure. If we need to go to them, we will. If we need to hold a baby sister in our arms to provide the space to speak, we will. If we need to meet before school, after school or during the day, we will. And, again, our families know this is an expectation. In this meeting, we listen. Alongside ensuring we all share the same hopes, we are seeking to understand the behaviour and to find support to prevent it reoccurring. Again, we talk to families and pupils about this at every opportunity – we tell our families explicitly that they may not always agree with our perspective and, if that occurs, to share that with us. As adults, we can find resolution by listening to one another. Our relationships with our families and our incredible community have been the base of any success we have had as a school. We treat those relationships as precious and when we make mistakes, which we do, we are honest about them and we say sorry. This builds reciprocity and respect.

If we see anything slipping or changing on a scale beyond individual pupils, we take decisive action – we are committed to self-criticism and see no utility in being defensive. We would rather be the architects of solutions than wardens of our systems. Those useless egos have been ransacked by morning practice long ago. Built into our culture is the familiarity of reinduction – we have a routine way to break our routines and we are unafraid to use it. To stop the whole school for a day and put things right through practice – always overcommunicating the purpose; always working together as a team. Our systems are not perfect, and we are always learning – together, grounded in evidence and shaped by a shared mission. Therefore, when we have the pleasure of welcoming visitors to our school, the pupils who guide the tours (given without training or staff supervision), are always in pairs.One pupil is simply the next pupil on the roll (all pupils have the opportunity) and the other is a pupil who has perhaps had a 'red line' or is struggling with the learning habits. The tour is part of their re-induction – both a way to let them know that they are part of our community, that we will continue to love and support them, and a way to allow them the opportunity to articulate what is so special about our school.

Managing behaviour is complex: the method is the message.

Crafting our school culture begins with being absolutely aligned on the purpose of our school; it is the sky that generates our daily climate, it is what we can all see and feel no matter where we are in the organisation or who we are talking to. Families and visitors should feel its warmth every time they are with us. It is our mission, it is our sky; we decide that the sun should always shine. Together, we turn abstract concepts into iterations. What is our school but our children? What is our school's culture but the values shared by our community?

There should be no hollow note, every interaction every day with every pupil needs to be reinforcing. The curriculum is the iteration of our culture; strategies are black type on white pages until they are made manifest by the words and actions of our team. We cannot create concrete edifices that deny agility – build it all but somewhere, suspended in the moment, there has to remain the potential to dismantle, to reshape, to de-clutter and clear away. That means no ego. It also means strength – we will do whatever it takes (tear it all down and start again) but we will do it as a team. No individual needs to pull so hard all the time; no one needs to break.

Culture is relationships; it is team.

When asked for our 'best bet' on the way to develop intentional culture, our thinking so far lies in the principles and procedures shared in this chapter. In summary (and simplicity): commit to simplicity, invest in explanation, listen hard, script in detail then practise and… repeat.

References

Boyce, A. S. et al. (2015) 'Which comes first, organizational culture or performance? A longitudinal study of causal priority with automobile dealerships', *Journal of Organizational Behavior* 36 (3) pp. 339-359.

Collins, J. (2001) *Good to Great*. London: William Collins Books.

Ermisch, J. and Del Bono, E. (2010) *Education mobility in England: the link between the education levels of parents and the educational outcomes of teenagers*. The Sutton Trust.

Goodman, A. and Gregg, P. (eds) (2010) *Poorer children's educational attainment: how important are attitudes and behaviour?* York: Joseph Rowntree Foundation.

Khattab, N. (2015) Students' aspirations, expectations and school achievement: what really matters?, *British Educational Research Journal* 41 (5) pp. 731-748.

Lencioni, P. (2012) *The Advantage: why organisational health trumps everything else in business*. San Francisco: Jossey-Bass.

Menzies, L. (2013) 'Lessons from Sway: What can DJ Sway teach us about 'levelling up' pupil aspirations', *The Centre for Education and Youth* [Online] 1 February. Retrieved from: www.bit.ly/3mTFeSt

Menzies, L. (2013) 'Educational aspirations: How English schools can work with parents to keep them on track', *Joseph Rowntree Foundation* [Online] 29 January. Retrieved from: www.bit.ly/3cDhCwB

Shafer, L. (2013) 'What Makes a Good School Culture?', *Harvard Graduate School of Education* [Online] 23 July. Retrieved from: www.bit.ly/2SdkXc9

Shaw, B., Menzies, L., Bernardes, E., Baars, S., LKMco, Nye, P., Allen, R. and Education Datalab. (2016) *Ethnicity, Gender and Social Mobility*. London: Social Mobility Commission.

Shaw, B., Baars, S., Menzies, L., LKMco, Parameshwaran, M., Allen, R. and Education Datalab (2017) *Low income pupils' progress at secondary school*. London: Social Mobility Commission.

Usable Knowledge (2016) 'Intrinsically Motivated', *Harvard Graduate School of Education* [Online] 11 September. Retrieved from: www.bit.ly/3jgpO8w

Author bio-sketches:

After leaving Ireland to study English at Clare College, Cambridge University, **Jenny Thompson** worked overseas in both Italy and India before becoming a teacher. Jenny moved into leadership as a SENCo and transitioned up from London to Yorkshire where she was accepted onto the Future Leaders programme. She initially joined Dixons Trinity in 2014 and subsequently became head of school. In 2017, Jenny was delighted to be appointed principal. She is now an executive principal at Dixons Academies Trust; she also works as a Behaviour Adviser for the Department for Education.

Throughout his career, from inner-city Leeds to Manchester and Bradford, **Luke Sparkes** has been committed to challenging educational disadvantage in complex urban settings in the north. His reputation was forged as founding principal of Dixons Trinity Academy in Bradford which in January 2014 became the first secondary free school to be judged Outstanding by Ofsted. Nationally, Dixons Trinity's pupil progress is amongst the very best. Luke has advised the Department for Education – writing and speaking widely on education. His influential expertise in school culture is shared through his work as a board member with the Confederation of School Trusts, Teach First's National School Forum and Ambition Institute's Schools Advisory Group. Now working as an executive director across Dixons Academies, one of the highest performing trusts nationally, Luke is shaping the future strategic development of the organisation.

LEADING A DEPARTMENT

SARAH BARKER

From the previous chapter, we can see that the culture of a school is the prerequisite. It is very hard to have an impact or even assess the impact of the leadership of curriculum, the levels of subject-specificity or the leadership of teacher development without getting culture right. But once we have, what remains to be done is hard to pinpoint and implement. In my view, it is hard to read Summer Turner's chapter as a senior leader in a school without concluding that we need to know a lot about a range of subjects and how we ensure that the curriculum is the progression model in different subjects. This is a massive task, but one that is essential we grapple with. So, this book now turns from culture back to curriculum.

Knowing about subject and phase leadership is a crucial aspect of wider school leadership. Both senior leaders and middle leaders need to know significant amounts about subjects. Commonly referred to as the 'engine rooms of the school' those leading departments or phases are often said to drive school improvement. In my experience, an element of getting out of the way of what subject experts are doing is some of the best support senior leaders can give, but how are leaders supposed to know if their middle leaders are performing well? And what do those middle leaders know?

Curricular leadership, as we have heard from Summer Turner, is really hard. Having spent a good proportion of my career believing senior curricular leadership was about asking good questions and assessing the quality of the response, I think that this was insufficient. If one is line managing a department, one needs to know a lot about the substance of that department – one needs a good enough knowledge of the academic subject, the school subject, and the relationship between them – and so much more.

In this chapter, Sarah Barker illustrates the complexity and difficulty of leading one core subject. This chapter is really useful for middle leaders in primary and secondary schools, to those who line manage those middle leaders, and those who lead or manage the line managers. It is an example of the level of complexity that we have to embrace to be the best possible school leaders – it would be a poorer chapter to attempt to do this generically because the challenges and problems manifest themselves very differently. However, the approach to challenges is one that all leaders can take from this chapter.

Sarah is, like many great school leaders, humble while being brilliant, and her exemplification of what a great head of English does here is fascinating.

Being a head of English in a secondary school is a messy, complicated affair.

Whether contractually or de facto, heads of English often find themselves responsible for whole-school literacy, EAL progress, reading interventions, SEND literacy needs, penmanship, staff literacy and oracy. They are expected to combine this kind of variety of responsibilities with the accountability for two GCSE qualifications for every child in each cohort. Some of these responsibilities bring joy and immense satisfaction – there is no better feeling than knowing that your team have brought about results for every child that will be listed on every formal application for life. English and mathematics are the cornerstone qualifications for successful adult life, and this responsibility is a constant presence in the minds of heads of English. Success in our subject can open doors, while failure means the start of adult life on the back foot. It is with this backdrop that heads of English lead their teams. The leader is a bridge from the team to school senior leaders, buffering pressures while striving to drive up standards and ensure that both pupils and colleagues are treated well and are provided with appropriate quality support to learn and to teach. This can be exhausting. Ofsted's 2018 Wellbeing and Workload Survey showed that '76% of teachers report that their job impacts negatively on their mental health' and the 2016 DfE teacher workload survey reported that teachers and middle leaders are working 54.4 hours a week.

It is no surprise, then, that we see the 'hero paradigm' (Gronn 2003) among our middle leaders, along with the old-fashioned underlying belief that we can reasonably expect to apply Great Man Theory to our middle leaders, when what we need is rational, competent, knowledgeable people at the helm of each faculty. English teams are complicated to lead. An array of varied subject knowledge, often meaning a paucity of knowledge in certain areas, means that the head of department or faculty may be faced with a team that has a variety of professional learning requirements so that they may competently teach a broad and rich curriculum. This is not helped by a prevailing attitude of genericism from some leaders and the orthodoxy of school leadership – where there is a focus on pedagogy at the expense of subject knowledge, and a belief that English itself is rather easy to teach. 'Anyone,' I was once told, 'can teach English. Anybody who has been teaching a few years has usually done a spell in an English classroom.' And thus, ten years ago, I was put in my place when arguing for subject-specialists across the key stages, in my ardent attempt to push up standards.

This trope of 'anybody can teach English' has resulted in the common solution in schools of plugging gaps on the English timetable with any colleague with a matching space on their schedule, regardless of responsibility level or knowledge-base. As I've suggested, even within the subject team the range of qualifications held by English specialists is vast. A well-qualified English teacher may well be an expert in Shakespeare, Romanticism and the Gothic, but struggle to teach grammar and punctuation. In 2010, Blake and Shortis found a wide range of degree subjects in a profile of PGCE English trainees, including English literature, media studies, drama/theatre studies, linguistics and cultural studies. In the recommendations of their report, they highlight that a point that 'emerged strongly' from their study is that 'there is a not a perfect match between any single undergraduate degree and the demands of teaching the subject English in secondary schools in England' (Blake and Shortis, 2010).

I would imagine that heads of science, mathematics and many other subjects face similar challenges, and I understand the issue is many multiples more complicated in primary schools. It is to this end that we see traits of the transformational leadership model in leaders, and specifically in heads of English, as they seek to increase the capacity of others to raise pupil attainment. Transformational leadership – that is as we have heard from Barker and Rees in their chapter – a model of leadership in which the leader works to motivate and empower their team members to bring about change and improved effectiveness but without explicitly prioritising subject knowledge. This model is normatively favoured by Western thinking about leadership – it is often pitted against the 'transactional' model of the 'carrot and stick'. However, for a school middle-leader, 'transforming' a team is often beyond our realm, reach and time-constraints.

A systemic misunderstanding of the subject, coupled with some non-specialist school leaders believing that they've done a good job at teaching English in the past, has contributed to the issue faced by heads of English: they are responsible for maximising the achievement and progress of entire cohorts, while simultaneously trying to ensure that every lesson across the faculty is delivered by a teacher with expert subject knowledge. There is an expectation that the head of English is an expert in leadership, pedagogy, all taught elements of the subject, as well as literacy beyond the bounds of English.

This leads to the core question for all school leaders that Barker and Rees raise in their second chapter: how can the leader – in this case, the head of English – manage an efficient and effective department, and what knowledge is needed to do so? The importance of the role, along with the complexity of trying to quality assure subject knowledge across English teams, will be considered and it is useful to consider Bereiter and Scardamalia's categories of knowledge in an attempt to open up the conversation as to how leaders can apply their knowledge to lead efficient and effective departments. These categories of knowledge, as outlined in their chapter, have not been picked apart and applied as discrete separate entities. For this chapter, it is helpful to see and understand that the knowledge types combine and interweave; they are complex and intrinsically connected within each leader. For example, a head of English may use informal knowledge of the team to decide on who will teach which class, which may be based on intricate formal knowledge of the course content, while using impressionistic knowledge when broaching these decisions with each team member.

Opening up a dialogue

If we consider a department that embraces a skills-based model of English teaching, we may see tasks alongside novels or plays such as writing a diary entry, writing a letter, producing a report or writing an article. Most non-specialist teachers would be able to manage this – after all, we're adults, living and functioning in a world where these things crop up in daily life. We all share a relatively sound functioning (if not formal) knowledge base of how to do such things. The same probably applies to reading a novel and discussing the themes and issues.

These, however, bear less relevance to the success criteria for formal qualifications in English language and literature than is reflected in many curriculum models in English. Of course, it's not just about the qualifications. For me, it's about pupils' empowerment and enrichment and for many breaking free from the shackles of disadvantage. I don't believe that writing a character's diary entry at the age of 12 will contribute to achieving these aims. It's a generic activity and offers little to the study of English.

Perhaps some teachers set these tasks as an exercise in empathy – maybe the thinking is that if pupils write about the character's thoughts and feelings, then they are demonstrating empathy. However, the really valuable insights in identifying thoughts and feelings comes through close textual analysis. Writing a diary entry does not help us to place ourselves into a character's position any more than hiding under the tables in a history lesson promotes empathy for those sheltering from overhead attacks at wartime. This sort of task is too simple for secondary English.

If there is a place for teaching personal expression through writing, then we need to equip our pupils with the ability to manipulate language to express themselves beautifully, clearly and accurately. This comes through careful study of the best writers, through explicit vocabulary teaching and through challenging and demanding responses to texts which transcend and extend upon the daily experience of our pupils. In short, the outcome of using language in a variety of interesting, appropriate and engaging ways is facilitated better by explicitly unpicking the knowledge that is used by those with expertise, that is implicit to them, and then ensuring this is taught explicitly so that all pupils can develop this 'skill'. This is not the only outcome of English of course, but it is, nonetheless, a curricular question as outlined by Summer Turner in her chapter and it requires a great deal of knowledge about the subject alongside knowledge of the team.

Using their formal knowledge of the subject area, and their informal knowledge of who best to deploy where, there are layers of approaches which could be considered by the head of English in this situation. Each layer has a different pacing and purpose:

- Curriculum (re)design
- Subject-specific professional learning opportunities

Curriculum (re)design

The head of English could – and often should – take brave steps in the design of their English curriculum, so that clear, rigorous strands run through the Key Stage 3 programmes of study, and feed into the knowledge needed to be prepared well for Key Stages 4 and 5. The design or redesign of the curriculum could be an opportunity to build a culture of excellence for both teachers and pupils. As we see traditional Key Stage 3 novels being taught in a more challenging primary curriculum, we need to adapt and update. If Year 7 pupils are arriving having already read the novels on our curriculum offer, then this is an opportunity for redesign and to increase further the breadth of experience and the challenge in the English curriculum.

This does not mean extended time for GCSE, or anything like it. It also does not mean that we should do this 'because of Ofsted' or 'because leaders say we must'. It means that we need to consider the demands of the specifications on formal qualifications and ensure that we do not do our young people a disservice with a watered-down, skills-driven approach to Key Stage 3. We should feel the moral imperative to *up the ante* in our curriculum. Every teacher in the team should know and understand what we teach and why we teach it, because if we can't articulate that then something has been lost and will be lost in attempting to ensure that the curriculum is the progression model. This lack of curricular understanding is less likely to enable the sharp and effective delivery of an ambitious curriculum. Teachers who are not experienced in the curricular development or inducted into the *how and why* are unlikely to be able to adapt to the complexities of 30 (or 150) pupils learning that curriculum. Rather than bemoaning the idea that Year 10 pupils know 'nothing' about life in Victorian England, or the Romantics, then we can shape their experience at Key Stage 3 so that they enter the GCSE years with a confidence – or automaticity, even – in such areas. There is life beyond Dickens for such enterprises; non-fiction texts, including primary sources and more contemporary works (*The Five: The Untold Lives of the Women Killed by Jack the Ripper* by Hallie Rubenhold, for instance) could enlighten and empower our young people's minds. Where, though, do we start with this mammoth job of curriculum design?

As Summer Turner outlined more generally, we can turn to Michael Young's (2014) concept of 'powerful knowledge' at this point, which is seen as a tool for social justice and equality. It is dynamic and flexible – we adapt and update it as our subject communities do. Powerful knowledge is bounded by three criteria:

1) It is distinct from the 'common sense' knowledge we acquire through our everyday experience.

We do not need to go to school to acquire this knowledge. Our English curriculum does not need to include 'common sense' knowledge, or skills that children will acquire in the workplace. Our English curriculum should seek to liberate children from their daily experience.

2) It is systematic.

Our English curriculum can be planned systematically so that links and connections can be made across the subject. This is crucial insofar as it provides pupils with the ability to make generalisations between concepts.

3) It is specialised.

Powerful knowledge has been developed by subject communities, such as novelists, artists, playwrights and academics in the field. Of course, these examples would look different in other subject areas, but in English, we can look to these groups for guidance on the best subject content.

When it comes to reworking the English curriculum, a good starting point is the end. Decide what you want your pupils to know and experience, and work out why you have made these decisions. This does not have to be driven solely by the next key stage. This is an opportunity to consider what the experts in our subject communities consider to be the best. Where are your gaps? Consider beyond the obvious – think about what you were reading as a teenager and consider whether you have lower expectations for the pupils you teach. Perhaps post-colonial literature is missing, or post-modernism with an explicit understanding of the whys and ways of the genre. It should be possible to step back, look at your existing curriculum and think 'is this really good enough?'

Whether you are looking at a spiral curriculum, in which concepts and knowledge are repeated and reinforced, or perhaps a strand model of the curriculum, where the core content is taught in-depth over a longer period, we can take the minds and hearts of our remarkably well-qualified colleagues to pull together a curriculum bursting with life-changing opportunities.

The practicalities

Informal knowledge of the team, including their breadth of subject knowledge, means that the delegation of this can be crafted for maximum effect. Of course, people need time, so the head of English needs to be able to negotiate this with senior leaders. We see time poured away in some schools: requirements for *all* staff to attend open evenings or an insistence that everybody attends generic learning about ICT systems, regardless of existing knowledge bases. Heads of English are in a position to negotiate this time with senior leaders, and if leaders want to maximise their curriculum development opportunities, they would do well to be receptive to such suggestions. There are ways to be creative here. Schools can and do manage to accommodate these models. In my current school, we ask heads of faculty to organise open evening attendance and to use the remaining staff as they see fit. Heads of faculty have designed their own feedback policies so that feedback is used for maximum impact within each subject domain. If you are a middle leader, discuss such an approach with senior leaders; a one-size-fits-all model of feedback is impractical and often means that teachers in some areas are faced with swathes of written marking that has little impact. Open up the conversation to see how you can gain some time for your team. Senior leaders need to work to be creative with time. A simple cost-analysis of insisting on every teacher attends every event, or attends generic professional learning, or updates displays every term will bring about eye-watering results.

If heads of department propose an alternative, then remember that s/he wants the best outcomes for the school too – after all, in the case of English this person carries the weight of a third of the school's progress measure! Loosening the reins, being creative with time, and trusting your faculty leaders to make the right choice is a strong bet. Staff retention is likely to be strong. Word will spread and recruitment is likely to be easier (and word really does spread among English teams across schools). Lastly – and this may seem like a long shot, but in my experience, it is a good one – results follow because the teachers will have the time to do the things that they want and need to do: plan, teach and give excellent feedback.

Subject-specific professional learning

Professional learning has too often been reduced to a generic model in schools. Brown et al (2016) evaluate the impact of the shifting nature of initial teacher education on subject knowledge and illustrate that, as the demands on schools shift, they 'may prioritise the immediacy of classroom practice or following centralised guidance' when delivering teacher-training.

Time is so precious, yet the model of bringing lots of well-trained smart teachers into one room to deliver a session on how to use, for example, the new whiteboard software or how to use a new management information system add-on, seems to dominate some institutions. That sort of information can be cascaded or – even better – sent out on email with an instruction sheet. We also see generic approaches to teaching and learning in some professional learning sessions, with little thought or nuance applied to the teachers in the room. Talk to any maths teacher who has had to endure an inset day on encouraging pupils to 'extend their written responses' and the problem becomes clear. Broad, one-size-fits-all approaches to differentiation have dominated professional learning across schools, with a tokenistic 'how would this work in your faculty?' activity to give the illusion of relevance. Perhaps you've sat through behaviour management sessions, watching your best behaviour manager politely nodding along, while knowing that your struggling teacher just needs to be backed up by a decent whole-school system? For me, the biggest frustration is the time and expense. A quick head count and a calculation of the average hourly rate will give a horrifying reality check of the real cost of avoidable generic approaches with minimal impact. Just think of how all of these resources could be redeployed into increasing subject knowledge. Think of how our lessons, content and curriculum would soar if we led departments full of teachers who all really, really knew their stuff.

The move to prioritise subject-specific professional learning focused on subject knowledge rather than generic pedagogical or systems-based teacher learning would likely yield improved affective factors in teachers too. Heads of English may feel that they do not have the authority or the autonomy to shift whole-school professional learning priorities, but even in a school where this is not open for discussion, there are opportunities to make this happen within the faculty. Consider each faculty meeting, perhaps one could surrender the agenda to allow for a session on a novel or a play. How much of the agenda can be shared electronically? If meeting time is too precious, then perhaps half of the meeting could go to this or – as my colleague, Kate Richards, designed – the '10-minute golden nugget'. This model could work well. It may take a brave subject leader to step away from 'the way we've always done it' but as it becomes a feature of meetings, then it'll become a joyous habit. And, of course, as we look around each English office and see the vast and impressive range of degrees held, we can rest assured that we really do have the brainpower among us to deliver enriching and high-quality subject-specific professional learning.

Heads of English and senior leaders could lead the way here on delivering these sessions, and then pass the baton to the team to continue sharing expertise. Heads of English could also liaise with senior leaders to negotiate the professional learning book-buying budget being extended to faculties. We expect teachers to read widely, but we should not expect them to spend their own money on such ventures. Stock up on texts to further the subject knowledge of the team and take the recommendations of what to read from the experts within the team. If you're stuck for ideas, then I have found the following texts to be excellent resources. This is just a starting point and I must emphasise that your own team will be in a better position to recommend apt choices for your context and, of course, senior leaders who line manage other departments should prioritise immersing themselves in the knowledge of those departments.

Books for Shakespeare

- *On Shakespeare's Sonnets: A Poets' Celebration* by Hannah Crowforth and Elizabeth Scott-Baumann (Bloomsbury Arden, 2016)
- *Shakespeare the Thinker* by A. D. Nuttall (Yale University Press, 2008)
- *Shakespeare's Language* by Frank Kermode (Penguin, 2001)
- *The Cambridge Companion to Shakespearean Tragedy* by Claire McEachern (Cambridge University Press, 2013)
- The Arden Shakespeare edition for any of your Shakespeare curriculum

Books for 19th century texts

- *Blake* by Peter Ackroyd (Vintage, 1996)
- *The Five: The Untold Lives of the Women Killed by Jack the Ripper* by Hallie Rubenhold (Black Swan, 2019)
- *Literary Remains: Representations of Death and Burial in Victorian England* by Mary Elizabeth Hotz (State University of New York Press, 2010)

Books for literacy

- *Thinking Reading: What every secondary teacher needs to know about reading* by James Murphy and Diane Murphy (John Catt Educational, 2018)
- *Reading Reconsidered: A Practical Guide to Rigorous Literacy Instruction* by Doug Lemov, Colleen Driggs and Erica Woolway (Jossey-Bass, 2016)
- *Closing the Vocabulary Gap* by Alex Quigley (Routledge, 2016)

Books for literary criticism and English pedagogy

- *A Companion to the History of the Book* by Simon Eliot and Jonathan Rose (Wiley-Blackwell, 2009)
- *The Art of Fiction* by David Lodge (Penguin, 1992)
- *The Point of Poetry* by Joe Nutt (Unbound, 2019)
- *A History of Black and Asian writing in Britain* by C. L. Innes (Cambridge University Press 2013)
- *How to teach English literature: Overcoming cultural poverty* by Jennifer Webb (John Catt Educational, 2019)
- *How to Teach: English: Novels, non-fiction and their artful navigation* by Chris Curtis (Independent Thinking Press, 2019)

The decentralisation of education in the current era has led to the loss of some local-authority led networks – at least, this is my experience in Bristol. For a short while, after the local authority-run English hubs were disbanded, we tried to continue to meet and network, but these efforts inevitably fell by the wayside. What has risen from the ashes, though, is a network of schools that are willing to share out their subject expertise in English. We no longer need to look in-house for all of our answers. Groups of schools are collaborating and sharing both lecture-style events (we have run a 'Grade 9 Jekyll and Hyde Workshop' recently which was three hours long and attended by five other schools) and the beauty of these is that teachers are attending to learn too. At our Jekyll and Hyde event, one teacher (Clare Doyle) made an audio file of the whole event on her phone – 'it was like being at university again!' she said. While over 100 pupils benefited from a high-brow lecture, over ten teachers also came to learn. Our lecturer for this was Robert Flitter, a phenomenal English teacher with a bachelor's and master's degree in history, who completed his master's dissertation on the flâneur. He took the pupils through a history of Victorian London, and all the historical elements of the novel. It was enlightening and powerful for all involved. This is the kind of dialogue that we could and should be opening up.

The English language dilemma

What exactly do we mean by 'English language'? I am not posing this question to dismiss the subject. I have strong ideas about what it means and entails. Discussions with other English teachers yield similar thoughts: a field which we can divide into semantics, grammar, discourse analysis and how we control and manipulate language for effect. The study of the English language is one of empowerment – we can teach pupils to recognise bias in writing and to know and understand why a well-crafted text is likely to achieve its aim. In teaching the mechanics of language, we can ensure that pupils enter the adult world being understood. Effective understanding of language enables us to form effective relationships and communicate well. Despite this, it is clumsily handled by examination boards, deprioritised by English teams, and conflated with 'literacy' by non-specialists. This is an example of a subject-specific challenge that heads of department might need to confront.

If we look at the English Language curriculum, and even the content of the current English language qualifications, how much of this do we actually include in our curriculum plans? A long-standing adage which I have heard regularly since my training in 2003 is 'we teach English language through English literature.' I am not sure that this is always true, though. I'm not convinced that we have clear idea of what it means to teach English language as a discrete subject, so this claim to 'teach language through literature' becomes the justification for a literature-only Key Stage 3, and an exam-question driven Key Stage 4. A further complication is the 'literacy across the curriculum' strategy, present in most schools. Literacy, of course, is everybody's responsibility. How, then, can we protect it as our own, and how can we ensure a high-quality curriculum within the faculty?

Start big. Pull apart the differences between English language, English literature and literacy. Of course, there will be crossovers – this will be more of a Venn diagram than three lists. Consider what is assessed at the end of each key stage. You may find that the content that the examination boards are assessing in English language bears a closer resemblance to English literature. Your own overview will indicate exactly what needs to be delivered in your faculty, and when and, perhaps, how. If you wish to teach language through literature, then high-quality linguistic analysis will be embedded within your literature units. The experts in your teams will be able to design such a curriculum (or where they can't, we must recruit or train them to be able to); this is where collaborative planning can really gain a foothold. You will also have identified the areas which should be promoted and taught across all subjects, which is our 'literacy across the curriculum' framework. Liaise with senior leaders to ensure that there is somebody to take ownership of this. It should not fall to the head of English – in fact, as a whole-school strategy, it should be a leadership role. You have the subject expertise within your team to advise on what this should look like, though.

Quality assurance in English: the book scrutiny

Heads of English will be guided by whole-school systems on the format and frequency of quality assurance. Whether it's the book scrutiny, or formal observations, or data analysis, we need to exercise caution when undertaking these activities in quality assurance. It's complex and tempting to simplify into tick-boxes, especially when both workload and accountability of a head of English are so high. Whether heads of English are scrutinising books, undertaking long observations with a generic focus, or analysing internal data, it would be worth considering that learning cannot be 'seen' and as Soderstrom and Bjork explain, 'the goal of instruction is to facilitate learning, which must be inferred at some point after instruction' (2013). Additionally, 'Learning, however, must be distinguished from performance, which is what can be observed and measured during instruction or training' (ibid).

This is a particularly important point when it comes to book scrutinies. The scrutineer can, possibly, glean some ideas about presentation and handwriting, pupil attendance, quantity of writing and other ostensible factors of a lesson. However, we must look to the research base to see that we cannot 'see' learning in books. This is because learning does not take place in books and – while this may sound obvious – I know of school leaders who are still making dubious comments about the quality of learning in books. Neat books with loads of writing and worksheets glued in perfectly are simply evidence that the pupil is busy. One of Coe's poor proxies for learning is 'students are busy: lots of work is done (especially written work)', yet the 'busy' book is too often hailed as being packed full of learning. It's not. It's just packed full of stuff. A book which is too busy can become a distraction, especially when it comes to revision. Peps McCrea's *Memorable Teaching* is a crucial text for reflecting on such areas of our practice. He writes, 'teaching is a zero-sum game. If it's not adding to the learning, it's subtracting from it' (McCrea, 2017, p. 24). This includes superfluous texts and images on slides and worksheets.

What, then, can we focus on? In 2019, Ofsted undertook a pilot study into book scrutinies. While the provenance of this study may be of concern to some, it is worth looking at their book scrutiny indicators – largely because they are compatible with a reduction in workload for both the teacher and the person carrying out the quality assurance.

Ofsted book scrutiny indicators for pilot study:

- Building on previous learning
- Depth and breadth of coverage

- Pupils' progress
- Practice

Detail of these indicators can be found in the 'Workbook scrutiny: Ensuring validity and reliability in inspections' report. Heads of English may find that the first and second indicators are particularly useful for faculty quality assurance processes. These indicators give us a chance to see whether – and how – the curriculum is being covered and sequenced. We can garner an understanding of the tasks set and the learning they are supposed to facilitate within our subject area and make a judgement as to whether these are appropriate to the class group. Again, each head of English needs to remember that some parts of our subject area need deep and rich discussion and so a book which is not packed with immaculate writing is not always an indication of a lack of learning.

All of this leads to more discussion on how schools can support with enhanced and deeper ways of strengthening this element of the formal knowledge of teams. While our subject association(s) are dwindling in membership, we can still turn to our subject communities as a collection of experts. Releasing teachers to undertake master's degrees in relevant subjects is powerful and grants access to the very materials that we can use to extend our knowledge. Schools should (and most can) support with this, whether financially or with the provision of time. It is important that heads of English feel confident to discuss and request support for these things. Whatever the finances, the core business of improving our pupils' life chances must take priority for senior leaders, executive boards and CEOs. A long-term view of investing in teachers in this way is transformative. Below is one outline of how this could look for heads of English, leading their team forward, unpicking the tangled complexities of their brilliant and complex – and brilliantly complex – teams.

	Year 1	Year 2	Year 3	Year 4	Year 5
Ongoing – internal	Monthly in-house English-specific learning	Monthly in-house English-specific learning	Monthly in-house English-specific learning	Monthly in-house English-specific learning	Monthly in-house English-specific learning
Ongoing – Outreach	Cross-LA/MAT/area Grade 9 workshop		Cross-LA/MAT/area Grade 9 workshop		Cross-LA/MAT/area Grade 9 workshop
Medium-term	Two teachers supported with MA English studies. Released during school time to study and granted a study day each long term.			Two teachers supported with MA English studies. Released during school time to study and granted a study day each long term.	
Long-term	Key Stage 3 curriculum review, develop, redesign – expert teachers assigned to units. Time given over from lower-impact school commitments.				

References

Blake, J. and Shortis, T. (2010) 'Who's prepared to teach school English?', *Committee for Linguistics in Education*. London: Kings College London.

Brown, T., Rowley, H. and Smith, K. (2016) 'Sliding subject positions: knowledge and teacher educators', *British Educational Research Journal* 42 (3) p. 494.

Higton, J., Leonardi, S., Richards, N., Choudhoury, A., CFE Research, Sofroniou, N., Owen, D., Institute for Employment Research and University of Warwick (2017) *Teacher Workload Survey 2016*. London: The Stationery Office.

McCrea, P. (2017) *Memorable Teaching*. Scotts Valley, CA: CreateSpace.

Ofsted (2019) 'Workbook scrutiny: Ensuring validity and reliability in inspection'. London: The Stationery Office.

Scott, B. and Vidakovic, I. (2018) 'Teacher well-being and workload survey: Interim findings', *Ofsted blog: schools, early years, further education and skills* [Online] 30 November. Retrieved from: www.bit.ly/2G8vNho

Snider, V. E. (2004) 'A Comparison of Spiral Versus Strand Curriculum', *Journal of Direct Instruction* 4 (1) p. 29.

Wise, C. and Bennett, N. (2003) *The future role of middle leaders in secondary schools: a survey of middle leaders in secondary schools in England*. London: National College for School Leadership.

Young, M., Lambert, D., Roberts, C. and Roberts, M. (2014) *Knowledge and the Future School: Curriculum and Social Justice*. London: Bloomsbury pp. 74-75.

Author bio-sketch:

Sarah Barker has been an English teacher for 16 years. She lives in Bristol and works at Orchard School. Sarah has led two English departments for the last ten years and been an assistant head for two years. She is now a teacher of English while completing her MA in English Literature. Sarah is interested in curriculum, pedagogy and research into how we can raise attainment for the most disadvantaged children. She blogs at roundlearning.org and tweets as @mssfax.

ASSESSMENT
BY MATT STANFORD

In 2015, as a new headteacher of a secondary school in Cambridgeshire, I looked at our assessment system. We had a combination of flight paths, replacement national curriculum levels that were, in fact, prose descriptors for each subject (i.e. just the same as levels), and a confusing amalgamation of formative and summative assessment that really acted as neither.

I knew from the writings of Daisy Christodoulou and Daniel Koretz that we needed to stop doing this, and if possible we had to do something better.

Fortunately, the history department, led at that time by Matt Stanford, had already stopped using national curriculum levels and so had a model. Matt was tired of generic approaches being foisted on his subject, and so he expertly led the school through a review of our assessment practices that allowed respect for subject disciplines. Matt is one of the most well-read people I know and – like many of the contributors to this book – very humble. He is open to suggestions and to the idea that we are unlikely to have the final word, but that we know enough to have a better approach than is the current orthodoxy.

As a result of Matt's work, all the schools that I have led since then have been significantly better – including those which he has not worked in himself, and my understanding of assessment theory, and the implementation of that theory, has been much better. He is also a phenomenal writer and I challenge you not to enjoy this chapter as a narrative, let alone as an education. When I was privileged to work with Matt, I was also privy to (and the subject of) a first-hand exemplification of 'managing up' – something that he did so skilfully because he was so knowledgeable about history and assessment.

A Clever Little Trick

An analogy by way of an introduction:

'There's a big trick being played with the small bulbs. The whole thing has to do with the financial-industrial plan...

'The factory had to fulfil the plan. Well, so they went and fulfilled it....

'Let's suppose that according to the plan they had to fill a production quota of a million candle power. Well, now just imagine – are they going to start producing this million in small bulbs? They wouldn't make it in two years, the devils. So they decided to get there with big bulbs. Whether you make small bulbs or big ones, the work is the same. But you don't need nearly so many. And so, those devils have settled on big bulbs. They're turning them out like pancakes.' (Zoshchenko, 1975, pp. 176-8)

In Mikhail Zoshchenko's satirical short story *A Clever Little Trick*, written in the Soviet Union at the time of the industrialisation drive known as the Five Year Plans, the protagonist complains that he can never find the right lightbulbs. The only ones he can get are super powerful ones that show up the cracks in the ceiling, give him headaches and burn through electricity at an alarming rate. The reason for the lack of sensible bulbs is revealed by the man who comes to read the electricity meter – the output of the lightbulb factory was simply measured in candle power.

At this time, Stalin believed that the economic backwardness of the Soviet Union left it and its revolution vulnerable to the predations of its capitalist neighbours. To defend itself, the Soviet government plunged the country into a forced industrial revolution, investing mind-bogglingly huge sums of financial and human capital into the creation of mines, steelworks, factories and railways. However, in the absence of the 'invisible hand' of the capitalist market to set production levels, how would the government, based in a Moscow, know how much or what was needed? How many tonnes of steel, how many screws, how many tractors would be needed to fulfil the plan? How, also, would the government know that its orders were being carried out? How would they know if their plans were being scuppered by the machinations of wreckers and saboteurs? The answer was simple – quotas were set centrally in Moscow. Every mine and every factory were given a target to meet every year, its output was measured and assessed and a judgement was made as to whether it had met its targets. Failure to meet these quotas would have serious, often lethal, repercussions for the managers of the Soviet system; time in the prison camps of Siberia often the reward for not fulfilling the plan. However, if targets were met, there were frequently financial and social rewards that could transform someone's life. There were huge incentives for managers to do everything they could to make sure the plan was fulfilled. Stakes were high. Accountability was absolute. And chaos reigned.

As in Zoshchenko's example, the system created some very perverse incentives. The reason that the protagonist can't find a useful lightbulb is that the lightbulb factory boss has a target set, not in thousands of lightbulbs but wattage, in candle power. The boss, wishing to avoid the Siberian Gulag and wishing to achieve the pay rise, has every incentive to meet the plan and produce the most illumination he can. If his factory can churn out high-powered bulbs, he can report to his bosses back in Moscow, with his hand on his heart, that his factory has exceeded the plan. All of this even though no one in Leningrad can find a decent bulb for their bathroom. While only a small percentage of school leaders are Stalin-like psychopathic despots, this story does model some of the issues faced by school leaders when thinking about assessment. As a school leader you probably do not have the capacity to have people deported to Siberian Gulags but you do the capacity to create acres of meaningless work, reward chance, incompetence and irrelevance, and generate oceans of unnecessary stress, fear and anger amongst your staff whilst never actually helping your institution achieve its desired aims. Just as in the Soviet Union, much damage can be done through the misunderstanding, misapplication and mismanagement of measurement systems.

In a school, the most important measurement system is the system that the school uses to assess pupils' knowledge and understanding. This chapter will seek to highlight some ways in which leaders can make these systems unhelpful and ineffective and suggest some ways in which leaders can hope to minimise the unintended consequences and perverse incentive of their systems and help their staff manage their use of systems that actually measure what they value. This will be done by asking the reader to reflect on some questions related to what, when, how and why pupils should be assessed in schools.

Do the teachers in your school know what they are trying to assess and does the curriculum of your school reflect that?

Subjects as a reflection of the domain; long-term memory, 'finger-tip' and 'residue' knowledge; the curriculum as progression model.

Questions about assessment are questions with intended outcomes. In the Soviet Union the end-goal was a communist utopia with industrialisation being seen as the path to its achievement. In a school it is about the education of young people and the curriculum is the path to achieving that.[1] Therefore, questions of assessment are, necessarily, questions of curriculum.

Just as leading a school is a domain-specific pursuit, so is leading a department or faculty in a school. This is not only because the teachers of design and technology face different practical challenges to, say, the teachers of Spanish, but because the school subjects are themselves derived from different academic domains. Subject leaders in schools must understand this and senior leaders must help them in this endeavour. Do you know if subject leaders and teachers in your school can answer the challenges set out by Alex Standish and Alka Sehgal Cuthbert in their book *What Should Schools Teach?*

'We think that all teachers and schools should know answers to the following questions: what does it mean to study a discipline and what is its value? Why is disciplinary knowledge important for the curriculum? What is a school subject and how are subjects related to disciplines? What different forms does knowledge take and what implications does this have for structuring the curriculum? How does disciplinary knowledge contribute to the education of children? Can and should all children learn disciplinary knowledge? What happens if children miss out on academic knowledge?' (Standish and Cuthbert, 2017)

If the teachers in your school do not know what they are trying to teach their pupils, they will not be able to assess it. If they do not have an awareness of, and some expertise in the domain of their subject discipline, then they cannot formulate a meaningful curriculum that represents an appropriate sample of that domain. If they cannot formulate a meaningful curriculum they cannot create meaningful assessments because they will not know what combination

---

1.   This idea of the curriculum as a path or journey is borrowed from Christine Counsell. Her blog series on curricular thinking for school leaders, although incomplete at the time of writing, is superb (Counsell, 2018a).

of substantive and disciplinary knowledge[2] they are looking for their pupils to demonstrate. If a subject leader is unable to do those things they will not be able to create or administer a curriculum that reflects a model of progression in their subject because they will not be able to say for certain which parts of that curriculum are more demanding than others for pupils, let alone what makes them demanding. The knock-on effect of this is that it unlikely that they will be able to justify the sequencing of the curriculum and the role of memory within that. Whether or not your school, like Ofsted, subscribes to Sweller, Ayres and Kalyuga's belief that 'learning is defined as an alteration in long-term memory' (Sweller et al, 2011),[3] it is highly likely that there are some things that subject leaders will want their pupils to retain, in detail, over a long period and other things for which it is more important to retain only a sense of. Christine Counsell has distinguished between these two types of knowledge as 'fingertip' and 'residue' knowledge. For Counsell, 'fingertip' knowledge is:

'the kind of detail that one needs in ready memory and that is acquired through familiarity after extensive enquiry. It does not matter if much of the detail then falls away. The second type [residue knowledge] can be likened to the residue in a sieve. It is not just the ability to remember that the Tudors came before the Stuarts and that they used parliament a lot. It is also the loose, amorphous objective of a 'sense of period'... Such a residue is bound to enrich current and future study by preventing anachronism and sharpening judgement, even after the particular stories and scenes have long receded.' (Counsell 2000)

Knowing what needs to be known by pupils at each stage is vital to the construction of curriculum and a good assessment system will be the measure not only of pupils' knowledge of that curriculum but of the subject leaders' ability to construct it in the first place.

---

2.   The best definition I have found of these concepts comes, again from Christine Counsell's work: 'Substantive knowledge is the content that teachers teach as established fact – whether common convention, concept or warranted account of reality. You might want pupils to know of crotchets, percentages, the Treaty of Waitangi, Debussy or prokaryotic cells. In calling this 'substantive', we are treating the material presented as givens. Disciplinary knowledge, by contrast, is a curricular term for what pupils learn about how that knowledge was established, its degree of certainty and how it continues to be revised by scholars, artists or professional practice. It is that part of the subject where pupils understand each discipline as a tradition of enquiry with its own distinctive pursuit of truth.' (Counsell, 2018b)

3.   For an interesting discussion on the definition of 'learning' see Willingham, 1998.

Do the subject leaders in your school understand how to assess what they want to assess?

Tests as proxies and samples; reliability of testing; multiple-choice questions as an example

Once subject leaders have decided what it is that they wish to teach, how it should be sequenced and what they wish to test in assessments they must consider how this is to be done. In his brilliant book, *Measuring Up – What Educational Testing Really Tells Us*, the American educationalist Daniel Koretz asserts: 'Test scores usually do not provide a direct and complete measure of educational achievement. Rather they are incomplete measures, proxies for the more comprehensive measures that we would ideally use but that are generally unavailable to us.' (Koretz, 2008, p. 9)

Once subject leaders have decided what their subject domain involves and have constructed a curriculum that is an appropriate proxy for the domain, they then need to give thought as to what part of the curriculum (and, therefore, what part of the domain) the assessments they set require are testing. If subject leaders are setting, for example, essays, are they looking for substantive and disciplinary knowledge in the pupils' responses to the questions? Do they understand what these mean more than 'AO1 and AO3 from the GCSE spec'? This must, even at key stages that end with a public examination, be wider than just the exam specification.[4] As Daisy Christodoulou states: 'Exams are only samples from wider domains, and because of this, there will always be ways of doing well on them that do not lead to genuine learning... The moment we start to target the exam, then the exam will stop being a valid measure.' (Christodoulou, 2016, p. 145)

If all pupils do is exam practice, unless the teacher is thorough enough so that they have drilled the pupils in every combination of exam-question-style

---

4.   Even though a GCSE examination has to be confined to that which is included in the specification and, therefore, give the impression that concerns about the wider 'domain' of the subject are irrelevant, there the very often domain-specific or technical ways in which terms are used that require teachers to think more deeply than just refer to the specification. For example, look at the difference between the use of the word 'explain' in religious studies and history GCSE specifications: for AQA Religious Studies A (8062) students must 'explain contrasting beliefs' (AQA 2017) whereas the OCR History A Explaining the Modern World (J410) students should be able 'to explain how historians... use the physical fabric of Kenilworth Castle... to understand the purpose of the site' (OCR, 2018). One is asking for examples and one is asking for 'reasons why'. Neither specification makes this distinction clear.

and point of content, there will be questions missed out. Understanding the fundamental concepts required by the specification will, usually, be of greater benefit than simply repeating exam questions. Even when the content of the test is well selected as a useful sample of the curriculum there are, of course, many ways in which the test itself can fall short of expectations. Koretz defines 'reliable' tests as those are that are consistent – a test is very reliable if one can rely on it to turn the same inputs into the same outputs. This does not necessarily mean that it is 'accurate' or even useful, only that one possible reason for its 'un-usefulness' has been addressed. (Koretz, 2008, p. 30-1)

Have subject leaders considered factors that might affect the reliability of the tests such as whether pupils all had the same opportunity to revise, whether they all sat the test in the same conditions, whether they all the same time to complete the tests, whether the teachers all gave the same emphasis to the different elements of the tests?[5]

Do subject leaders in your school have a clear understanding of why children are being tested?

Assessment for learning; assessment for performance management.

Since the 1990s, Dylan Wiliam in has been writing about the use of assessment for learning in education. While this has been much abused and misunderstood in the English education system it still, if understood correctly, can provide positive results. One of the things that Wiliam has done is to highlight the work of Ruth Butler, who explored the impact on pupils' progress of comments with and without grades on their work. What Butler and Wiliam found has implications for the subject leaders' thinking about the purpose of testing. If the test is purely to see what pupils know, then there is no requirement to think about the ways in the feeding-back of the test might help a pupil improve. However, if the point of the test is to help pupils learn then this is the most important part of the whole exercise.

Do subject leaders have a clear understanding of what they are asking pupils to do with the feedback they receive and when and why they might, or might not, share grades, ranks or scores with their pupils? Do they have a clear understanding of the distinction between summative and formative assessment and are they, and their pupils, aware of when they are doing each?

---

5.   For a more thorough discussion on this question, see chapter 7 of Koretz (2008).

Similarly, are individual pieces of work, tests, single sets of grades and so on, being used by subject leaders to judge the performance of teachers? Have you considered what impact raising the stakes of these tests will have on the reliability of the data? Have you considered what perfectly understandable, if undesirable, behaviours might be encouraged by this metric? When is using assessment data valid way of judging a teacher's performance? How do you avoid creating a system where the rational response of the participants is to create only one type of lightbulb?[6]

Do you have a clear picture of who needs to know what about your assessment system?

Validity; what pupils, teachers, subject leaders, senior leaders and external auditors need to know about 'how your pupils are doing'.

The partner of reliability in education testing is validity. Validity is not a measure of a test but a measure of the inferences made from the results of a test. In other words, it is a question that pertains to the people who are looking at the test results. Too often, information that is perfectly useful in one way is used to make invalid, or partly valid, conclusions. For example, a percentage grade on a maths test covering algebra might be a useful piece of data to see is a pupil has understood a new mathematical concept. However, if compared to a higher grade on the previous test on, say, geometry there are many schools in which a 'data manager' or school leader might make an invalid inference that the pupil has stopped making progress in mathematics even though their understanding of algebra has developed.

School leaders need to think very carefully about who needs to know what information about which parts of pupils' performance on assessments. The following are some questions that might be useful to consider:

- Do pupils need to know how well they did on an assessment?

Yes and no. Thought should be given as to whether the test is summative or formative. If the assessment is designed to be formative, improve a pupil's attainment, then the most important thing is that pupil knows what they need

---

6.   This tendency of the test to corrupt that which it purports to assess is known as Campbell's law after the work of the American sociologist Donald Campbell. For more on this and the educationalist E. F. Lindquist's analysis of its effects on education see Chapter 4 of Koretz (2017).

to do differently to improve their result. Every teacher can conceive of situations where it might prove unhelpful to let a pupil know just how well or badly they have done. Have the teachers in your school and their subject leaders considered these questions when giving feedback on tests? Similarly, if your teachers are trying to assess a pupil's understanding of a sample of the domain of a subject, this is a difficult thing to do. Reducing this task to 'child-friendly' mark schemes or similar things can often obscure the complexity of the assessment and, therefore, impede the reliability of that assessment. I would argue that mark schemes are for teachers and formative feedback is for pupils.

If the assessment is summative, purely to report the current state of a pupil's knowledge, understanding or performance, then have teachers thought about what kind of numbers or grades actually convey useful information about a pupil's attainment? What might be the benefits of reporting to a pupil the results of a cross-country race in minutes and seconds as opposed to the rank she finished? Does the pupil need to know what the average time was? Would it be better to report the mean, median or (possibly in other contexts) modal average? When might knowing the centile or quartile which her time falls into be more useful? Similarly, have teachers given consideration to what data-set might these statistics be drawn from? If one class, taught by a former weight-lifter, do the cross-country in the driving sleet of December, why might their data skew the 'summative' results of the class who were taught by the former Olympic distance runner who chose a mild, sunny afternoon in May for her class's run?

There might well be merit in a pupil knowing that her time was in the bottom quartile of the class in a cross-country run. However, this *summary* of their performance is not on its own going to help the pupil *form* better results. It may act as a 'wake-up call' that spurs a better performance but it might, just as equally, foment resentment, anger, frustration or self-disgust. After all, she probably noticed that three-quarters of the class were back before her and might not feel that she needed to be told again. However, formative feedback offering expert advice on posture, strengthening exercises and gait is much more likely to improve her running time. If that is the aim, then teachers should carefully consider when, how and why summative results are shared with pupils. Summative data is not formative data and everyone involved in assessment in schools must understand this.

Do teachers need to know how well a pupil did on an assessment?

Yes. However, they shouldn't only be relying on the formal assessment system to make this judgement. Teachers are trained professionals and, as such, they will make many judgements about the performance of the pupils in their charge, whether these are based on perceptions of behaviour, conversations with pupils, class discussion, reading a pupil's book, data from external sources, conversations with other members of staff, 'formal assessments' such as tests, essays or performances or public examinations. As professionals, they should acknowledge that these are all part of the way in which a teacher assesses a child's knowledge of the curriculum.

Does a subject leader need to know how well a pupil did on an assessment?

Yes and no. Subject leaders should be able to use the assessment and reporting systems in your school to find out that information fairly quickly and easily. However, it would seem unreasonable to ask them to know about the current performance of any pupil at the drop of a hat. This is because assessments of pupils' progress is – as discussed above – complicated, requirements like this will encourage the collation and maintenance of collections of useless data. A subject leader might be able to very quickly lay their hands on marks from a recent assessment but if they claim that they can find out how a child they do not teach is doing in a matter of seconds, they are probably looking at data that cannot tell them anything particularly useful.

Teachers should keep information about their pupils. This information should be made available to subject leaders and senior leaders if required. However, it should be kept for the teacher, in ways that are most useful to each individual teacher. Your teachers should have the freedom to create 'messy markbooks' (Counsell and Carr, 2014). You want your teachers to be expert in the very technical subject of the progress of the pupils they teach and technical documents to support experts are, almost by definition, difficult to understand.

Does a senior leader need to know how well a pupil did on an assessment?

Yes and no. Instead of collating marks from individual tests and assessments, school leaders might be better off spending their time supporting pupils to behave, coaching teachers to trying to understand the principles of assessment, dealing with parents, or giving space for curricular thought. For instance, even if a head knew what percentages Year 8 got on their tests in drama without at least some understanding of the questions Standish and Cuthbert asked subject disciplines, without a knowledge of whether the curriculum was a reasonable sample of the domain, without knowing whether the test was written, administered and marked in ways that would help generate reliable data, what possible valid conclusions could be drawn from this information? As with subject leaders, unless there are issues where a particular pupil's work is of importance, a senior leader needs only to know if the subject leader knows whether the teachers know how well a child is doing.

Do your assessment system, line management systems, quality assurance systems and reporting systems allow this to happen?

If there are problems, how might you find out where the weak link in the chain is? How might inflexible, 'data-driven' models (for example percentages of grades) mask real problems? (When might you be acting like the Soviet central planner who is delighted with the output of the Leningrad lightbulb factory?)

Do parents and carers need to know how well their child did on an assessment?

Yes. It goes without saying that any piece of data held by a school should be available to parents and carers if asked for, there is merit in thinking about what information is volunteered. There may be very good reasons to explicitly ask parents and carers to acknowledge that they have seen the summative grade awarded to an individual English essay. However, if that English essay is just one data-point in a wider assessment of a pupil's progress, is that made clear by your assessment and reporting systems?

It is vital parents and carers should know what is being taught, how much of that their child has learned and what practical steps they can take to support the child to help them learn more. Might there be benefits for asking parents and carers to acknowledge that they have seen their child taking steps to address points made in formative feedback?

Do your assessment and reporting systems allow these things to happen?

A model of an assessment system

The following is a description of an assessment system used at Cottenham Village College, a high-performing comprehensive secondary school in England.[7] While this model was not perfect, it did embody many of the principles outlined previously.

---

7.   This is a description of the assessment system used at Cottenham Village College. It was largely designed by Geraint Brown, Stuart Lock and Matt Stanford but with the help and input of many of the staff at that school.

1. For Key Stage 3, teachers and subject leaders design curricula with the intention of making the curriculum the progression model.[8] For Key Stage 4, they work from the best GCSE specification available to them.

   1.1 The focus of multiple whole-staff training sessions has been used to build the staff's capacity to do this. This has included looking at the ideas of substantive and disciplinary knowledge, the educative, utilitarian and moral reasons for selecting curriculum content and thought about how this knowledge is retained.

2. While there is a whole-school policy given guidance about the frequency of marking and feedback, responsibility for deciding what this looks like in the different subjects falls to those subject leaders.

   2.1 Subject leaders to set out a clear rationale for assessing what they are assessing and how this is done and these are added as appendices to the assessment policy.

   2.2 Out of respect for the differences between the hierarchical and cumulative nature of different subjects, the number of prior experience pupils might have of subjects, timetable restrictions and teacher workload, there are no school-wide deadlines nor 'data-drops' which require the uploading of grades for individual pieces of work. This also removes the temptation of subject leaders or assistant heads to (mis)use that data to make judgements about the performance of the staff and pupils. There are, however, two exceptions to this:

---

8. The idea of the curriculum 'being the progression model' is simply the idea that the things that at taught later are more difficult or require more knowledge than those taught earlier. The Associated Board of the Royal Schools of Music 'grade' exams are a very good example of this: a 'pass' at Grade 2 is a better result than a 'distinction' at Grade 1. This is because the range of things on which the candidate might be tested (i.e. the curriculum) at Grade 2 includes all of the theory and exercises from Grade 1, all of the physical strength and dexterity needed for the Grade 1 performance pieces as well as new theory and exercises and new performance pieces that are harder than those of the earlier grade. So a candidate achieving a 'pass' at the higher grade has made progress in her piano playing despite getting a lower grade because the content of the curriculum is more challenging – in other words, the curriculum is the progression model. For a practical example of what this looks like in one subject in a secondary school see Stanford (2019).

○ A baseline test around the beginning of the year.

□ What form this takes is left to the professional judgement of the subject leader – baselines in English which Year 7 pupils have been studying since day one of school will look different to those in, say, Spanish, which many pupils will never have studied before in their lives, or religious education in which pupils from different primary schools may have studied different parts of different world religions.

□ While this is required in the first half term of the year, it only has to be reported to subject, rather than school, leadership.

○ A summative end-of-year exam.

□ This will be described in detail.

3. Summative 'Attainment Grades' that are clearly and deliberately de-coupled from the assessment of individual pieces of work are reported to parents and carers twice a year.

3.1 These 'Attainment Grades' are not the grades that pupils received for individual pieces of work. Instead they are designed to reflect the teachers' professional judgement about how much of the curriculum (meaning both substantive and disciplinary knowledge) has been learned by the pupil. These judgements are based on the following level-descriptors:

A	The pupil has performed exceptionally well in all aspects of the subject's curriculum so far, demonstrating comprehensive knowledge and understanding. Their learning is usually well above the average.
B	The pupil's performance has been at least good in all aspects of the subject's curriculum so far, demonstrating very secure knowledge and understanding. Their learning is usually above the average.
C	The pupil has performed at least competently in all aspects of the subject's curriculum so far, demonstrating sound knowledge and understanding. Their learning is usually around the average.
D	The pupil has performed at least at a basic level in all aspects of the subject's curriculum so far, demonstrating elementary knowledge and understanding. Their learning is usually slightly below the average.

E	The pupil's performance has been weak in most aspects of the subject's curriculum so far, demonstrating limited knowledge and understanding. Their learning is usually well below the average.

3.2 These descriptors are designed to inform teachers' professional judgements in a 'best fit' model. They are not to be further sub-divided or criterion-referenced. While departments should take opportunities to moderate their judgements through comparison and discussion, explicit evidence of this is not required at any reporting stage. This is designed to allow the teacher to use any of the evidence available to them, soft, hard, numerical or impressionistic to inform their judgement. For example, if a pupil delivers a stunning Shakespeare soliloquy in an end-of-unit drama 'exam' but is unable to get a laugh in a piece of classwork on slap-stick and does terribly on the 'fun quiz' on Brecht, the teacher can weigh up all of that data in making their judgement. In short, the grade should reflect what can be learned about the pupil's knowledge from all of the tools in the teacher's 'assessment toolbox' and everything recorded in their 'messy markbook'.

3.3 These grades are designed to be easily comprehensible – an 'A' is really good, a 'C' is good and an 'E' is problematic.

3.4 The grades are not designed to tell parents and carers or school leaders what has been learned: only how much has been learned. They are flags not maps.

3.5 If parents and carers want to know more about how the judgements were made by individual teachers, those conversations can, of course, happen. Often the report itself is the stimulus, for those more detailed, nuanced and helpful conversations.

3.6 These grades are reported to parents and carers alongside grades that illustrate judgements about the pupil's progress. Currently, the grades that are used are:

- ▫ Exceeding expectations;
- ▫ Meeting expectations;
- ▫ Slightly below expectations;
- ▫ Well-below expectations.

These grades are derived from a comparison of prior attainment data that is available. This has included the beginning of year baseline test, Key Stage 2 attainment data, MidYIS tests, reading age test data, CAT scores and any previous year's school attainment data.

3.7 Pupils are also awarded grades that are designed to show something about their attitude to learning, Currently, they are awarded one of the following grades for 'Effort', 'Organisation' and 'Homework':

- Excellent;
- Good;
- Need for improvement;
- Cause for concern.

3.8 These written communications are further supported with parents' evening meetings and the reporting of 'achievement' and 'behaviour' points. Teachers are also contactable by parents and carers, usually through the mediation of a form tutor, year head or subject leader, if further clarification is needed.

4. The summative exam at the end of the year is different from the rest of the assessment and reporting system. The summative exam should test a wider sample of the curriculum than other 'assessments' during the year.

4.1 Whereas as other assessments will, in almost all cases, lead to some formative feedback that requires the pupils to take specific actions to ameliorate their knowledge and/or reflect on their performance. There is no such requirement for the summative, end-of-year test. It is summative.

4.2 The construction of the end-of-year test is subject to the judgement of the subject leader but it should be constructed with an eye to the assessment of the following for their subject:

- Substantive and disciplinary knowledge;
- 'Residue' and 'fingertip' knowledge;
- Knowledge taught in previous years and knowledge that will be taught in subsequent years.

4.3 The results of this test are reported to parents and carers are a percentage alongside the median performance of the cohort. There is not an attempt to 'translate' these grades to 'GCSE grades' because the exams are not GCSE exams. The only sound inference one can make about the performance of a pupil in that exam is about the performance in that exam. If the exam is constructed to test a reasonable sample of the curriculum and the curriculum represents a reasonable sample of the domain, then it is valid in-and-of-itself. If the exam is not constructed in that way, the leadership of the school needs to ask itself why that is the case – guessing about how a pupil will do in a different type of test in, at least, two years will not make any of the data more valid or reliable.

How might a school leader go about implementing this?

The 1st of July, 1916 was one of the bloodiest days in British military history. Around 57,000 men were killed or wounded on the first day of the Battle of the Somme.[9] The tactics of the British generals had failed, leading to men being asked to walk, in bright sunshine, across open fields towards enemy machine guns. Even half-an-hour into that disastrous day, battalion commanders were telephoning their divisional headquarters asking if there was to be a change of plans in the face of the obvious mounting catastrophe. The answer was no. Although some of these men could see the carnage unfolding in front of them, the generals' plan did not give them the authority to take the initiative, protect their men's lives or even make a more effective assault on the enemy line.

In contrast, in the spring of 1918, the German nearly won the First World War with very different tactics. Instead of a massed assault, the commanding officers of smaller, highly trained, units were set objectives by their generals but they were given the freedom to adjust their tactics as they went along in response to the circumstance they found themselves in. This is an example of a long-standing Prussian military tradition called 'Auftragstaktik' (known in the UK as 'mission command' tactics), which was based on the ideas of the general Helmuth von Moltke the elder. Moltke wrote: 'The higher the authority, the shorter and more general will be the orders be. The next lower command adds what further precision appears necessary. The detail of execution is left to the verbal order, to the command. Each thereby retains freedom of action and decision within his authority.' (Moltke, 1996, p. 185)

---

9. For more detail, see Middlebrook (1984).

The only reason that the German offensive failed to win the war was that the high command was not able to maintain the supply to the front lines of men and material needed to take full advantage of the initial breakthroughs. If you will excuse the analogy, I think that this approach has much to commend it when thinking about school leadership.

It is true that the assessment system outlined is a high-trust model but where the senior leadership of a school does not trust the professional judgement of the middle leadership, they are not going to make things better by by-passing the expertise that should be there with a bureaucratic, managerial system. The best outcome in those circumstances will be lions being led by donkeys. There is always an irony about writing about assessment practice for teachers. Assessment is what teachers do all the time in myriad different ways, formal and informal and yet, when it comes to the assessment of assessment much of the expertise we gather as professionals is junked in favour of something that will generate 'hard' data points: flight paths, 'groups' statistics, tick sheets, forms with a fixed number of boxes to be filled, pass/fail work scrutiny exercises, graded lessons, generic targets, and pupil voice exercises with inflexible question set. I fear that this is because we have allowed pressures from local authorities, trusts, governments, Ofsted, league tables, value-added scores, cohort data, Progress 8, performance-related pay and others to raise the stakes of our assessments of ourselves and our colleagues. This raising of the stakes has had the same impact it always has – it undermines the reliability of the data and the validity of the inferences that can be drawn from it.

Senior leaders can determine the metrics by which subject leaders will be judged. They are in charge of measuring the output of the lightbulb factory and they need to use more sophisticated measurements than only candle power. Just as a leader would expect a teacher to have a variety of data to assess a pupil's understanding, senior leaders need a variety of data about their subject leaders' understanding – they are the locus of expertise and should guide senior leaders through what is unique and particular about their subject, their curriculum and its assessment. If a school values the curriculum as a collection of samples from different subject domains, and assessment as reflecting a sample of that, then schools should allow the person with the better knowledge the freedom and responsibility to manage the assessment of that system.

Towards a system of 'guilds'?

There is an enduring tension in school leadership. Senior leaders need to allow their middle-leadership the freedom to know their job and to do their jobs well it would be impossible for senior leaders to be expert in all of the things taught in a school. However, they need to know that their middle leaders are expert. From a position of ignorance, senior leaders must judge expertise. Any attempt to make subjects conform to standard models undervalues and undermines that which makes them unique and therefore that which give them value. You might make a pretty display by pinning butterflies to a board but you will not see them do much flying afterwards. How can this position be reconciled? There are a number of ways in which we, in our daily lives, are encouraged to put our trust in a service or product the creation and the workings of which we are ignorant. One of the simplest is the appeal to authority; something that we see everyday. Before the modern period, the idea of a monarch's head on a coin acts as a guarantee – the trust in the size weight and purity of the metals in the coin directly related to the trust in the authority of the monarch. We can still see this in the Royal Warrant badges that are printed on goods and packages telling you that, for example, the Queen's chosen condiment supplier is Heinz. (If it's good enough for Her Majesty…) The same principle operates with the Kitemarks that tell us that a product has been tested to conform to a given British Standards Institution safety standard.

What are these teaching Royal Warrants and Kitemarks? In days gone by, they were simply the Qualified Teacher Status and the Postgraduate Certificate of Education. The guarantor of the quality of the teaching 'product' was the university who endorsed the qualification. At the time of writing UCAS is advertising 571 courses (gov.uk, 2020) to become a secondary history teacher alone, the idea of the reputation of the guarantor standing for the reputation of their alumni is gone. However, before the modern period, there were other guarantees of quality of work. In medieval Europe, after the Church and the monarchies, the most powerful institutions were the guilds. One need only look at the guildhalls in many towns and cities to see their influence.[10] These organisations were groups of craftsmen or merchants who were engaged in the same trade. They were granted a monopoly to control the production of those goods and, therefore, acted as a cartel to control prices. However, they also controlled trading standards and education. It was not in the guild's interest to allow substandard goods to be sold in their jurisdiction as it reflected badly on them. Similarly, they were responsible for the training of young men from apprentices, through journeymen to the masters through the production of their masterpiece.

---

10   Membership of a 'Livery Company' guild such as the Worshipful Company of Fishmongers still grants its members the Freedom of the City of London and the right to drive sheep across London Bridge!

Is there room in the English education system for a guild system today? Should we, as a profession, be working towards a system of professional bodies that are responsible for the training, review and continued professional development of our subject specialists? If the senior leader is, by necessity, ignorant of the expertise needed to teach geography, could a system be built whereby the quality of their work is guaranteed by a Worshipful Company of Geographers (or, perhaps the Royal Geographic Society or the Geographical Association for in the absence of a guild, membership of a subject-association is a good start for someone looking for a guarantee of quality. For example, the Historical Association runs a Quality Mark scheme that will assess the performance of a school's history department[11]).

What form these 'guilds' might take, what their relationships might be to government, local authorities, universities, MATs, subject associations, professional bodies, trade unions and schools would need to be clarified. However, it might just provide the answers that English schools need.

References

AQA (2017) GCSE Religious Studies A 8062 Specification', *AQA* [Online] 10 November. Retrieved from: www.bit.ly/3n3dafu

Butler, R. (1988) 'Enhancing and undermining Intrinsic motivation; the effects of task-involving and ego-involving evaluation on interest and performance', *British Journal of Educational Psychology* 58 pp. 1-14.

Christodoulou, D. (2016) *Making Good Progress? The Future of Assessment for Learning*. Oxford: Oxford University Press.

Counsell, C. (2000) 'Historical knowledge and historical skills: a distracting dichotomy' in Arthur, J. and Phillips, R. (eds) *Issues in History Teaching*. London: Routledge

Counsell, C. (2018a) 'Senior Curriculum Leadership 1: The indirect manifestation of knowledge: (A) curriculum as narrative', *The Dignity of the Thing* [Online] 7 April. Retrieved from: www.bit.ly/3cIs7if

Counsell, C. (2018b) 'Taking Curriculum Seriously', *Impact* [Online] September. Retrieved from: www.bit.ly/3cF0SoG

---

11. More information about the Historical Association's Quality Mark scheme can be found on their website at www.history.org.uk

Counsell, C. and Carr, E. (2014) 'Using time-lines in assessment', *Teaching History* 157 pp. 54-62

GOV.UK (2020) *Find postgraduate teacher training.* Retrieved from: www.bit. ly/347QIcq

Koretz, D. (2008) *Measuring Up: What Education Testing Really Tells Us.* Cambridge, MA: Harvard University Press.

Koretz, D. (2017) *The Testing Charade – Pretending to Make Schools Better.* Chicago: University of Chicago Press.

Middlebrook, M. (1984) *The First Day on the Somme: 1 July 1916.* London: Penguin.

Moltke, H. K. B von. (1996) *Moltke on the Art of War.* New York: Presidion Press.

OCR (2018) GCSE (9-1) *Specification HISTORY A (EXPLAINING THE MODERN WORLD) J410.* Retrieved from: www.bit.ly/30kaosn

Standish, A. and Cuthbert, A. S. (2017) 'Introduction' in Standish, A. and Cuthbert, A. S. (eds.) *What Should Schools Teach?* London: UCL Institute of Education Press.

Stanford, M. (2019) 'Did the Bretons Break? Planning increasingly complex 'causal models' at Key Stage 3' in *Teaching History* 175 pp. 8-15.

Sweller, J., Ayres, P. and Kalyuga, S. (2011) *Cognitive Load Theory.* New York: Springer-Verlag.

Wiliam, D. (1998) *Enculturating learners into communities of practice: raising achievement through classroom assessment.* ECER Paper. London: King's College London.

Willingham, D. (2017) 'On the Definition of Learning...', *Daniel Willingham* [Online] 26 June. Retrieved from: www.bit.ly/2HwLqzp

Zoshchenko, M. (1975) *Nervous People and Other Satires.* Bloomington: Indiana University Press.

Author bio-sketch:

Matt Stanford is the director of the Schools History Project and teaches history at Cottenham Village College in Cambridgeshire, where he was head of department when they were awarded the Historical Association's Gold Quality Mark. He has had several journal articles published, presented at national conferences and led CPD sessions for a variety of audiences including teachers in secondary and primary schools and both trainees and mentors for the Cambridge University PGCE programme. You can find him tweeting as @stanf80.

LEADING TO FLUENCY

BY THE READING APE

There is no more important task for school leaders than to ensure that every child can read. If a child leaves any of my schools unable to read, I have failed. Moreover, the earlier a child can read, the more enhanced their life chances. But of course, it isn't as simple as that. In coming to understand how we lead in a primary school, and when we try to get pupils who are struggling to catch up in a secondary school, I've come to appreciate the breadth and depth of research into the teaching of reading. Unlike most other aspects of schools that we lead, there is an extensive research base that can be bewildering.

The best resource I've encountered is the Reading Ape blog. I can think of no better place for school leaders to encounter and develop their understanding of how pupils learn to read. The links with achievement milestones at age 11 and 16 are stark and important for us to understand and grasp. I now demand, partly as a result of the Reading Ape's contributions, that all leaders in my schools understand what good teaching of reading looks like, including a firm understanding of the best possible curriculum and assessment.

I asked The Reading Ape to contribute to this book as I wanted the Ape to share their insights and how they might support leaders. I feel privileged that they agreed.

'My name is Zira. I am ten years old. I cannot read. My teacher is nice and works with me a lot and finds books for me and tries to teach me to read. I know the books are for younger children. They have lots of pictures. I can remember some of the words because they appear a lot in the books. When I can't remember a word, I sound out the first letter. My teacher helps me to do this and encourages me to look at the pictures to see if there is a picture of something that starts with the sound or I try to guess a word that makes sense. Sometimes I guess right and my teacher is happy. Sometimes I guess wrong and I know my teacher is disappointed. Mostly, I just wait until my teacher tells me the word. When I can remember the whole of the book, we move on to another book. This is scary. Although some words look familiar it takes me a long time to remember any of them. We keep working until I can remember all of them. My friends read books without pictures. Just loads of words. I have no idea how they remember all of them, but I do know that I will never be able to remember enough words to read their books.'

Zira was taught, in the final year of primary school, by an experienced teacher and was able to read no better at the end of the year than at the beginning. The teacher despaired at Zira's lack of progress. She just couldn't get it. The teacher would tell Zira the word on one line, but Zira would fail to recognise the same word on the very next line. It was a hopeless case but at least the teacher tried and was very patient. It was a little puzzling to the teacher that Zira was very good at listening comprehension. The teacher taught Zira a few 'tricks' that enabled her to score some marks on the SATs paper at the end of Key Stage 2, but she went off to secondary school that summer unable to read fluently and with a SEND label that was never removed. The Year 6 teacher was comforted with the knowledge they had all done their best but there was clearly something wrong with Zira.

There was nothing wrong with Zira. Her teacher fitted the identified profile of many primary teachers: well-versed in children's literature but not knowledgeable in the basic concepts of the English language (Maleteta Joshi et al, 2009). Zira could have been taught to read. Every piece of knowledge that would have enabled her to read is in existence.

1. Humans are inherently programmed to communicate orally – speaking is a biologically primary process (Geary, 2007). Reading, however, is not.

The ability of humans to communicate orally has developed over millions of years with diverse language possible from about one hundred thousand years ago (Jablonski and Aiello, 1998). It appears that language has an instinctive, inherent foundation and that there exists a universal grammar (Chomsky, 1965; Bickerton, 2018). Nonetheless, this is an aural and oral instinct that has evolved as the human brain has developed and not in a smooth progression but as 'a mosaic structure of cognitive vestiges from earlier stages of human emergence' (Donald, 1991).

Written language has been in existence for around five thousand years which is not an evolutionary period. Thus, the brain cannot have evolved to write and read; writing and reading have evolved to the constraints of the human brain (Dehaene, 2015), 'reshaping and reusing old parts for new purposes' (Egan, 2004). 'Learning to read is not like acquiring one's native language, no matter how much someone wishes it were so' (Perfetti, 1991).

Reading must be learned.

It can also be taught. Schools can teach reading. Primary schools can ensure reading is taught to fluency. Primary school leaders should not assume that primary school teachers know how to do this. Secondary school leaders should not assume that primary schools have taught reading to fluency even when standardised scores suggest this.

2. Reading begins with speech.

Infants detect minimal contrasts in words. For reading and writing, however, children require a conscious awareness of sounds within words (Lieberman et al, 1974). Phonological awareness – sensitivity to and the ability to manipulate the sound structure of language – is a crucial precursor to reading. This then assists the most potent causal factor in the acquisition of word recognition (Blachman, 2000): phonemic awareness – the ability to distinguish phonemes, the smallest units of linguistic sound within words.

Phonological awareness and phonemic awareness are the greatest early indicators of reading outcomes.

They can be promoted through the oral and aural familiarity with rhyming texts along with experiences with specific detection and segmentation tasks which should begin before any early reading instruction and continue during the initial years of learning to read (Bradley and Bryant, 1983).

Assessing phonemic awareness for early readers will give leaders an indication of pupils' preparedness for decoding instruction.

3. Humans cannot read by remembering the shape of words.

The human brain has a capacity of between 2000 and 5000 logographs – characters or symbols representing meaning (Leong, 1973, Gough and Hillinger, 1980; Akamatsu, 2006). The average educated adult has a vocabulary of 100,000 words (Pinker, 2003). Reading is not logographic deciphering.

Symbolically encoded languages like Chinese and Japanese have evolved syllabic elements to help relieve the logographic memory ceiling. They take many years of study to learn to decipher. Chinese children are expected to recognise only 3500 characters by the age of 11 (Leong, 1973), and it takes 12 years of study to learn 2000 logographs in Japanese kanji (Gough and Hillinger, 1980; Akamatsu, 2006). The brain can decode alphabetically encoded words written in upper- and lower-case (and with practice mixed-case) equally quickly (Polk and Farah, 2002). There are two implications: firstly, that we do not recognise words by their shape (the same word written in upper- and lower-case looks completely different, as does a handwritten word and a printed word) and secondly, that letters do not float independently but that strings of letters are unconsciously bound together.

An alphabetically encoded language is NOT symbolic.

Any instruction that promotes the learning of words as shapes is fatally flawed and will always fail once the limit of logographic memory has been reached. The use of flashcards promotes logographic recognition, with children often remembering stain patterns on the card to identify the word (Stanovitch, 1986). Early reading schemes that systematically repeat words (that are not decodable using a child's current learned phonic knowledge) specifically encourage whole-word recognition.

The removal of any early reading instruction, programme or practice that distracts from a learner's focus on the alphabetic principle and that may promote word shape recognition as a strategy for reading, will enhance early reading provision.

4. The alphabet was invented once in human history and has not been improved upon (Havelock, 1976).

The first recordable codes for language used symbols to represent words (Daniels and Bright, 1996). These logographic forms of writing kept hitting the buffers of human memory capacity no matter how they adapted. Even with a mixture of syllables and symbols, reading and writing required huge feats of memory and only a very few were able to master the process. The Phoenicians, by adding vowels to the developing Seirite sound to letter code, created the first fully phonetic alphabet. They were now able to transcribe unambiguously and accurately the spoken words of any language using fewer than 30 symbols. This system operated well within the confines of human memory and was thus learnable by anyone able to master the system of codification. This lever of civilisation (Breasted, 1926) made universal literacy a possibility.

For any language encoded using an alphabet, the letters are key.

Alphabetically encoded languages are far easier to learn to decode that symbolically/syllabically encoded languages. Languages that have high levels of orthographic transparency – most sounds are represented by one letter – are easier to learn to decode: ancient Greek and Latin, Italian, Spanish, Finnish. English has the most opaque orthography but is still encoded using an alphabet.

5. English has developed into the most complex alphabetic code.

Perhaps if we had stuck to Latin, then it would take our children the four months it takes Italian children to learn to decode, we would have the almost non-existent levels of dyslexia reported in Italy (Dehaene, 2015) and could perhaps delay formal education for a year or two. However, the entwining of Old English with Norman French, with many spellings erratically selected by Flemish printers, resulted in the least transparent alphabetic code that, with effective teaching, takes up to three and half years to learn to decode.

44 sounds have to be represented using only 26 letters. This results in two vital principles (and problems):

- One letter can represent more than one sound.
- A sound can be represented by more than one letter.

The 44 sounds can be spelt using around 200 letter combinations. This is the heart of the complexity of the English alphabetic code. English has, nonetheless, been encoded using an alphabet.

Despite its complexity, English is an alphabetically encoded language. All words in English are encoded using the alphabet.

80-90% of words in English follow a regular encoding with the others following more complex patterns and of the recognised one hundred high frequency 'irregular words' only 28 do not conform to the regular code (McGuinness, 2004). No word in English is completely phonologically opaque. Suggesting to emergent readers that some words are 'tricky 'and 'just have to be learned' denies the alphabetic principle and may be confusing (McGuiness, 1999). All words in English are encoded using the alphabet. The encoding may have become complex because of historical language mutations but there is always some precedential transparency that gifts the letters rather than the word shape greater deciphering agency. Even words like 'stomach' provide accurate phonological cues and would be far more difficult to read if represented as a random sequence of letters – 'omtshca' (Tumner and Nicholson, 2011).

6. English is a complex code, but the decoding and encoding of that code can be taught.

Learning the variety of letters that represent the same sound and the variety of sounds that can be represented by a single letter takes time, patience and regular practise. The evolved complexity of the English alphabetic code resulted in the teaching of it not being systematised until the 18th century and the learning of it left to chance. The children of the English merchant classes learned to read Latin and Greek before English so had considerable code knowledge gifted from these more orthographically transparent languages. The poor were taught the alphabet (with one sound associated with one letter) and then had access to a modest canon of religious texts that they learned by heart – often giving the appearance of reading. As there was little to read, the resultant widespread illiteracy made little difference. When one of them did manage to teach themselves to read, Thomas Cromwell, he ended up running the country – perhaps why the English elite have been so suspicious of universal literacy.

In 1665, Blaise Pascal (Rogers, 2002) devised a system of atomising the sound and letter correspondences of French (which has an opaque orthography) that by encouraging pupils to blend the identified sounds enabled them to decode whole words. This concept of synthesising sounds represented by letters into words is the foundation of synthetic phonics.

If the correspondences between letters and sounds (grapheme-phoneme correspondence) are taught sequentially beginning with the simpler correspondences (the basic, simple or initial code) with the more complex correspondences (the complex or extended code) introduced later, the whole alphabetic code can be taught systematically: Systematic Synthetic Phonics. The inverse process of segmenting words into their phonemes and then associating the appropriate graphemes can be taught at the same time eventually enabling effective encoding and spelling. The efficacy of systematic phonics instruction is supported by an overwhelming catalogue of research dating back to the early 20th century. The conflicting research has been driven by poorly designed studies carried out by prominent educational academics that focused on fluency and reading comprehension than decoding (Diack, 1965; Terman and Walcutt, 1958; Chall, 1967; McGuinness, 2004).

In an alphabetically encoded language, the letters and groups of letters represent sound. Learning to decode words by blending (synthesising) the sounds represented by letters together is the start of reading. It is recommended this start at the beginning of a child's Reception year (Holdaway 1979; Stanovich and West 1989) and continue systematically until the whole of the English alphabetic code has been mastered.

The teaching of SSP requires the possession of considerable subject knowledge and expertise by teachers and leaders of reading.

7. Not all phonics instruction is systematic.

Analytic phonics, resorting to phonic strategies when whole-word, syntactic and contextual strategies have failed, is not systematic and developed as a result of the ineffectiveness of the aforementioned strategies. It is predicated on a reader having a large bank of memorised words, performs poorly when compared to systematic phonics instruction and commonly results in the monitoring adult reading the unknown word (Watson and Johnston, 2004). This should not be confused with the incidental use of phonic strategies when readers with considerable code knowledge need reminding of elements of the code to enable them to attack unknown words.

The requirement of a large bank of memorised words is also a prerequisite for phonics programmes and systems that require the reader to decode unknown words by the use of associative letter patterns in known words. The concept of onset and rime phonics is founded upon the reader ignoring the opening grapheme's phoneme, the identification of the subsequent letter pattern through association with a known word, the replacement of the opening phoneme of the known word with the actual phoneme and the blending of the replaced phoneme with the identified letter pattern's sound. If that seems complicated for a single syllable word, then the cognitive gymnastics challenge to decode a polysyllabic word may, for a struggling reader with a poor word memory bank, be insurmountable.

Doing 'phonics' is not enough – SSP is far more effective at promoting decoding automaticity than analytic phonics (Johnson and Watson, 2005). Any instruction or programme that permits gaps in code knowledge to form is not systematic.

8. The Year 1 Phonics Screening Check (DfE, 2012) is important, useful and flawed.

The phonics screening check has been hugely influential in the promotion and adoption of SSP. It is the only national reading assessment outside of EYFS that does not assess reading by testing reading comprehension. Therefore, it has a significant element of analytic capability. It is, nonetheless, flawed. Firstly, it mixes real words with pseudo-words. This means it is unable to assess whether the real words are being decoded or recognised from memorised word-shape: tests using pseudowords alone, the Bryant Test of Basic Decoding Skills (1975) for example, are far more valid (Gough, 1983).

Secondly, the Screening Check does not screen the entire code. This of itself is not an issue as children may reasonably not have mastered the entire code by the end of Year 1. However, by placing the assessment in Year 1, it may have encouraged the conclusion of phonics instruction for children who attained or exceeded the threshold score – the assumption being that they had mastered phonics. Even full marks on the screening is not an indication of mastery and was never intended to be so. This phenomenon was highlighted when the Year 3 phonics screening pilot was undertaken by the DfE (2017). 49% of the Year 3 sample failed to achieve the threshold score. The proposal to adopt a Year 3 phonics screening was dropped after union pressure (naht.org.uk, 2017). Whether the 49% of children who failed to reach the threshold ever learned to read was not monitored.

The phenomenon of older pupils having significant gaps in code knowledge is exacerbated by the complexity of unlearning the inefficient decoding strategies associated with poor reading (Ehri, 2004).

Many children enter Key Stage 2 and Key Stage 3 with insufficient code knowledge to attain reading fluency.

Children who are instructed and assessed in phonics until mastery have the chance to become fluent readers (and better spellers). The assessment resources are available, simple to use and free. Key Stage 2 and Key Stage 3 teachers who are fully cognisant with the phonics code can teach it systematically to mastery and, more importantly, able to facilitate phonic word-attack strategies for pupils who are building code knowledge and encountering unknown words.

Clear teaching, repetition and practice are essential along with further practise decoding texts aligned to the code taught and learned (decodable texts). Decodable texts may appear to have tenuous storylines and not fulfil the 'love of reading' criterion. This is because they are driven by relevant code knowledge and not plot and narrative imperatives. They are resources for practice.

No child who cannot read will ever love reading.

There is considerable research to suggest that encoding (writing by hand) during phonics instruction greatly assists the development of spelling (Cunningham and Stanovitch, 1990) and that systematic phonics instruction greatly assists spelling efficacy (McGuinness, 2004; Castles, Rastle and Nation, 2018; Bowers and Bowers, 2018; Ouelette, Martin-Chang and Rossi, 2017).

Pseudoword assessments are readily available to school leaders, have high reliability factors and can be quickly administered (e.g. Bryant Test of Basic Decoding Skills, 1975). Progress to phonics mastery can be monitored and recorded, but note that linking any assessment with teacher performance management risks invalidating the assessment (Deming, 1994). Where leaders ensure all teachers (particularly in Key Stage 2) in primary schools have high levels of code knowledge, word-attack support for pupils is enhanced.

9. There is no such phenomenon as 'reading readiness'.

The concept that children who struggled to learn to read at an early age were just not ready and should have the instruction delayed until they were older was an integral part of Dewey's (2017) constructivist pedagogical paradigm. This concept of 'reading readiness' was intuitively attractive, discredited by early research (Wilson et al, 1938) but maintained traction such that 'delay as a teaching technique' developed into common educational parlance (Anderson and Dearborn, 1952).

Delaying the teaching of the decoding of English inhibits reading progress.

Children who have begun English reading instruction in their first year of formal schooling and before the age of six are more likely to become fluent readers (Holdaway 1979; Teale 1984; Stanovich and West 1989).

10. 'But what about children who don't learn to read by phonics?'

To ignore that alphabet when teaching the decoding of English is inexplicable (Daniels and Diack, 1953). If the code is not specifically taught, then the only option for an emergent reader is to decipher it for themselves. It is estimated that between 24% and 75% of children can do this (McGuiness, 1999; Adoniou, 2017; Turner and Burkard, 1996). To be able to do this requires access to a significant variety of texts and adult support. Nearly all children who start in Reception with highly developed reading skills are from families with a high socio-economic profile (Hughes and Stainthorp, 1999). This reverse code-cracking is possible for a few, inefficient for most and, for some, impossible. Decoding is far easier when we have the code, as Alan Turing found.

It is much easier to decode English if the code is explicitly taught.

For an alphabetically encoded language to be read, the code must be learned. There is no alternative. The International Dyslexia Association places the cause of dyslexia primarily in phonological processes – it will take longer, require more patience and probably greater teaching skill, but the code will still have to be mastered for fluent reading to manifest.

Leaders whose teachers have an awareness of how much of the alphabetic code their pupils have mastered and what remains to be mastered will allow pupils to become fluent readers. Pupils who have already mastered the alphabetic code are not impeded by phonics instruction but are supported in their spelling – an ironic slant on Pascal's wager.

11. '…teaching children to decode by giving primacy to semantic-contextual and syntactic-contextual cues over graphemic-phonemic cues is equivalent to teaching them to read the way weak readers read!' (Pressley, 2006)

Goodman's (1967), Smith's (1975) and Clay's (1991) whole language approach to reading was linked to Chomsky's (1965) model of inherent oral language acquisition and suggested that semantic and contextual cues, not alphabetic decoding, drive the reading process. This top-down theory of information processing – psycho-linguistic guessing – is incompatible with the speed of processing required for fluent reading (Rayner and Pollatsek, 2013) and was undermined by MRI scanning research (Dehaene, 2015).

Smith and Goodman's whole language approach was adopted by the state of California for seven years which resulted in 60% of Californian nine and ten-year-olds being unable to gain an even superficial understanding of their books and dropped to the bottom of the United States reading league tables (Turner and Burkard, 1996). New Zealand adopted a whole language approach to early reading instruction. 20% of six-year-olds in New Zealand were soon unable to read and required one-to-one Reading Recovery tuition – a programme developed by whole language advocate Clay (1985) that follows the same principles of the approach that failed the children in the first place. Most of these children made little progress (Chapman, Tunmer and Prochnow, 2001).

By the end of Year 2, 2000 memorised logographs are sufficient to read many simple books and will give many young children the appearance of very fluent reading – far more fluent than their decoding peers. The 'Year 3 dip' – or 'Grade 4 slump' as it is known in the USA (Chall, 1983) – in reading, emerges as a result of the necessity for increased reading vocabulary capacity for more demanding texts along with the reduction in visual cues as books become more text-rich. With the memory threshold for logographs replete, and with an incomplete code knowledge, children must resort to contextual cues, picture cues, syntactic cues or guesswork.

The theory that reading, like oral language, is intuitive, absolves teachers from having to teach it and school leaders from having to lead it (Peal, 2004). Mixed methods of teaching reading are inefficient but maintain considerable traction.

Research by the NFER (Walker and Bartlett, 2013) found that 67% of teachers believed that a 'mixed methods' approach to the teaching of reading was the most effective. A survey by the NAS/UWT in 2013 (politics.co.uk, 2013) showed that 89% of teachers believed that children needed to use a variety of cues to extract meaning from text confirming the results of Sheffield Hallam University's research two years earlier that revealed 74% of primary school teachers encouraged pupils to use a range of cueing systems that included picture clues (gov.uk, 2011).

Leaders should not underestimate the intuitive attraction and traction of 'mixed methods' and should guard against it. Several ubiquitous programmes of reading instruction are either based upon or include elements of mixed methods instruction.

12. Words can be read more quickly than letters. The development of the Word Superiority Effect (Reicher, 1969) is crucial for reading fluency.

When American PhD student James Cattell (Anderson and Dearbourne, 1952) discovered in 1885 that adults could read a short sentence in the same time it took them to read three unrelated words, he deduced that words were more memorable than letters. He went on to reason that we do not read words by the serial decoding of individual letters but that we read whole words, not individual letters. If that were true then that leaves phonics, with its teaching of serial phoneme decoding and blending to identify words, entirely redundant. However, Cattell had tested adults who were fluent readers. This was a critical flaw. The ability to decode words at speed to automaticity is a function of decoding mastery and the result of developing the word superiority effect (Reicher, 1969).

Automatic word recognition is not reliant on word shape but the recoding of letter patterns and their associated sounds. Orthographic processing is contingent on phonological processing with reading fluency dependent on the acquisition of word-specific orthographic representations (Perfetti, 2007). Persistent decoding practise leads to an inherent understanding and recognition of legitimate letter patterns. Once orthographic processing is viable for a reader (as a result of numerous fixations), the word superiority effect (Reicher, 1969) becomes evident and the counter-intuitive phenomenon of the word being perceived before its component letters is manifest (Ehrlich and Rayner, 1989). This may seem absurd but consider the misspelt word 'diffrence' that may be read as 'difference' before the misspelling is identified (Rayner and Pollarsek, 2013). Or try reading letter groups on car number plates – they appear as merely random letters until a group of letters conform to a legitimate word pattern, and suddenly we read a word (even a pseudoword). The word superiority effect is only evident once decoding automaticity is attained by a reader. Prior to this, an emergent reader can only decode using phonological processing (Stanovich, 2000). Any initial reading instruction that does not enable a reader to decode sounds in sequence and encourages the continued practise of decoding will require the pupil to either decipher the code by themselves or achieve the pseudo-fluency of logographic processing (McGuinness, 1999).

Although the word is the smallest unit of meaning, it is only a deep and full knowledge of letter patterns and their associated sounds that make up the alphabetic code which enables the decoding of the word. Automaticity, the perception of detailed orthographic representations necessary for fast, efficient word recognition is primarily self-taught during independent reading (Share, 1995). Languages with shallow orthographies require only two exposures to unfamiliar words for automaticity to be activated (Share, 2004) whereas English, with its deeper orthography, requires at least four exposures (Nation et al, 2007). Younger children, however, do benefit from greater numbers of exposures (Bowey and Muller, 2005).

Children require time to phonologically recode words on their own during instruction if automaticity is to develop (Share, 1995).

When a child hesitates when attempting to decode, they must be afforded sufficient time to attempt a phonological recoding. Even failed attempts facilitate some level of orthographic learning (Cunningham et al, 2011) especially when the teacher can refer to the alphabetic coding structure rather than merely read the word for the child to repeat. This is a crucial factor. Without teacher input and monitoring, sustained silent reading showed almost no positive effects in developing orthographic processing because there was no way of ensuring a child's investment in the reading. Monitored and leveraged whole-class reading was more effective (NICHD, 2000).

Leaders who ensure that all teachers of reading can refer to the alphabetic code structure when assisting word-attack of unknown words, enhance pupils' likelihood of achieving reading fluency.

13. Automaticity is not fluency.

Whilst at the decoding stage of reading development, a learner is recognising letters and letter combinations but accessing the attendant sounds associated with those letters from long-term memory thus enabling the working memory to then blend those sounds. The word may then be retrieved from long-term memory or, if not present in the brain's lexicon, merely be read without meaning.

As the speed of decoding increases, letter patterns are accessed and recognised more rapidly from long-term memory, the word superiority effect (Reicher, 1969) becomes apparent and decoding automaticity emerges. At this point in a reader's development, the long-term memory is privileging legitimate sound to letter pattern correspondence to attempt correct or valid pronunciation. Access to the lexical pathway (Dehaene, 2015) will be restricted by vocabulary knowledge which for early readers will be necessarily constrained by chronological and experiential maturation. This may manifest itself in the regularly observed and unfairly criticised 'barking at print' (Rosen, 2012) phenomenon and 'the [...] unnatural monotony of sound' (quoted in Diack, 1965) noted by 19th century HMIs, with the resultant absence of speed, accuracy and prosody associated with reading fluency.

This obsession with fluency led teachers in the late 19th century to ensure their pupils memorised texts to perfection to ensure they appeared fluent when inspectors visited (Lawson and Silver, 1973). It didn't help that teacher pay progression was linked to pupils' reading fluency – a further warning of invalidating assessments by tethering them to performance management (Deming, 1994). This slow and sometimes stuttering recoding is an expected and normal phenomenon (Kuhn and Stahl, 2003). The Roman pedagogue, Quintilian (Quintilian and Watson, 1913), by demanding that reading be, 'at first sure, then continuous and for a long time slow' (p. 14), gave his charges the space to practise decoding to automaticity.

Automaticity is sometimes regarded as the 'missing link' between decoding mastery and reading fluency (Laberge and Samuels, 1974).

Automaticity is essentially self-taught (Share, 1995) through regular fixation on words through reading texts at instructional level but can be assisted through the techniques of repeated reading and assisted reading. Children require the opportunity to practise reading texts at their instructional level to promote automaticity. Timetabling is the most effective means to embed regular practise (Fullan, 2015). There is growing evidence that repeated reading of a text with an exemplification of fluency and regular verbal feedback and scaffolding from a teacher leads to gains in reading rate, accuracy and prosody in passages not previously read (Kuhn and Stahl, 2004). Assisted reading, whereby the instructed reader reads slightly behind the fluent reader has also indicated strong improvements in fluency as does any assisted practise which includes strong elements of scaffolding and feedback from a stronger reader (Rasinski et al, 2011). The selection of text is vital, with its level of complexity requiring a correlation with the expertise of the instructor (Kuhn and Stahl, 2004).

Leaders and teachers can assess automaticity quickly and easily using tests that measure whether pupils can, within a short fixation, read age-related words (eg. The Appalachian State University Word Recognition Inventory). Note that linking any assessment with teacher performance management risks invalidating the assessment (Deming, 1994).

14. Reading fluency requires the presence of three interrelated elements.

Once decoding has become automatic and the decoding of words swift, the long-term memory supports reading through rapid deciphering along with lexical recognition and identification. This liberates working memory to attend to the *prosody, rate* and *accuracy* associated with fluent reading. Prosodic reading is the ability to make oral reading sound like authentic oral speech (Rasinski et al, 2011) and requires a significant reading speed with high levels of accuracy (both indicating evidence of the word superiority effect). All three elements must be present for reading to be fluent. When encountering longer unknown words with more complex phonetic patterns, the cognitive process will revert to its decoding model, evidenced by the slower sounding out of phonemes and associated blending of syllables to decipher the word. This phenomenon is evident even in very experienced readers (Dehaene, 2015), as when most adults read 'pneumonoultramicroscopicsilicovolcanoconiosis'.

Fluency instruction accounts for less than five minutes per day of teaching in primary classes and of all the major components of reading, fluency teaching is given the least amount of time (Gamse et al, 2008).

Repeated and assisted reading greatly improves reading rate, prosody and accuracy (Kuhn and Stahl, 2004). Reading speed, accuracy and prosody can also be easily and quickly assessed.

Reading rate assessments produce a words-read-per-minute score along with an accuracy percentage (eg. DIBELS form the Oregon State University). Rasinski et al (2016) suggest that words-per-minute scores are significantly correlated with academic outcomes and are a strong predictor of university entrance (including which university – the higher the reading rate, the more prestigious the university).

Prosodic reading can be taught and assessed. Miller and Schwanenflugel (2008) found that developing more mature pitch and intonation in early primary school readers was associated with faster developing comprehension achievement. Perhaps more significantly for primary schools, meaningful correlations were found between prosody and performance in standardised silent reading comprehension tests (Rasinski, Rikli and Johnston, 2009). Dowhower (1987) found that where repeated reading instruction focused feedback on phrasing sensitivity for prosody, fluency improved. Several small-scale studies, where a theatrical presentation with a focus on prosody and expressive delivery of reading was the culmination of practice, have found substantial gains in reading speed and reading expressiveness (Martinez, Roser and Strecker, 1999).

Prosody can be measured. Discrete prosody tests measure prosodic reading through an interpretive rubric that produces a quantitative score. They are simple and quick to administer and valid (Miller and Schwanenflugel, 2006) – e.g. (Rasinski, 2010) Fluency Rubric – available online. Once again, linking any assessment with teacher performance management risks invalidating the assessment (Deming, 1994).

15. Reading comprehension tests conflate a variety of reading elements.

Establishing the intended purpose and meaning of a non-present communicator is the intention of reading (Thorndike, 1917). To enable this, readers require sufficient decoding expertise to release working memory to attend to the cognitive demands of extracting meaning from text. Comprehension is an unstable construction that changes moment by moment (Pearson, 2001). If, as Kamhi (2007) suggests, reading comprehension is a complex mix of higher-level mental processes dependent on specific knowledge in content area, then a comprehension score may not reveal much about a pupil's progression to reading fluency. It will conflate decoding ability, automaticity, rate, accuracy, content knowledge as well as social and cultural experiences.

A reading comprehension test is unable to reveal that a child has not yet mastered the phonic code. A pseudoword assessment can reveal this.

Assessments which focus on specific elements of reading progression are readily available and provide more forensic detail for formative evaluation than a reading comprehension score. A pupil still mastering the phonic code will not have sufficient working memory available to extract all but the most superficial meaning from a comprehension test text. A comprehension test, in this case, indicates no specific remedial or developmental action.

However, support in mastering the code will not only improve the pupil's decoding ability but will also have a direct and equal effect on comprehension (Gough and Tumner, 1986) – this research produced 'The Simple View of Reading' which concluded that decoding and reading comprehension are separate but correlated.

What the research suggests – checklist for leaders

- Promote and assess phonological and phonemical awareness before and during early decoding instruction.
- Ensure the selected phonics programme is systematic and teaches ALL of the code.
- Establish for learners that English has been encoded using the alphabet and the code can be learned. Avoid undermining the principle of the alphabetic code with references to 'tricky' words.
- Regularly assess all pupils' code knowledge using pseudoword tests until they have mastered the entire code – this might be years after the phonics screening check. Assess pupils in Key Stage 2 for gaps in code knowledge. Fill the gaps.
- Ensure pupils learning the code have the opportunity to practise code knowledge with decodable texts – this will also help the development of the word superiority effect.
- Ensure teaching and texts avoid the promotion of multiple cueing strategies for reading – decoding only.
- Ensure all teachers (especially Key Stage 2 teachers) are fully cognisant with the selected phonics programme.
- Ensure attempts by pupils to decode unknown, or misread words are supported by references to the code and that unknown words are not merely read for pupils. This requires considerable subject knowledge and expertise, particularly in upper year groups where phonics is not taught daily.
- Ensure pupils have ample opportunity to achieve automaticity by reading texts at an instructional level.
- Teach reading automaticity through repeated and assisted reading.
- Assess reading automaticity.
- Slow, stuttering, deliberate reading is an expected phenomenon for pupils developing automaticity – you may have to explain this to inspectors.
- Teach prosodic reading.
- Assess prosody.
- Teach reading fluency through repeated and assisted reading.
- Assess reading fluency – accuracy, rate and prosody.
- Highlight words-per-minutes rates as there is a strong correlation with academic outcomes.
- Focused assessments will enable timely and relevant intervention – specific code knowledge, automaticity and reading fluency.

- Avoid invalidating assessments by linking them to teacher performance management.
- Avoid comprehension tests as a forensic reading assessment tool.

For secondary leaders

- Statutory Key Stage 2 reading data may not reveal the full extent of pupils' progress to reading fluency.
- Some pupils will join your school without having achieved reading fluency. Assess where they are in terms of their progress to fluency (see above) and work from there.

What Zira might have said:

'My name is Zira and I am ten years old. I am not great at reading. In class we all read the same book. I cannot read as fast as the rest of my class, and I don't read with that much expression. I have always read more slowly than my friends, but I am much faster than I used to be. Sometimes I don't recognise a word, and I have to break it up into the sounds that the letters are representing and then blend those sounds together. This can be difficult because I know that the same letter often represents more than one sound, and the same sounds can be represented by more than one letter. I do know all of the possible sounds and their letters, I just sometimes don't know which one it is. This can be frustrating because sometimes I just can't work it out. When this happens, my teacher tells me what the sound is and what the letters are that are representing the sound. Then I can usually blend the sounds together to read the word. My teacher makes me do it again. If I do this a few times, then I can usually read the word when it comes up again. It can be a bit slow, but I get there in the end. I am definitely getting faster, I know this because my teacher tests my speed and lets me know that I am getting faster.'

...and, yes, I was Zira's teacher.

References

Adoniou, M. (2017) 'Misplaced faith in phonics and the phonics screening check', *Education Journal* 313 pp. 25-27.

Akamatsu, N. (2006) 'Literacy acquisition in Japanese-English bilinguals' in Joshi, M. and Aaron, P. G. (eds) *Handbook of orthography and literacy*. Mahwah, NJ: Eribaum.

Anderson, I. and Dearborn, W. (1952) T*he Psychology of Teaching Reading*. New York: Ronal Press.

Bickerton, D. (2018) *Language and Species*. Chicago: University of Chicago Press.

Blachman, B. (2000) 'Phonological awareness' in Kamil, M. L., Mosenthal, P. B., Pearson, P. D. and Barr, R. (eds) *Handbook of Reading Research* (Vol. 3). Malwah, NJ: Eribaum.

Breasted, J. (1926) *The Conquest of Civilisation* (1st ed). New York: Harper Bros.

Bowers, J. and Bowers, P. (2017) 'Beyond Phonics: The Case for Teaching Children the Logic of the English Spelling System', *Educational Psychologist* 52 (2) pp. 124-141.

Bowey, J. and Muller, D. (2005) 'Phonological recoding and rapid orthographic learning in third-graders' silent reading: A critical test of the self-teaching hypothesis' *Journal of Experimental Child Psychology* 92 (3) pp. 203-219.

Bradley, L. and Bryant, P. (1983) 'Categorizing sounds and learning to read – a causal connection', *Nature* 301 (5899) pp. 419-421.

Castles, A., Rastle, K. and Nation, K. (2018) 'Ending the Reading Wars: Reading Acquisition From Novice to Expert', *Psychological Science in the Public Interest* 19 (1) pp. 5-51.

Chall, J. (1967) *Learning to read* (1st ed). New York: McGraw Hill.

Chapman, J. and Tunmer, W. (2016) 'Is Reading Recovery an Effective Intervention for Students with Reading Difficulties? A Critique of the i3 Scale-Up Study', *Reading Psychology* 37 (7) pp. 1025-1042.

Chomsky, N. (1965) *Persistent topics in linguistic theory*. New York: International Council for Philosophy and Humanistic Studies.

Clay, M. (1991) *Becoming literate* (1st ed). London: Heinemann.

Clay, M. (1995) *Reading recovery.* Portsmouth, NH: Heinemann.

Cunningham, A. and Stanovich, K. (1990) 'Early spelling acquisition: Writing beats the computer', *Journal of Educational Psychology* 82 (1) pp. 159-162.

Cunningham, A., Perry, K. and Stanovich, K. (2001) 'Converging evidence for the concept of orthographic processing', *Reading and Writing* 14 (5/6) pp. 549-568.

Department for Education (2017) 'Year 3 Phonics Screening Check pilot'. Available at: www.bit.ly/2F5ZyyU

Department for Education (2011) 'New phonics check will identify thousands of children needing extra reading help', *gov.uk* [Online] 16 September. Available at: www.bit.ly/36GD5nc

Dewey, J. (2017) *The School and Society.* Dinslaken: Anboco.

Deming, W. E. (1994) *Out of the Crisis.* Cambridge, MA: The MIT Press.

Diack, H. (1965) *In spite of the alphabet: a study of the teaching of reading.* London: Chatto and Windus.

Dehaene, S. (2015) *Reading in the brain.* New York: Penguin Books.

Donald, M. (1991) *Origins of the modern mind.* Cambridge, MA: Harvard University Press.

Dowhower, S. (1987) 'Effects of Repeated Reading on Second-Grade Transitional Readers' Fluency and Comprehension', *Reading Research Quarterly* 22 (4) p. 389.

Egan, K. (2004) *Getting it wrong from the beginning.* New Haven: Yale University Press.

Ehri, L. (2004) 'Teaching Phonemic Awareness and Phonics' in McCardle, P. and Chhabra, V. (eds) *The Voice of Evidence in Reading Research* (1st ed). Baltimore: Paul H. Brookes Publishing Co.

Fullan, M. and Fullan, M. (2013) *The New Meaning of Educational Change.* Milton: Taylor & Francis.

Geary, D. (2007) 'Educating the evolved mind' in Carlson, J. and Levin, J. (eds) *Educating the Evolved Mind: Conceptual Foundations for an Evolutionary Educational Psychology.* Charlotte, NC: Information Age Publishing, IAP.

Goodman, K. (1970) 'Reading: A psycholinguistic guessing game', *Journal of the Reading Specialist* 6 (4) pp. 126-135.

Gough, P. (1983) 'Context, form, and interaction' in Rayner, K. (ed.) *Eye movements in reading: Perceptual and language processes.* New York: Academic.

Gough, P. and Tunmer, W. (1986) 'Decoding, Reading, and Reading Disability', *Remedial and Special Education* 7 (1) pp. 6-10.

Gough, P. and Hillinger, M. (1980) 'Learning to read: an unnatural act', *Bulletin of the Orton Society* 30 (1) pp. 179-196.

Havelock, E. (1976) *Origins of Western literacy* (1st ed). Boston: Harvard University Press.

Hepplewhite, D. (2016) 'Phonics Teaching – is it 'fit for purpose'?', *Teaching English* [Online] Summer issue. Available at: www.bit.ly/2SsrJLB

Holdaway, D. (1979) *The Foundations of Literacy.* Sydney: Scholastic.

Hughes, D. and Stainthorp, R. (1999) *Learning From Children Who Read at an Early Age.* London: Routledge.

Johnston, R. and Watson, J. (2004) 'Accelerating the development of reading, spelling and phonemic awareness skills in initial readers', *Reading and Writing* 17 (4) pp. 327-357.

Kamhi, A. (2007) 'Knowledge Deficits: The True Crisis in Education', *The ASHA Leader* 12 (7) pp. 28-29.

Kuhn, M. and Stahl, S. (2003) 'Fluency: A review of developmental and remedial practices', *Journal of Educational Psychology* 95 (1) pp. 3-21.

LaBerge, D. and Samuels, S. (1974) 'Toward a theory of automatic information processing in reading', *Cognitive Psychology* 6 (2) pp. 293-323.

Lawson, J. and Silver, H. (1973) *A social history of education in England.* London: Methuen and company.

Leong, C. (1973) 'Hong Kong' in Downing, J. (ed.) *Comparative Reading.* New York: Macmillan.

Liberman, A., Cooper, F., Shankweiler, D. and Studdert-Kennedy, M. (1967) 'Perception of the speech code', *Psychological Review* 74 (6) pp. 431-461.

Lloyd-Jones, M. (2013) *Phonics and the Resistance to Reading* (1st ed). London: Howl Books.

McGuinness, D. (2004) *Early reading instruction.* Cambridge, MA: The MIT Press.

McGuinness, D. (1999) *Why our children can't read, and what we can do about it.* New York: Simon & Schuster.

Malatesha Joshi, R., Binks, E., Hougen, M., Dahlgren, M. E., Ocker-Dean, E. and Smith, D. L. (2009) 'Why elementary teachers might be inadequately prepared to teach reading', *Journal of Learning Disabilities* 42 (5) pp. 392-402.

Martinez, M., Roser, N. and Strecker, S. (1999) '"I never thought I could be a star": A readers theatre ticket to reading fluency', *The Reading Teacher* 52 pp. 326-334.

Miller, J. and Schwanenflugel, P. (2008) 'A Longitudinal Study of the Development of Reading Prosody as a Dimension of Oral Reading Fluency in Early Elementary School Children', *Reading Research Quarterly* 43 (4) pp. 336-354.

National Institute of Child Health and Human Development (2000) *Report of the National Reading Panel: Teaching Children to Read.* Washington, DC: US Government Printing Office.

Nation, K., Angell, P. and Castles, A. (2007) 'Orthographic learning via self-teaching in children learning to read English: Effects of exposure, durability, and context', *Journal of Experimental Child Psychology* 96 (1) pp. 71-84.

Naht.org.uk. (2017) 'Abandoning phonics retests Year 3 children will be welcomed by school leaders, says NAHT', *NAHT.org* [Online] 15 December. Retrieved from: www.bit.ly/2I0aizZ

Ouellette, G., Martin-Chang, S. and Rossi, M. (2017) 'Learning From Our Mistakes: Improvements in Spelling Lead to Gains in Reading Speed', *Scientific Studies of Reading* 21 (4) pp. 350-357.

Pearson, P. (2001) 'Life in the radical middle: A personal apology for a balanced view of reading' in Flippo, R. F. (ed) *Reading researchers in search of common ground.* Newark, DE: International Reading Association.

Perfetti, C. (1991) 'The Psychology, Pedagogy, and Politics of Reading', *Psychological Science* 2 (2) pp. 70-83.

Perfetti, C. (2007) 'Reading Ability: Lexical Quality to Comprehension', *Scientific Studies of Reading* 11 (4) pp. 357-383.

Pinker, S. (2003) 'Language as an adaptation to the cognitive niche', in Christiansen, M. and Kirby, S. (eds.) *Language evolution: States of the art.* New York: Oxford University Press.

Polk, T. and Farah, M. (2002) 'Functional MRI evidence for an abstract, not perceptual, word-form area', *Journal of Experimental Psychology: General* 131 (1) pp. 65-72.

NASUWT (2013) 'NASUWT: Research shows teachers concern over phonics', *politics.co.uk* [Online] 15 February. Available at: www.bit.ly/2SsrJLB

Pressley, M. (2006) 'What the future of reading research could be'. Paper presented at the International Reading Association Reading Research conference in Chicago, IL.

Quintilian. and Watson, J. (1913) *Quintilian's institutes of oratory.* London: G. Bell & Sons.

Rasinski, T., Reutzel, R., Chard, D. and Linan-Thompson, S. (2011) 'Reading Fluency' in Kamil, M., Pearson, P., Birr Moje, E. and Afflebach, P. (eds) *Handbook of Reading Research* (Vol. 4). New York: Routledge.

Rasinski, T., Chang, S., Edmondson, E., Nageldinger, J., Nigh, J., Remark, L., Kenney, K., Walsh-Moorman, E., Yildirim, K., Nichols, W., Paige, D. and Rupley, W. (2016) 'Reading Fluency and College Readiness', *Journal of Adolescent & Adult Literacy* 60 (4) pp. 453-460.

Rasinski, T., Rikli, A. and Johnston, S. (2009) 'Reading Fluency: More Than Automaticity? More Than a Concern for the Primary Grades?', *Literacy Research and Instruction* 48 (4) pp. 350-361.

Reicher, G. (1969) 'Perceptual recognition as a function of meaningfulness of stimulus material', *Journal of Experimental Psychology* 81 (2) pp. 275-280.

Rogers, B. (2002) *Pascal.* New York: Routledge.

Share, D. (2004) 'Orthographic learning at a glance: On the time course and developmental onset of self-teaching', *Journal of Experimental Child Psychology* 87 (4) pp. 267-298.

Share, D. (1995) 'Phonological recoding and self-teaching: sine qua non of reading acquisition', *Cognition* 55 (2) pp. 151-218.

Smith, F. (1975) *Psycholinguistics and reading.* New York: Holt, Rinehart and Winston.

Stanovich, K. (1986) 'Matthew Effects in Reading: Some Consequences of Individual Differences in the Acquisition of Literacy', *Reading Research Quarterly* 21 (4) pp. 360-407.

Stanovich, K. (2000) *Progress in understanding reading: Scientific foundations and new frontiers* (1st ed). New York: Guildford Press.

Stanovich, K. and West, R. (1989) 'Exposure to Print and Orthographic Processing', *Reading Research Quarterly* 24 (4) p. 402.

Terman, S. and Walcutt, C. (1958) *Reading: chaos and cure.* New York: McGraw-Hill.

Thorndike, E. (1917) 'Reading as reasoning: A study of mistakes in paragraph reading', *Journal of Educational Psychology* 8 (6) pp. 323-332.

Tumner, W. and Nicholson, T. (2011) 'The development and teaching of word recognition skill' in Kamil, M., Pearson, P., Birr Moje, E. and Afflerbach, P. (eds) *Handbook of Reading Research* (4th ed). New York: Routledge.

Turner, M. and Burkard, T. (1996) *Reading fever.* London: Centre for Policy Studies.

Walker, M. and Bartlett, S. (2013) *Evaluation of the Phonics Screening Check: First Interim Report* (1st ed). London: NFER.

Wilson, F. T., Flemming, C., Burke, A. and Garrison, C. (1938) 'Reading progress in kindergarten and primary grades', *Elementary School Journal* 38 pp. 442–449.

Author bio-sketch:

The Reading Ape is fallible. Blogs can be read at thereadingape.com. The Reading Ape tweets as @TheReadingApe.

PRIORITISING TEACHING CHILDREN TO WRITE

BY DANIELLE V. DENNIS

While there is a wealth of research about early reading, which has been systematised and organised to produce some effective strategies across schools in the UK and wider, the teaching of writing is still much harder to synthesise to a body of knowledge. A primary headteacher I know well said to me recently that 'we think we're close, but no one has really nailed how to teach writing'.

It is also the case that the writing assessment at Key Stage 2 in the UK is via teacher assessment. While there is some moderation, this being internal teacher assessment means that it is treated as reading's poorer relation. But writing is harder than reading. Encoding is harder than decoding. And teaching it is hence (arguably) a lot harder.

There is some limited research to unpick on the teaching of writing, but even much of that is 'noise'. As school leaders, it is really hard to know what one must know, and in planning this book I knew this chapter would be one of the hardest to write. Danielle taught at my own children's school, bringing a synthesis of academia and pragmatism to curriculum and explicitly to literacy. She is well-placed, therefore, to be able to advise us on what leaders need to know about the teaching of writing and, hence, I gave her this chapter which she later described to me as 'fiendishly difficult'. She's right, it was, but it was illuminating to me to read it and I think it will be for all school leaders too.

While much attention has been given to research on the teaching of reading, and how pupils' learn primary reading, there is a dearth of scholarship on primary writing. Because of this, the teaching of writing in the primary years is treated with much broader strokes, lacking reference to the component skills children need to build expertise in the process. Writing is often used as a summative assessment, or final evaluation, of primary children's knowledge of both process and content with little emphasis on the explicit teaching or practice which children require to become proficient. Hochman and Wexler (2017) suggest that one of the biggest problems in classrooms is that teachers often assign writing without teaching it.

Between the ages of three and five, young children progress through a series of approximations to writing. Byrnes and Wasik (2009) describe these as phases, including:

- Phase 1: non-figural graphics such as scribbling and wavy lines;
- Phase 2: strings of circles or pseudo-letters, often written as distinct units;
- Phase 3: samples that contain actual letters they know.

In other words, children understand that graphemes (a written symbol that represents a sound, or letters) carry meaning and intend to convey their messages through the use of approximations until they are explicitly taught the alphabetic principle and able to match graphemes with phonemes (smallest unit of sound). This is not dissimilar to a child that picks up a familiar book and 'reads' it by telling a story they've memorised. The child understands that the print carries meaning and tells the story well before they have pieced together the component skills of reading.

Typically, there is a lag in the development of writing ability compared to a child's reading ability (Byrnes and Wasik, 2009). While these two areas of literacy develop alongside each other, it is the reading that generally informs the writing, and therefore a child's ability to communicate through writing advances at a slower rate. Byrnes and Wasik (2009) report a lag of three to four years between using schemata to comprehend stories and using them to write stories, and this lag is even greater for expository texts. Many primary schools, however, ask children to write texts that are as complex as those they are reading, which is incongruent with what we know about children's literacy development and may serve to hinder their capacity as competent writers across genres. In this chapter, I highlight what we know about children's writing development and discuss our best bets for leaders to ensure that the teaching of writing in the primary years is most effective.

What we know about how children develop as writers: alphabetic principle

Much like reading, acknowledging the role of the alphabetic principle in writing development is essential to supporting young children's abilities. Phonemic awareness, phonics, fluency and vocabulary each play important roles in writing development. These skills must be explicitly taught alongside extensive reading, making it essential that the teaching of reading and writing is thoughtfully planned to complement each other rather than viewed as discretely separate endeavours, which is too often the case in primary schools.

Ehri and Roberts (2006) note that while phonemic awareness is conceptually separate from letters and spellings of words, its function is to enable novices to connect speech to print. Phonemic awareness refers to the ability to manipulate phonemes in spoken words. Segmenting, blending and deleting phonemes supports children to understand the way spoken language works, which builds into the overarching concepts included within phonological awareness, such as rhyming and syllabic operations. As children begin to learn letter names – a key component of writing development – they can map both their phonemic and phonological awareness to their understanding of creating meaning through writing.

Although decoding develops before encoding, it is the knowledge of phonics, combined with phonemic and phonological awareness, that allows children to structure the written text. As children become more proficient decoders, they are better able to practise encoding words they can fluently read. In early phases of encoding, children will 'use but confuse' their knowledge of phonics and spell words incorrectly as a consequence (Bear et al, 2016). Often these incorrect spellings are decodable and, therefore, carry meaning. Although sometimes eschewed in much comment amongst educators on social media, these inventive spellings develop as children begin to encode words for the purpose of making meaning. In multiple studies of inventive spelling, the practice was '... coupled with impressive awareness of and attention to the phonemic structure of words' (Adams, 1990).

Inventive spelling and the role of orthographic knowledge

Inventive spellings are a useful assessment tool for teachers to understand children's connections between phonemes and graphemes to determine which must be explicitly taught for children to use it correctly moving forward. In other words, children will naturally invent spellings as they are learning to encode. As teachers assess this practice, they are better able to provide children with explicit instruction in word analysis and consonant blending, which is a necessary complement to children's independent orthographic intuitions (Adams, 1990). Richgels (2003) found that children were more likely to use the correct spelling of a word if it was explicitly taught after they attempted to apply their knowledge of grapheme-phoneme correspondence.

According to Beck and Beck (2013), '[w]ritten English has four major components: (1) phonology, the sounds in speech; (2) orthography, the spelling system; (3) semantics, word meanings; and (4) syntax, how words fit together in sentences' (p. 122). Simply put, orthography is a language's spelling system or the system by which writers order letter sequences when encoding oral language. Beck and Beck believe orthographic knowledge can develop at roughly the same time as children are learning phonics, but as noted earlier children will then decode before encoding words based on orthographic principles and will likely make errors (inventive spellings) in their efforts to encode. Bear et al (2016) view these errors as predictable based on the way children progress in their orthographic development. As such, they suggest that teachers offer spelling instruction that builds on this development rather than by teaching spelling words from seemingly random sources, which are again likely mapped on to words children can decode rather than building on their encoding abilities. They further posit that this orthographic development overlaps with semantics and that syllables, suffixes, bases and roots are also features children 'use but confuse' resulting in misspellings that should then be explicitly taught based on the orthographic stage children are working within. Suffice to say that orthographic knowledge builds upon itself and the teaching of spelling should be informed by that development. To get the teaching of writing right, we must acknowledge the role of orthographic development and how knowledge manifests through it.

Orthography, semantics and knowledge

Children should be asked to write about what they know, not about what they like. From the standpoint of motivation theory, the more children write about what they know the more likely they are to be motivated to write and may, therefore, 'like' it, but we take a misguided approach in education when we assume children will write so long as they can choose to write about something they like. For school leaders, this means the scope and sequence of the curriculum must be considered alongside children's writing development and that how writing is taught requires careful consideration. This is one argument for both teaching writing alongside extensive reading and explicit instruction of subjects to build children's knowledge of content across a range of concepts, and these arguments connect orthography and semantics to knowledge because children become more familiar with word meanings and spellings as they are taught and provided time to practise more complex ideas. Two principles offered in *The Writing Revolution* address the connection of subject knowledge. The first states, '[w]hen embedded in the content of the curriculum, writing instruction is a powerful teaching tool' and the second says, '[t]he content of the curriculum drives the rigor of the writing activities' (Hochman and Wexler, 2017, p. 8).

Byrne and Wasik (2009) conceive of writing development as the '…coalescing of knowledge and processes, rather than the acquisition of separate components' (p. 269). Relatedly, Puranik and Lonigan (2014) theorise three dimensions accounting for emergent writing skills (p. 455-6):

1. Conceptual knowledge: children's understandings of the purposes of writing, knowledge about the functions of print, and knowledge of writing concepts;
2. Procedural knowledge: children's knowledge of the specific symbols and conventions involved in the production of writing;
3. Generative knowledge: children's emerging ability to compose phrases and sentences in their writing.

It takes time to develop the knowledge and processes children need to produce extensive text, both fiction and non-fiction, and yet we often ask them to use writing, from a very young age, as a summative assessment tool. Instead, viewing writing as a formative assessment tool addresses neurodevelopmental constraints and allows teachers to better recognise how both knowledge and processes are advancing. This can happen by giving greater credence to smaller units of text and focusing children's attention on sentence-level practise. Doing so encourages children to construct discriminate parts of writing through deliberate practise and building those into cohesive communication. Hochman and Wexler (2017) posit that '[s]entences are the building blocks of all writing' (p. 8) and recommend children be provided with consistent opportunity to practise sentence-level strategies. Practise is likely to engender fluency and the automatisation of writing skills frees working memory to attend to meaning or the orthographic and semantic components that are developing.

Knowledge and the writing process

Byrne and Wasik (2009) refer to the structural and functional aspects of writing where the structural includes developmental changes in working memory capacity and knowledge resources and the functional includes changes in the writing process. When explicitly taught subjects across the curriculum, children's bank of knowledge improves with age and experience. This leads to increased fluency at the level of text generation and helps writers overcome the limits of working memory.

Both groups of authors discuss the importance of teacher scaffolding during the writing process to make the process more fluent, so children are better able to articulate their knowledge using domain-specific semantic and orthographic knowledge. Scaffolding leads to higher quality writing and increases children's ability to '...gain independent, explicit control over their genre knowledge' (Beringer et al, p. 293). Scaffolds also expand children's abilities to write across multiple genres. Beringer et al encourage teachers to introduce expository writing in early grades (e.g. Key Stage 1) so long as sufficient teacher modelling and scaffolding is in place to assist children in text generation. However, Byrne and Wasik (2009) found that young children are better able to write expository text that asks them to report, rather than analyse, and suggest that children need opportunities to demonstrate fluency in generating text that reports before being asked to analyse. Similarly, it is unlikely that children will be able to transfer writing skills from one subject to another until they have received substantial amounts of explicit writing instruction (Hochman and Wexler, 2017). Further, findings from studies reported by Byrne and Wasik suggest that young children have a more difficult time creating and writing for an imaginary audience than older children.

Writers and writing environments

Reporting on multiple studies, Byrne and Wasik (2009) propose that models show two kinds of variables affecting the writing process: (1) characteristics of individual writers and (2) characteristics of writing environments.

Individual writers

Psychologists argue that four components explain outputs of the writing process: (1) motivation factors, (2) knowledge structures in long-term memory, (3) cognitive processes, and (4) working memory (Byrne and Wasik, 2009).

Motivation factors: Motivational aspects of writing are goal-directed. A change in goals will lead to a change in writing output. To engage in writing regularly, children must have positive attitudes toward the process and themselves as writers. Byrne and Wasik (2009) explain that children need to believe '...writing affords them more benefits than costs' (p. 253). Even for the most proficient writers, writing is a challenging task. As such, we should judge developing writers, not by the standards of an adult, but rather by what is developmentally appropriate for their stage of writing progress (Beringer et al, 2002). We then build appropriate scaffolds that we explicitly teach, which allows children to build their understanding of the writing process and develop more positive attitudes regarding their abilities as writers.

Knowledge structures in long-term memory: Byrne and Wasik (2009) list five knowledge structures writers must employ to successfully craft a piece of writing. They suggest that when a writer is lacking any of the five the output will differ in quality. The five knowledge structures are (1) task schemas, (2) topics, (3) audiences, (4) genres, and (5) language. Task schemas are the knowledge writers have of past writing experiences and understandings of the expected outcome of the piece. Topics are the knowledge writers have of the content needed to complete the writing product. Audiences change depending on the schemas and topics writers are addressing, and a writer needs to consider who they are writing the piece for and what knowledge the audience has of the topic. Genres have distinctive structures that writers typically first learn by reading and then must be able to emulate. Language includes knowledge of grammar, syntax and semantics.

Cognitive processes: Reading skills are at the center of writing production. However, Hayes (1996) clarifies that writers read to evaluate in order to revise text they generated. Hayes notes three cognitive processes that support writing: text interpretation, reflection, and text production. Text interpretation is essentially the preparation phase of writing. This is when writers acquire the knowledge needed to build mental representations of the text. Reflection aligns with the planning process and involves decision and inference making. Text production is the translation of text interpretation and reflection into the writer's product.

Working memory: There are three phases of text production that are impacted by working memory. The first is the formulation phase where writers plan what they will say in their work. This leads to the execution phase when the writer enacts the plan developed in the formulation phase. Finally, during the monitoring phase, the writer reads and revises the work produced. Depending on the ability of the writer to engage in the writing process and/or to have the requisite knowledge to write fluently about the topic, working memory will affect each of the phases.

Writing environment

Writing is contextual: The audience, medium, and individuals who are present change as an author moves from one context to another. Hayes (1996) found that these changes affect the writing process in important ways. A meta-analysis of 32 studies showed that a change in medium, from paper to computer, resulted in higher quality pieces from all writers, but especially weaker writers (Byrne and Wasik, 2009). Considering such a shift when working with young children must be done cautiously as extensive instructional time would be needed to first teach them word processing skills. However, this does lead to a question about the purpose of the task and how we might elicit children's understandings of the content before asking them to write about it.

Hochman and Wexler (2017) note that the two most important phases of the writing process are planning and revising. This supports the notion that more proficient writers continually re-read and revise their work (Hayes, 1996), which suggests that children require numerous opportunities to read and revise their writing. Studies indicate that such revision should not always occur individually. Rather, collaborators are essential in the shifting context of the writing environment. As Beringer et al (2002) remind us, '[w]riting may be conceptualized as a social activity in which writers not only compose for an audience but also co-construct through dyadic discussion – goals, plans, content, strategies, and even initial and revised versions of text' (p. 293). There are benefits to teacher-as-collaborator just as there are benefits to children collaborating with one another. Again, purpose and intentionality are important considerations when deciding who is best suited to collaborate during the revision process. Dyson (2003) refers to this as social mediation and highlights the importance of oral language in writing. Although Dyson does not relate this directly to revision, she offers that writing is a '...communicative event, the relationship between oral and written language – and between a child's constructed meaning and a written message – is not initially, or exclusively, a direct one' (p. 128). This is not to suggest that we simply turn children loose to communicate their ideas. Rather, we provide explicit scaffolds or frameworks for them to follow to keep our purpose – planning or revising – at the fore of their conversations.

Concluding thoughts

Six main points drive the message of this chapter on primary writing instruction:

1. The teaching of writing in the primary grades must shift from being primarily summative to being primarily formative. When developing a scope and sequence for primary writing instruction, school leaders need to consider how smaller units of writing (used as formative approaches to gauging children's progress) build into summative works over time.

2. Teachers and school leaders must understand how children develop as writers and plan teaching based on the phases they build on in that process. For their part, school leaders must ensure teachers know that the teaching of writing is almost entirely formative and that professional learning is prioritised to ensure that the difficulties of teaching young children to write are considered.

3. As in reading, the teaching of the alphabetic principle for writing cannot be understated. Phonemic and phonological awareness and phonics not only support children's decoding but also their developing encoding skills (though those do lag behind decoding). School leaders will need to ensure all teachers understand how the alphabetic principle develops, how decoding and encoding are explicitly taught, and how to assess children's writing to support progress toward more sophisticated works.

4. Children use inventive spelling and it should be used as an assessment tool for teachers to determine how to build their orthographic knowledge, which is developmental and sequential. Leaders ensure that teachers understand how to use inventive spelling as an assessment tool.

5. Children write about what they know and, therefore, connecting writing to subject knowledge will augment children's ability to write for multiple purposes. Thus, school leaders must consider how children develop as writers and create explicit ways for teachers to embed writing instruction within and across subject areas.

6. Individual writers and writing environments affect the writing process in myriad ways and the purpose and intentionality with which we address those impacts children's development as writers. Working with both year groups and subject leads, school leaders should develop plans for writing environments across the school that includes a variety of ways for children to practise and discuss their writing.

Suggested reading

School leaders interested in augmenting their knowledge of primary writing might consider the following texts for future reading:

Bear, D. R., Invernizzi, M., Templeton, S. and Johnston, F. (2016) *Words Their Way: Word study for phonics, vocabulary, and spelling instruction* (6th edition). Boston: Pearson.

Words Their Way focuses on the developmental sequence for teaching orthographic knowledge. This is an excellent book to use for a book study with teachers because it provides both the why and how for word study whilst clearly describing children's development as proficient spellers.

Beck, I. L. and Beck, M. E. (2013) *Making Sense of Phonics: The Hows and Whys.* New York: Guilford.

Although this book does not emphasise the teaching of writing, having deep knowledge of phonics will support teachers in understanding children's inventive spelling to determine the necessary teaching that needs to occur. There is, however, substantial discussion on teaching phonemic awareness, which is useful for developing both decoding and encoding abilities in young children.

Byrnes, J. P. and Wasik, B. A. (2009) 'Chapter 9: The Development of Writing Skills' in *Language and literacy development: What educators need to know.* New York: Guilford.

This entire book is excellent. It provides overviews of the research related to language and literacy development in a very accessible manner. Chapter 9 is one of the strongest descriptions of writing development currently available to teachers and leaders.

Hochman, J. C. and Wexler, N. (2017) *The Writing Revolution: A guide to advancing thinking through writing in all subjects and grades.* San Francisco: Jossey-Bass.

Shifting from assigning writing as a summative task to teaching writing in a formative manner can be challenging for some teachers. Reconsidering ways to explicitly teach writing is necessary when making this transition, and *The Writing Revolution* provides clear principles and strategies for doing so. Leaders should support teachers by asking them to read about a strategy, practise using it in class, discussing with colleagues, and practising further. The strategies provided are scaffolded so it is not recommended that teachers attempt to incorporate too many at one time, especially as they are first learning to use them in their teaching.

References

Adams, M. J. (1990) *Beginning to read: Thinking and learning about print.* Cambridge, MA: The MIT Press.

Bear, D. R., Invernizzi, M., Templeton, S. and Johnston, F. (2016) *Words Their Way: Word study for phonics, vocabulary, and spelling instruction* (6th edition). Boston: Pearson.

Beck, I. L. and Beck, M. E. (2013) *Making Sense of Phonics: The Hows and Whys.* New York: Guilford.

Beringer, V. W., Vaughan, K., Abbott, R. D., Begay, K., Coleman, K. B., Curtin, G., Hawkins, J. M. and Graham, S. (2002) 'Teaching spelling and composition alone and together: Implications for the simple view of writing', *Journal of Educational Psychology* 94 (2) pp. 291-304.

Byrnes, J. P. and Wasik, B. A. (2009) *Language and literacy development: What educators need to know.* New York: Guilford.

Dyson, A. H. (2003) 'Writing and children's symbolic repertoires: Development unhinged' in Neuman, S. B. and Dickinson, D. K. (eds) *Handbook of Early Literacy Research* (pp. 126-141). New York: Guilford.

Ehri, L. C. and Roberts, T. (2006) 'The roots of learning to read and write: Acquisition of letters and phonemic awareness' in Neuman, S. B. and Dickinson, D. K. (eds) *Handbook of Early Literacy Research* (vol. 2). New York: Guilford, pp. 113-131.

Hayes, J. R. (1996) 'A new framework for understanding cognition and affect in writing' in Levy, C. M. and Ransdell, S. (eds) *The science of writing: Theories, methods, individual differences, and applications.* Mahwah, NJ: Erlbaum, pp. 1-27.

Hochman, J. C. and Wexler, N. (2017) *The writing revolution: A guide to advancing thinking through writing in all subjects and grades.* San Francisco: Jossey-Bass.

Puranik, C. S. and Lonigan, C. J. (2014) 'Emergent writing in preschoolers: Preliminary evidence for a theoretical framework', *Reading Research Quarterly* 49 (4) pp. 453-467.

Richgels, D. J. (2003) 'Invented spelling, phonemic awareness, and reading and writing instruction', Neuman, S. B. and Dickinson, D. K. (eds) *Handbook of Early Literacy Research*. New York: Guilford, pp. 142-158.

Author bio-sketch:

Danielle V. Dennis is Professor of Literacy Teacher Education and Policy and Director of the School of Education at the University of Rhode Island, USA. Danielle also serves as professor-in-residence at Cottenham Primary School where she leads the Powerful Knowledge, Powerful Pedagogy (@powerfulknowped) research project that studies the professional development needs of teachers and school leaders as they develop and implement a knowledge-rich curriculum.

LEARNING AND MEMORY

BY DYLAN WILIAM

When I became a school leader, I hadn't considered any aspect of cognitive science. In fact, in common with many, I hadn't encountered it. I certainly would have shied away from considering memory as important. It was only when I was confronted with a definition of learning that intentionally rests on remembering that I, in turn, began to confront the orthodox view that somehow implicitly separated teaching from what is being taught and the expectation that it is to be learned and remembered.

As well as being one of the most prominent and articulate defenders of education research, Dylan Wiliam exemplifies an approach that is informed and persuaded by research. If reliable studies challenge his pre-existing beliefs, as evidenced by social media, he is open to confronting those beliefs – including when the conclusion is something he finds uncomfortable. As a result, he exemplifies an era I hope our profession is moving into, and one that we need to embrace all the more as school leaders.

As an author, speaker, educator and critic, Dylan has been incredibly influential in schools, and here he unpicks what school leaders need to know about how pupils remember what has been taught.

The problem

'I taught it, they just didn't learn it.' There are two ways of interpreting this sentence. The first is that it is the epitome of a bad teacher or one who is satisfied that as long as the content has been 'delivered' in some sense, then if the pupils did not learn it, that is the fault of the pupils. However, there is another way to interpret this sentence that reveals an important insight into teaching and learning.

The teacher taught something to her or his pupils, the pupils satisfactorily completed the tasks they were assigned and could demonstrate the relevant skills at the end of the activity and the next day – and perhaps even the day after – only for the pupils to be unable to reproduce the same evidence of learning two weeks later. What's going on here? Did the pupils learn it or not? The answer depends on how you define 'learning'.

Paul Kirschner, John Sweller and Richard Clark suggest that learning is 'a change in long-term memory' (2006, p. 75). Many people object to this definition because they assume that a change in long-term memory refers only to rote memorisation of facts but long-term memory includes anything that we remember for the long-term, such as what our children look like or how to ride a bicycle. If we do not have to relearn or restudy something each time we need to recall it, it is in long-term memory. As Kirschner, Sweller, and Clark (p. 77) go on to say, 'The aim of all instruction [i.e., all activities planned by the teacher] is to alter the contents of long-term memory. If nothing has changed in long-term memory, nothing has been learned.' With this definition, if pupils can do something at the end of a lesson but cannot do so some time later then no learning has taken place. What makes teaching so challenging is that the way that educational experiences (or, indeed, experiences of any kind) get translated into long-term memory is not well understood, seems to be rather unpredictable, and is often counterintuitive.

What makes this issue even more serious is that most teachers and school leaders – either in the UK or elsewhere – get little or nothing in their pre-service preparation programmes about how human memory works which, when you think about it, is rather odd. After all, as teachers, we are in the memory business. We want our pupils to remember what we are teaching. As a result, much of what happens in schools is driven by models of learning and memory that are, at best, uninformed by what research in cognitive science tells us about how learning takes place and, at worst, is actually inconsistent with that research.

What we know about how memory works

Most people's beliefs about how memory works are similar to the 'law of exercise' first articulated by Edward Thorndike in 1913, which comprises the 'law of use' and the 'law of disuse'. The idea is that if we use the things we have learned then memory is strengthened, and if we do not use them then memory is weakened. If we are unable to recall something we once knew we assume that the memory has been so weakened that the memory has gone entirely. For example, the vast majority of people educated in England within the last five decades will have studied French for at least a few years and it is practically certain that they would have been taught the French word for 'ear'. If you cannot remember the French word for 'ear' then it is natural to assume that the memory has gone – the lack of use has caused the memory of that word to decay entirely.

However, if I showed you a list of ten parts of the body in French, most people would be able to pick out the French word for 'ear' immediately, which would not be possible if the memory had faded entirely. The memory is still there, it's only difficult to retrieve.

This distinction between how well something has been learned, and how easy it is to retrieve at any particular time, is at the heart of the 'new theory of disuse' developed by Robert and Elizabeth Bjork (Bjork and Bjork, 1992). Any item in memory has two characteristics: storage strength (how well something has been learned) and retrieval strength (how easy that item is to retrieve at any given moment). One important assumption of this theory is that while retrieval strength can go up and down, storage strength can only increase – if you have ever learned something, the memory is always there, but what might be difficult is retrieving it at any given moment.

There are two important sets of experimental findings from the work of the Bjorks and other memory researchers that have particular relevance for education. The first is that storage strength is increased both by restudying an item or by successfully retrieving it from memory, but that retrieval has a bigger impact on storage strength than restudy.

Retrieval improves long-term learning more than restudy

This is an important – and rather counterintuitive – finding. Most people's models of memory are rather like the idea of reading data from a hard disk. When data is read from a hard disk, the hard disk itself is not changed. But human memory does not work like that. When we successfully retrieve things from memory, that makes the memory stronger. This is important because it explains the power of what is sometimes called 'the testing effect'.

Many people believe that our pupils are tested too much in school, and one common quote that is used in objecting to the amount of testing in our schools is that 'weighing the pig doesn't fatten it'. However, in terms of learning this claim is quite wrong. When pupils are tested on something, they are forced to retrieve things from memory and that retrieval practice actually strengthens the memory. In fact, practice testing is one of the most strongly supported strategies for improving learning in all of psychology (Dunlosky, Rawson, Marsh, Nathan and Willingham, 2013).

A particularly powerful illustration of the testing effect comes from an experiment conducted by Henry 'Roddy' Roediger and Jeffrey Karpicke

(Roediger III and Karpicke, 2006) where 180 undergraduate students read one of two passages of English text, each of which contained 30 idea units: 'The Sun' (256 words) or 'Sea Otters' (275 words). All students were given seven minutes to read the assigned passage and then spent two minutes doing multiplication problems (so that they would have to think about something other than the passage for a while). The students were then randomly divided into three equal groups, with different patterns of study (S) and testing (T), with two minutes spent on multiplication problems between each study or testing session:

SSSS: students spent three seven-minute periods re-reading the passage.

SSST: students spent two seven-minute periods re-reading the passage, and one seven-minute period completing a test on the contents of the passage.

STTT: students spent three seven-minute periods completing a test on the contents of the passage.

Students then completed a questionnaire in which they were asked to rate (on a seven-point scale) how interesting and readable the passage they read was and how much they would remember of the contents. The results are shown in table 1.

	Rating		
	Interesting	Readable	Remember
SSSS	3.8	2.5	4.8
SSST	4.1	2.5	4.2
STTT	4.6	2.8	4.0

Table 1: Student ratings from questionnaires

Students were then tested on their knowledge of the passage they had read. Half the students were tested after five minutes and half the students were tested a week later. The results are shown in table 2.

	After 5 minutes	After 1 week
SSSS	83%	40%
SSST	78%	56%
STTT	71%	61%

Table 2: Proportion of idea units recalled

When students were tested five minutes after the learning session, those who had read the passage four times recalled more than those who had read the passage three times and then been tested, who in turn recalled more than those who had read the passage just once and been tested three times. However, when students were tested a week after the learning session, this order was reversed. Those who had read the passage just once and been tested three times recalled more of the passage more than the other two groups. The retrieval practice provided by the test enhanced long-term learning more than the restudy provided by the opportunity to read the passages again.

This result is all the more interesting because, as shown in table 1, those who read the passage four times were more confident than the other two groups that they would remember the contents of the passage. The increased familiarity with the passage provided by the chance to read the passage several times made the students think they were learning more, whereas they were, in actual fact, learning less. This is an example of a quite general phenomenon which is that learners (and their teachers!) often express a preference for approaches to learning that are more effective in the short term but lead to less effective long-term learning (Bjork, 1994).

There is an additional benefit from practice testing and that is that when pupils find out that an answer they thought was correct is actually incorrect then they tend to remember the correct answer for longer than if they had just guessed an answer. Moreover, the more confident that pupils are that their answers are correct, the bigger the learning effect of being corrected. This is quite a surprising finding as previously, researchers had believed that when pupils had more confidence in their answers, their ideas would be more resistant to change, whereas quite the reverse seems to be true. This phenomenon was given the name of 'hypercorrection' effect by Brady Butterfield and Janet Metcalfe who summarise this effect by saying 'Errors committed with high confidence are hypercorrected' (Butterfield and Metcalfe, 2001, p. 1491).

The second set of experimental findings is that the increase in storage strength produced by restudying something or successfully retrieving it from memory is greater when retrieval strength is low. In other words, when something is less familiar the effects of restudying it are greater and when something is harder to retrieve from memory then the effect of successfully retrieving it from memory on long-term retention is greater.

Restudy and retrieval increase storage strength more when retrieval strength is *low*

One immediate implication of the idea that restudy and retrieval improve storage strength more when retrieval strength is low is that studying material in blocks (what is sometimes called 'massed practice') is less efficient than spacing the same amount of study time over several study sessions (what is sometimes called 'distributed practice'). A particularly compelling demonstration of this effect is provided by a recent experiment carried out by Doug Rohrer and his colleagues in five middle schools in Florida (Rohrer, Dedrick, Hartwig and Cheung, 2020). Each of the 15 teachers recruited for the experiment taught at least two, and in most cases, four or more, parallel 7th grade (Year 8) classes. In addition to their regular studies, pupils completed eight worksheets over 14 weeks, with a review worksheet ten days later. Each of the worksheets covered two sides of a single sheet of paper and contained eight problems.

Half of each participating teacher's classes were allocated to receive 'blocked' practice. For these classes, all the worksheets focused on a single topic with worksheet 2 focusing on graphs, worksheet 4 on inequalities, worksheet 6 on expressions and worksheet 8 on circles. The other four worksheets contained a variety of problems on other topics such as probability, angles and volume, and each worksheet contained a range of problems on different topics. The other half of each teacher's classes were allocated to receive 'distributed' practice so that each worksheet contained one question on each of the four focal topics (graphs, inequalities, expressions, and circles) and four questions on the other topics (i.e. probability, angles, and volume).

Approximately five weeks after completing the review worksheet, which contained one problem on each of the focal topics with four other problems, pupils were asked to complete a test with four problems on each of the four focal topics (graphs, inequalities, expressions, and circles). The average score for the 389 pupils getting blocked practice was 38% (median 31%). The average score for the 398 pupils getting distributed practice was 61% (median 62%). The difference between the two groups was equivalent to an effect size of 0.83 standard deviations or, to put it another way, an average pupil assigned to the distributed practice group scored at a level achieved by only the top 20% of those getting blocked practice. Moreover, this positive effect was found for each of the 15 teachers.

This is a striking result because, due to the design of the experiment, each teacher taught both the blocked practice and the distributed practice groups, so the quality of teaching was the same for all pupils. Two of the teachers reported that their pupils took much more time to complete the interleaved worksheets but the other 13 teachers said that the interleaved worksheets took only slightly more time for pupils to complete. And yet, by distributing the practice, so that pupils came back to a topic when it was less familiar, so that retrieval strength was low, the same amount of study time produced a bigger impact on long-term learning.

Of course, we should not place too much weight on just a couple of studies but the benefits of practice testing and distributed practice are two of the most strongly supported learning strategies in all of psychology. One particularly useful review of research was produced by a group of psychologists that investigated whether any particular learning strategies were effective 'across the board'. They looked for strategies that were effective across different kinds of material to be learned (vocabulary, science definitions, mathematics concepts, maps, diagrams, narrative texts, expository texts), different kinds of learning conditions (discovery learning, direct instruction, collaborative learning), different kinds of pupil (different ages, knowledge level, motivation, self-efficacy, interests) and that were effective with different measures of learning (cued recall, free recall, essay writing, portfolios, achievement tests and classroom assessments). They looked in detail at ten strategies, including summarisation, highlighting/underlining key passages of text, re-reading and self-explanation. The two strategies that were effective across all the different situations that they explored were practice testing and distributed practice (Dunlosky et al, 2013).

Implications for practice

The findings of how our memories work described above are somewhat counterintuitive and reinforce the importance of domain-specific knowledge for effective leadership. As in many areas of human experience, many of our intuitions about what kinds of practices are most effective are wrong with the result that the limited time we have to teach our pupils is being used ineffectively and inefficiently.

Many schools have dispensed with formal testing entirely and many others use tests and examinations only at the end of a term or a school year to indicate how much pupils have learned even though we have known about the power of practice testing for over a hundred years. Some resist using practice testing because they are concerned about increasing pupil anxiety even though regular practice testing appears actually to reduce text anxiety (Agarwal, D'Antonio, Roediger III, McDermott and McDaniel, 2014).

Perhaps the most important insight here – at least as far as implementation is concerned – is that pupils do not gain any additional benefit from practice testing when a teacher records a score in a mark-book. The benefits come from retrieval practice, when pupils take the test, and from hypercorrection, when pupils find out that an answer they thought was correct is actually incorrect. The best person to mark a practice test is, therefore, the person who just took it. That is why pupils are likely to benefit substantially from increased use of what I call 'zero-stakes' tests, where pupils complete tests under test conditions, are then given the scoring key so they can mark their own test and do not have to tell the teacher how they did unless they want to.

There is also often resistance to the idea of distributed rather than blocked practice because teachers believe that their pupils would prefer to spend a substantial amount of time on one topic. This may well be true, of course, but they are likely to remember less of what they are taught. It is also worth noting that in the study by Doug Rohrer and his colleagues, approximately half the teachers reported that their pupils dislike blocked practice *more* than distributed practice, while half the teachers said there was no difference. As far as we can tell, therefore, the use of practice testing and distributed practice represent two of the 'best bets' for how to improve educational outcomes for our pupils without spending more money or increasing teacher workload. Although, as ever, the research provides only a broad indication that these two strategies are likely to be effective, rather than a blueprint for how these ideas can be implemented. For example, a certain amount of blocked practice may be useful when pupils first learn about a concept or skill, and as pupils get nearer to formal tests and examinations such as Key Stage 2 tests and GCSEs, the benefit of distributed rather than blocked practice may be smaller. Also, it is worth noting that most studies on distributed practice have provided pupils with regular corrective feedback on their work and this may be a necessary ingredient of effective distributed practice.

The research on distributed practice shows that two one-hour sessions separated by an interval long enough for pupils to begin forgetting what they learned in the first session will result in better long-term learning than a two-hour session. The problem, of course, is that material of different kinds (e.g. conceptual versus verbal) may be forgotten at different rates so, for the time being at least, teacher judgement will be essential in putting these ideas into practice.

In terms of practical steps, perhaps the first thing to do is to make sure that teachers are aware of the research on the power of practice testing and distributed practice while making it clear that how these ideas are implemented in practice will require a considerable amount of professional judgement.

One concrete option is to encourage teachers to try using either distributed practice or practice testing for just one topic. For example, if a term's work in mathematics would normally cover seven topics, with two weeks per topic, then six of the topics could be blocked, and one of the topics could be distributed over the term (e.g. one lesson per week or fortnight, depending on the length of the mathematics lessons). It would then be possible to see whether pupils performed better at the end of the term on the distributed topic than on the blocked topics. Similarly, a teacher might use 'zero-stakes' tests in the teaching of one or two topics, with the other topics taught traditionally, and then, when pupils take an end-of-term or end-of-year test or examination, it will be possible to see if pupils are getting better marks on those topics taught using distributed practice or practice testing.

In primary schools, rather than having a 'maths hour', the research discussed above suggests that it may well be more effective to have two separate 30-minute sessions, one early in the day and one late in the day. This is to give children a chance to begin to forget what they learned in the morning (or more precisely, so that retrieval strength has begun to decline) so that the second session leads to better long-term learning (i.e. increased storage strength) than would be the case with a one-hour block.

Another implication of this research is that it may be more helpful to have more frequent, shorter lessons in a secondary school timetable rather than fewer, longer lessons. While having seven or eight lessons of 35 to 40 minutes in a day (as was common 50 years ago) involves a lot of pupil movement, it does mean that pupils will spend more time studying material when retrieval strength is low. In other words, it may be worthwhile for schools to investigate the trade-off between the loss of teaching time that is caused by increased pupil and teacher movement and the increased long-term learning that results from pupils spending more time studying material when retrieval strength is low. Where schools retain longer periods in the timetable (e.g. periods of 55 to 75 minutes), teachers should be encouraged to break these periods up into smaller units, with a different focus in each one. For example, a single 55-minute mathematics lesson might include 25 minutes on probability, 5 minutes of mental arithmetic practice and 25 minutes on the angles in circles. While these ideas might seem to be better suited to more academic subjects, it is important to realise that the findings about the benefits of distributed practice have been found to apply just as well for physical skills, including motor coordination.

The idea that learning is a change in long-term memory also brings into question the idea of looking for 'progress in a lesson'. Of course, leaders need to observe teaching in their schools and give feedback to teachers about their practice, but it is important to bear in mind that identifying good teaching is extraordinarily difficult because it requires predicting how much of what is happening in a lesson right now will be remembered in two or three weeks. If this were not hard enough – because storage strength is increased more when retrieval strength is low – learners need what Robert Bjork calls 'desirable difficulties' in learning (Bjork, 1994, p. 193). These are situations where retrieval is more difficult and, therefore, likely to have a greater impact on long-term learning. What this means is that lessons that look very effective may be ineffective and lessons that make pupils struggle may cause pupils to remember more. As psychology professor Daniel Willingham says, 'memory is the residue of thought' (Willingham, 2009, p. 54).

As one demonstration of the difficulty of identifying effective teaching from observation, a group of 165 experienced school leaders viewed videos of eight teachers. Four of the teachers had been especially effective over the last three years (with their pupils making significantly above average progress) and four of the teachers had been less effective over the same period (with their pupils making significantly less than average progress in each of the last three years). The leaders were asked, after they had watched the videos, to decide which of the teachers were from the more effective group and which were from the less effective group. The average number correct for the 165 leaders was 3.85 (Strong, Gargani and Hacifazlioğlu, 2011). In other words, they would have done better by flipping a coin.

The key takeaway here is that observing teaching is not a particularly effective way of determining whether and, if so, what pupils are learning and, consequently, periodic assessment is not only desirable but also absolutely essential. Moreover, to prevent the creation of a culture of 'learning and forgetting' in which pupils are tested only on what they have learned over the previous two or three weeks, assessment needs to be *synoptic*. In other words, even an end of unit test should ideally test pupils' retention of material from previous units, and perhaps even previous years. Not only will the results of such assessments provide valuable retrieval practice for pupils, but they will also provide leaders with valuable information in two ways. First, and perhaps obviously, they will provide information about whether pupils are really learning what they are being taught. Second, and just as important, pupils' performance on such review assessments provide valuable evidence about the alignment between what pupils are being taught and what is being assessed. After all, low scores on a test may not mean that the pupils are not learning anything, but rather that what they are learning is not being captured by that particular test.

A chapter of this length, inevitably, skates over the surface of complex issues and the further reading listed will provide the interested reader with far more detailed treatments of the issues outlined here. Nevertheless, even a basic understanding of the importance of practice testing and the benefits of distributed rather than blocked practice provides leaders with powerful tools for helping pupils remember more of what they learn in school.

Further reading

One of the most welcome developments in recent years is that cognitive psychologists are producing research findings that have real, direct and immediate relevance to classroom practice. In this chapter I have provided a rather brief overview of some of the educational implications of the 'new theory of disuse' but there are many other areas of research that school and system leaders need to know about to lead effective instructional improvement. One particularly exciting area of research is cognitive load theory which looks at the factors that influence whether and how educational experiences get translated into long-term memory, and provides important insights into the importance of instructional design and sequencing, although implementing these ideas requires substantial subject expertise.

For the specific topic of this chapter, there are five books that are both readable and that provide useful and rigorous overviews of the state of current research on learning and memory.

Agarwal, P. K. and Bain, P. M. (2019) *Powerful teaching.* San Francisco: Jossey-Bass.

Boser, U. (2017) *Learn better: Mastering the skills for success in life, business, and school, or, how to become an expert in just about anything.* Emmaus, PA: Rodale.

Brown, P. C., Roediger III, H. L. and McDaniel, M. A. (2014) *Make It Stick: The Science of Successful Learning.* Cambridge, MA: Belknap Press.

Carey, B. (2014) *How We Learn: The Surprising Truth About When, Where and Why It Happens.* New York: Random House.

Didau, D. and Rose, N. (2016) *What Every Teacher Needs to Know About Psychology.* Woodbridge: John Catt Educational.

While each of these books covers a lot of the same ground, they do so in different ways, with different perspectives and – given that a better understanding of how pupils learn will have a substantial impact on how effective any leader's efforts will be – it is probably worthwhile to read all five.

References

Agarwal, P. K., D'Antonio, L., Roediger III, H. L., McDermott, K. B. and McDaniel, M. A. (2014) 'Classroom-based programs of retrieval practice reduce middle school and high school students' test anxiety', *Journal of Applied Research in Memory and Cognition* 3 (3) pp. 131-139.

Bjork, R. A. (1994) 'Memory and metamemory considerations in the training of human beings' in Metcalfe, J. and Shimamura, A. P. (eds) *Metacognition: Knowing about knowing.* Cambridge, MA: MIT Press, pp. 188-205.

Bjork, R. A. and Bjork, E. L. (1992) 'A new theory of disuse and an old theory of stimulus fluctuation' in Healy, A. F., Kosslyn, S. M. and Shiffrin, R. M. (eds) *From learning processes to cognitive processes: Essays in honor of William K. Estes* (vol. 2). Hillsdale, NJ: Lawrence Erlbaum Associates, pp. 35-67.

Butterfield, B. and Metcalfe, J. (2001) 'Errors committed with high confidence are hypercorrected', *Journal of Experimental Psychology: Learning, Memory, and Cognition* 27 (6) pp. 1491-1494.

Dunlosky, J., Rawson, K. A., Marsh, E. J., Nathan, M. J. and Willingham, D. T. (2013) 'Improving students' learning with effective learning techniques: Promising directions from cognitive and educational psychology', *Psychological Science in the Public Interest* 14 (1) pp. 4-58.

Kirschner, P. A., Sweller, J. and Clark, R. E. (2006) 'Why minimal guidance during instruction does not work: An analysis of the failure of constructivist, problem-based, experiential, and inquiry-based teaching', *Educational Psychologist* 41 (2) pp. 75-86.

Roediger III, H. L. and Karpicke, J. D. (2006) 'Test-enhanced learning: Taking memory tests improves long-term retention', *Psychological Science* 17 (3) pp. 249-255.

Rohrer, D., Dedrick, R. F., Hartwig, M. K. and Cheung, C. N. (2020) 'A randomized controlled trial of interleaved mathematics practice', *Journal of Educational Psychology.*

Strong, M., Gargani, J. and Hacifazlioğlu, O. Z. (2011) 'Do we know a successful teacher when we see one? Experiments in the identification of effective teachers', *Journal of Teacher Education* 62 (4) pp. 367-382.

Willingham, D. T. (2009) *Why don't students like school: A cognitive scientist answers questions about how the mind works and what it means for your classroom.* San Francisco: Jossey-Bass.

Author bio-sketch:

Dylan Wiliam is Emeritus Professor of Educational Assessment at UCL (University College London). In a varied career, he has taught in urban public schools, directed a large-scale testing programme and served several roles in university administration including dean of a school of education. In addition, from 2003 to 2006, he was senior research director at the Educational Testing Service in Princeton, New Jersey. Over the last 20 years, his work has focused on supporting teachers all over the world to harness the power of assessment to support learning.

PROFESSIONAL DEVELOPMENT THROUGH INSTRUCTIONAL COACHING

BY JON HUTCHINSON

I've been lucky enough to meet Jon Hutchinson on several occasions and have benefitted from his clear articulation of the process of developing teachers at his school, Reach Feltham. As a fellow-member of the advisory group developing the Early Career Framework, Jon often used reflections on his own development and how that had been accelerated at his school to unpick what is required by teachers and, particularly, those at the start of their careers. Reach Feltham is one of a few schools that has metaphorically torn up the orthodoxy to try to do things better. The insights from many of their leaders and teachers have challenged the system to be better.

If it is true – as often quoted – that an education system cannot be better than the quality of its teachers and that a school leader needs to have her or his eye on the central business of teaching and learning, then we must improve professional learning for teachers. It has a bad name – ineffective, performative and irrelevant. I've experienced many attempts to improve using a coaching model, and the challenge is often implementation. The testimony of those that work at Reach Feltham is that it is different, and there is a better way. I asked Jon to write this chapter because knowing more about effective teacher development, using a beacon school as an example, is something I believe will make more effective school leaders and, consequently, more effective schools. I have read and used this chapter in my own school and I'd be surprised if readers don't find it equally useful.

'Did you hear, Pat? Did you hear what Coleman found? It's all family! Schools make no difference; families make the difference!'

The year is 1966 and we're in the cafeteria at Harvard University. Seymour Lipset, Professor of Sociology, has just burst in, revealing the findings of the Coleman Report to his friend Daniel Patrick Moynihan, Professor of Education and Urban Politics. Lipset's excitement is well-placed – Coleman's extraordinary conclusion would send shockwaves across the western world.[1] In the UK, Basil Bernstein echoed the verdict in his essay 'Education Cannot Compensate for Society' (1970). The regrettable situation led Barbara Heyns to declare that education research had pipped economics to the unenviable position of the 'dismal science' (1986, p. 186).

Do schools make a difference?

Thankfully, over the next 50 years, educational researchers responded to the pessimists by declaring, in the words of Ben Goldacre, 'I think that you'll find it's a bit more complicated than that'. As far back as 1979, Rutter et al found that successful secondary schools could secure as many as 'four times as many (examination) passes than those at the least successful school' (p. 19), even after controlling for differences in intake. Criticism followed along methodological lines, leading to more sophisticated statistical modelling. In short, education can be analysed through different 'levels'. These are commonly grouped into the district level, the school level, the teacher level and the pupil level. There are background pupil factors that schools, as Coleman suggests, cannot really influence and yet consistently account for the majority of differential pupil outcomes. Socio-economic status is one, but there are others, many of which are intertwined and dynamically related. It is these factors that account for the majority of variation in pupil outcomes, probably accounting for around 50% of pupil attainment.

What about the other half? Over the last few decades, one conclusion has arisen time and again from such studies: the 'teacher effect' far outweighs the 'school effect' (Muijs and Reynolds, 2000; Nye et al, 2009; Teddlie and Reynolds, 2000). It is difficult to place a single percentage on the variation of teacher effect on the variation of pupil gains, but Nye et al (2004) suggest somewhere between 7% and 21% (p. 239). This is much larger than the effect of the school on pupil attainment, meaning there is more variation within a school than between schools. As the authors put it:

---

1. It has been suggested that Coleman did not, in fact, make the assertion that schools made little difference to student achievement, and that rather his conclusions were misinterpreted (Nye, Konstantopoulos and Hedges, 2006; Alexander, 2016).

'differences among teachers is substantial in comparison to the variance between schools. In reading, the between teacher variance component is over twice as large as between-school variance component at grade 2 and over three times as large at grade 3. In mathematics, the pattern is similar [...] Thus [...] which teacher a student happens to get within a school matters more than which school the student happens to attend.'

More than this, and perhaps most significantly, Nye et al (2004) found that there is a larger teacher effect for pupils with low socio-economic status. So, if we want to improve pupil outcomes – particular the outcomes of the most disadvantaged pupils – and if we want to *make a difference*, then we are best off focusing our attention on teachers. Supporting teachers to improve is the biggest lever to improve outcomes that we have available to us.

What is the state of teacher professional development?

Unfortunately, despite such conclusive findings, the lamentable state of effective professional development for teachers (or rather lack thereof), has remained something of a dirty secret within schools. As Antoniou and Kyriakides (2013, p. 2) put it: 'Despite the recognition of the importance of teacher professional development, most training opportunities remain fragmented, poorly aligned with curricula, and inadequate to meet teachers' needs and priorities for improvement.' In case you were worried the authors were pulling their punches, they go on to summarise research from Ball and Cohen (1999): '... each year schools, districts, and educational systems spend a considerable amount of money and resources on in-service seminars and other forms of professional development, which are intellectually superficial and don't consider the knowledge base of effective teaching and how teachers could better learn and implement such practices' (Antoniou and Kyriakides, 2013, p. 2).

Upon reading this diagnosis, I was reminded of an 'in-service seminar' that I had been sent on during my first year of teaching. Since I would be teaching in Year 6 for the first time, that crucial SATs year, I was afforded the opportunity to visit the local authority to receive some bespoke training. During a mathematics session on probability, our trainer spent a good chunk of time demonstrating how it was possible to remove the label from a can of meatballs and replace it with a dog food label. This, he went on to explain, would mean that during the lesson you could open the 'dog food' and start to scoff the meatballs down! When I tentatively enquired as to how we could actually, you know, improve our teaching of probability (a topic my class found very hard) he winked at me and said 'Trust me, the kids will *love it* when you eat the "dog food".'

I'd like to say that this was an isolated incident, but I have learned in the subsequent years that it's possible to walk into any staffroom in the country, ask the first teacher you find and you will hear a CPD horror story just like it.

What do we know about effective teacher development?

Taken together, the above may read like a counsel of despair but all is not hopeless. The Department for Education assembled an expert group in 2015, tasked with addressing just this problem which led to the publication of a new Standard for 'Teachers' Professional Development' in 2016. In the accompanying letter to the Minister for Schools, the group emphasised: 'From the start, we were clear that the standard needed to be based on the best available evidence about what makes professional development effective – and that it should communicate this in a clear and usable way to everyone in the teaching profession' (Department for Education, 2016a).

The importance of leadership in achieving this aim was repeatedly stressed. The standard is made up of four criteria, setting the requirements for successful teacher professional development (Department for Education, 2016b):

1. Professional development should have a focus on improving and evaluating pupil outcomes.
2. Professional development should be underpinned by robust evidence and expertise.
3. Professional development should include collaboration and expert challenge.
4. Professional development programmes should be sustained over time.

The authors conclude by stating that all of this must be underpinned by a fifth part:

5. Professional development must be prioritised by school leadership (ibid).

In the accompanying implementation guidance (Department for Education, 2016c), the group also distinguishes between professional development activities and professional development programmes, concluding that the former are less likely to have a lasting impact on pupil outcomes. Ongoing programmes, on the other hand, are deemed more likely to 'sustain and embed practice' (ibid, p. 5).

What is teacher expertise?

Peps Mccrea (2018) argues that when we talk about developing teachers, we are really talking about moving them along the spectrum of proficiency and towards mastery. However, he goes on to argue that we are limited in our capacity to systematically develop this since 'we don't yet have a clear consensus around what this [expert teaching] entails' (p. 3). Offering a way forward, Mccrea argues that 'Developing teacher expertise is largely a process of helping teachers build their mental models in four distinct, but related, domains' (ibid, p. 6, but paraphrased):

1. **Path** – how to best present and sequence knowledge to pupils.
2. **Pupils** – what pupils know and do not know, as well as what motivates them.
3. **Pedagogy** – how pupils learn and how to catalyse learning within the classroom.
4. **Self-Regulation** – how to evaluate and iterate their own practice, considering their own biases.

More than this, though, expert teachers' knowledge in the above domains is organised differently to novices. The knowledge is extensive, actionable, fluent and meaningful. It may be apparent, here, that such an understanding of expertise is highly domain-specific. This is one key conclusion drawn by David Berliner, perhaps the world-leading authority on teacher expertise. Expertise in teaching A Level biology does not transfer to expertise in analysing Shakespeare's sonnets, as we discover as soon as we are tasked with a cover lesson outside of our subject. Expertise also struggles to transfer to new groups of pupils, as anyone who has ever moved schools can attest.

These sophisticated – yet domain-specific – mental models, Berliner points out, allow expert teachers to 'represent problems in qualitatively different ways to novices', and also 'perceive more meaningful patterns'. Much of this activity is automated and seemingly invisible to an outside observer. Helping teachers to develop these mental models is clearly crucial then, but on its own it is not enough. We want teacher behaviours in the classroom to change for the better. We want action. One mechanism that shows tremendous promise is 'instructional coaching', which Kraft et al (2018) identify as an essential feature of PD training that facilitates 'teachers' ability to translate knowledge and skills into actual classroom practice' (p. 551). Building mental models is crucial for developing expertise, but without action we're left with what philosopher Allan Watts terms as 'all retch and no vomit'.

How do we develop expertise within teachers?

At the researchEd national conference in 2018, Sam Sims argued that instructional coaching is 'currently the best-evidenced form or professional development we have' (Sims, 2019). Not to be confused with generic coaching models, which take a non-judgemental, reflective and facilitate approach to development, *instructional coaching* is closer to what a sports coach does.

Let's take athletics as an example. When a running coach is attempting to improve a sprinter's performance, she will begin by observing the athlete's 100m dash. Then, a very small tweak will be identified. Perhaps they notice that the athlete's torso is at a slight angle when it should be vertical. Feedback on this small change will be communicated before the better approach is modelled. Lastly, the athlete will be given an opportunity for extensive, deliberate practise aimed only at achieving this small sub-goal. Corrective feedback will be provided throughout the practise session. We can take the same approach to teaching and although only applied within education relatively recently, there is ever-expanding literature on the practice. Reviewing replicated controlled trials, meta-analyses, A-B testing and systemic research programmes, Sims concludes that 'I have looked hard at the literature and I cannot find another form of CPD for which the evidence is this strong' (ibid).

There are, however, different models and programmes of instructional coaching. How do we know which ones retain fidelity to the research evidence set out by Sims? Helpfully, 'five tenets that help distinguish coaching from other forms of PD' (CPRE, 2018) are set out by Matthew Kraft, Associate Professor of Education and Economics at Brown University, who has spearheaded much of the research in this area. They are: individualised, intensive, sustained, context-specific and focused. It is worth taking each of these in turn and briefly expanding them to gain a clearer picture of exactly what we are talking about when we talk about coaching.

First, coaching must be individualised. Teachers in any school will be at different stages of their practice with different priorities of what they need to do to improve. Whilst an NQT teaching a GCSE music lesson may require support in modelling proficiency to her pupils, an experienced Year 4 teacher will likely need something different. There is no quicker way to irritate busy teachers than to make them sit through an irrelevant CPD session. Built into this model is the idea that every teacher can improve, but that a one-size-fits-all approach is unlikely to develop all teachers. Coaching, therefore, is one to one with meetings based on individual, micro-observations (or drop-ins) of lessons.

Second, coaching is intensive. This means that a coach will meet their teacher at least every few weeks and probably weekly. Any longer than this and the gains that are initially achieved will likely be lost. Coaching meetings identify the area for development and allow lots of practise, then close the feedback loop in the classroom soon after. This does mean that coaching requires an investment in terms of time (from both teacher and coach). Third, coaching is sustained usually over a year, more likely indefinitely. Since the assumption is that every teacher can always improve, it makes no sense to cease coaching as this implies that some God-like level of teaching has been achieved. Coaching moves away from the one-off lesson observation and grand judgement and towards a cycle of low stakes, incremental improvement.

Fourth, coaching is context-specific, and the particular class or classes are set in the centre of the development process. It may be that a new cohort coming in has particular difficulty with following whole school routines, or a particular class has extremely high levels of prior attainment and require lots of additional challenge. Coaching can and should account for this. Lastly, coaching is focused. Action steps for improvement should be achievable almost immediately, and certainly within the time frame of the next meeting. Coaching conversations themselves are not rambling, general chats but are instead deliberatively selective. Great coaches consider what they won't talk about as much as what they will, selecting the highest leverage action step for improvement and zoning in on that.

What does this look like in a busy school?

We then have fertile ground in which to work. However, the preceding findings need to be translated into policy and action at the school level by leaders. This presents a clear and present danger; as soon as a good idea turns into a policy in schools, lethal mutations can abound. It is worth noting that every time you choose to do something, as a school, you are choosing not to do something else. Colleague's time is precious and it can only be spent once. At Reach, we've interpreted the research and as a leadership team developed a shared language around the principles revealed by the literature. Putting this into action requires us to move through three phases as set out by Harry Fletcher-Wood in *Developing Teacher Professional Development for Change* (2018):

1. Set a clear goal.
2. Identify clear needs.
3. Align professional development to goals and needs.

The dynamic nature of such an approach is both necessary and frustrating. It means that there will never be some perfect CPD offer. Schools are full of moving parts and so professional learning must respond accordingly, constantly evolving to meet the needs of the school, pupils and teachers. For us, coaching is a good bet, and so the bulk of what remains in this chapter will focus on describing how we've developed the way we do it over the last seven years. We can never be completely certain of our choices – education is far too complex for that – but given what we've set out above, it seems safe to assume that instructional coaching will improve teaching on an ongoing basis and that pupils outcomes (both cognitive and affective) will raise as a result.

Coaching also forms an important part of our culture; there are no superhero teachers at Reach. Each week our headteacher gets an action step, just the same as our trainees. We are embarked in a collective endeavour – it's a team effort. We care about our staff enough to want them to develop and support them to get there, no strings attached. When I first joined Reach I remember Principal Ed Vainker telling me 'If you aren't getting coached, then you shout about it. It is your right to get better. It is my responsibility to make sure that you do; it's a promise I'm making you'. This culture of continuous, incremental improvement is still the same today. So when recruiting new teachers, we ask them to teach the same 20-minute lesson twice on the interview day. After the first lesson, an observer will give them a short coaching session, which might result in an action step to, for example, use whole-class questioning to check for understanding before the independent task. The interviewee then quickly adapts their plan with the 'coach' and has another go with a different class, trying to put the action step into play.

This serves two purposes. First, it tells us if the prospective teacher is 'coachable' – how readily and swiftly are they able to take on feedback and adapt their practice as a result. We are far less interested in how 'good' a teacher is and far more concerned with their capacity to improve. Second, it gives the candidate a taste of what it will be like to teach at Reach. If successful, they will be receiving weekly coaching sessions and so they must be comfortable with the process. We have leant heavily on Paul Bambrick-Santoyo, Ark Teacher Training, Ambition Institute and Doug Lemov, to arrive at a model of coaching that we're happy with. Originally, we used a six-step process, but increasingly found this to be bloated and woolly – meetings took too long and the longer a meeting is, the more likely it will be cancelled. Now, then, we have just three steps to each coaching conversation: see it, name it, do it.

Let's break down exactly how coaching works at Reach. Every single teacher has a coach who will 'drop-in' on their coachee once a week. This is usually no longer than ten minutes and often coaches will record the teaching on a tablet ready to review together later. Shortly after the drop-in, the coach and coachee will meet for a coaching meeting. The 'see it' phase relates to seeing the gap in their practice, as well as 'seeing' what their practice could be like. It could be as simple as talking over children instead of waiting for silence, delivering too many instructions in one go or not jotting the steps of a complex procedure on the board. Using video is helpful here as the teacher can be shown themselves. This can be a little awkward to begin with and we always check teachers are comfortable with it first (some say no, which is fine). So just as the athletics coach will model exactly how to hold your body vertical whilst sprinting, the coach may model the independent task, but jotting the steps to the procedure whilst doing so. The coach and coachee will then name this change in practice, which we call an 'action step'. It is helpful if the coachee formulates it in their own words, but keeping it brief is important. Good action steps are focused, measurable and achievable. Our example above may have been, 'To write the steps to success on the board whilst modelling a new procedure.'

The final stage is the part that is most commonly missed out but is the most important bit. Do it. When Benedict Cumberbatch's Dr Strange is quizzed as to how he became a doctor, he responds with: 'Study and practice. Years of it.' In a sense, that is all that is being advocated here, but when was the last time that you systematically rehearsed a tiny component of your teaching repertoire? It is easy to go through our teaching careers with the lesson being the practice, which means kids never get to see the final performance. At Reach teachers don't practise until they get it right, we practise until we can't get it wrong, just like we expect of our pupils.

So, after naming the action step, it's paramount that you practise together, (Lampert, 2010) taking it in turns to be the teacher or the child. It feels weird to begin with, but just as an actor will have whispered 'To be or not to be?' into the bathroom mirror a thousand times before asking the same question to the audience, teachers shouldn't try out their move for the first time in front of Year 9 on a Friday afternoon. Deliberate practise develops that fluency and automaticity of core practices, whilst the chance to rehearse and refine 'high-leverage practices'.

Though this process may sound intimidating, it is worth stating that our coaching is no-stakes. It is completely unattached to any sort of performance management but choosing the correct coaches is important, and the relationship between the coach and coachee is critical. At our school, everyone wants to be coached by Tilly, our deputy head, who is equal parts the loveliest human on earth and a forensic teaching analysis machine. You trust that she will make you better and you trust that she'll make you feel good about it. Teachers at Reach go out of their way to get Tilly in their classroom because they *want* her to tell them what to do differently. That's the kind of school I love to work in.

Which other professional development ingredients should I add?

Of course, coaching is only the 'form' of professional development, the mechanism. It does not tell us about the substance or the content. It would be perfectly possible to implement an instructional coaching programme and give teachers systematic but dreadful feedback. This could be feedback which was not grounded in any sort of evidence around how pupils learn, or how to create wonderful classroom cultures, or what valid and reliable assessment practices look like. Perhaps you've received feedback like this once or twice yourself?

For this reason, coaching is only part of our offer around professional development at Reach. The whole package currently looks like this:

Professional development	Description	Purpose	Example
Teacher coaching	Individualised, one to one feedback on teaching practice provided by a dedicated coach, occurring weekly.	Supporting all teachers to improve so that they, in turn, drive high pupil attainment.	A coach observes the start of a maths teacher's lessons and notice pupils enter unsettled, so during coaching meeting practices 'threshold' with the teacher, standing at the door and shaking each child whilst handing them a 'Do Now' task to complete.
Whole-school CPD	Share whole-school priorities and policies, alongside the rationale and strategies that have been developed to help achieve these.	Meeting the goals of the school development plan through collective endeavour.	Training on Doug Lemov's whole-class 'control the game' reading technique, to ensure pupils are reading aloud in all lessons.
Subject-knowledge development	Departments meet fortnightly to discuss the content that they are teaching, common misconceptions, and how to best present material to pupils in a coherent manner.	Teachers' subject knowledge has been identified as the most important factor in securing positive pupils outcomes (Coe et al, 2017).	Reading Geoffrey Hill's literary criticism of Carol Ann Duffy, and considering how this debate would best be presented to A Level English students.
Leadership coaching	Middle leaders are given one to one meetings every other week to share the work they are doing to address the school priorities. Senior leaders provide feedback and action steps.	Middle leaders are the engine house of a school, but require regular support to flourish. Senior leaders can point to knowledge bases and expedite sound decisions-making through coaching.	A head of music explains that one teacher is not responding to feedback during coaching meetings and failing to meet action steps. A senior leader will rehearse the conversation that the head of music will have with the teacher.
Professional reading	A short educational research summary email is sent weekly to staff, and a well-stocked, ever-expanding CPD library is available.	Develop teachers mental models around education to serve as the foundation for action and impact.	Teachers are as likely to be spending their PPA time reading *Making Good Progress* by Daisy Christodoulou as they are marking pupils work.
Wider professional development	Any activity or programme identified by a teacher which may lead to an improvement in their mental models and, therefore, teaching.	Allow all teachers to pursue professional development that interests them and will enrich our organisational knowledge and practice.	A master's degree in education. A talk by a specialist. A professional qualification course.

209

In a lovely metaphor, Harry Fletcher-Wood sets out how each of these elements could be considered an ingredient, but need to be combined to make a whole meal. For each teacher, that combination will be slightly different and will likely change over time. To take an example, we believe that a thorough understanding of the emerging field of cognitive science is crucial to our teachers securing long-term knowledge and understanding across the curriculum. Cognitive load theory has become our standard model, which is referred to in meetings, conversations and development sessions across phases and departments. To ensure all teachers had a strong understanding of this model of learning, we recently emailed a link to the free, online course 'Cognitive Science for Teachers Level 1', provided by Seneca Learning. Several teachers immediately emailed back with their certificates – they had already completed the course of their own volition. It was immediately necessary to adapt our offer.

Perhaps this is culture eating strategy for breakfast, or perhaps strategy cooked up something too delicious for teachers to ignore. Promoting a culture of saying 'yes' when it comes to professional learning is critical, though. It was this policy that meant that when I arrived at Reach, I was given half a day off each week, paid, to attend lectures for the master's degree in education that I was completing. Go into any classroom and there is a good chance that the teacher will be working on something unique and interesting, often with an expert outside agency. This is not only good for that teacher, it enriches our school. In short, being clear about what you value as a leadership team and making it as easy as possible for teachers to develop along those lines, building their own sophisticated mental models and practising putting it into action, is the best way to secure a happy workforce and amazing pupils outcomes. If we can foster this as a profession, the impact could be transformational. As emphasised by the DfE's expert group, leaders have unique role and a solemn responsibility to spearhead this work. They are well placed to, not least because they are more likely to have developed a finely tuned bullshit detector, exercising professional scepticism towards the more outlandish claims and the snake oil that boomerangs cyclically from chancers hoping to make a quick buck. Always remember that your teachers' time is a precious resource and respect that fact by refusing to encroach on it with whim or fancy.

Conclusion

Clearly, there is work to do. The opening section of this chapter outlined the complexity and difficulty in developing robust and ongoing professional development. In a long list of priorities, for leaders and teachers alike CPD often drops down the agenda. Many an initiative has tried and failed to bridge the gulf between the knowledge base from educational research and related disciplines and what teachers think and do in their classrooms. But we can conclude with a more optimistic summary. It is my genuine belief that we stand on the precipice of a paradigm shift within education, ready to mature as a profession and engage in systematic, theoretically-underpinned and empirically informed professional development.

There is a groundswell of grassroots demand, exemplified through the success of researchEd conferences. An independent 'what works' clearing house – the Education Endowment Foundation – is flourishing, testing interventions through randomised controlled trials and producing increasingly nuanced and sophisticated reports to disseminate key findings. The national inspectorate has developed a new inspection framework which is underpinned by a deep and wide-ranging review of research literature. The Chartered College of Teaching publishes a regular award-winning journal for teachers. The new Early Career Framework will ensure that all new teachers are trained in line with the best available evidence around teaching, learning, assessment and classroom management. Organisations such as Ambition Insitute are offering qualifications for teachers at every stage of their career, again grounded in evidence. So, if we're careful, we just might ensure that no new teacher will ever have to sit through a dog food CPD session again.

References

Alexander, K. (2016) 'Is It Family or School?: Getting the Question Right', *RSF: The Russell Sage Foundation Journal of the Social Sciences* 2 (5) pp. 18-33.

Antoniou, P. and Kyriakides, L. (2013) 'A Dynamic Integrated Approach to Teacher Professional Development: Impact and Sustainability of the Effects on Improving Teacher Behavior and Student Outcomes', *Teaching and Teacher Education* 29 (1) pp. 1-12.

Ball, D. L. and Cohen, D. K. (1999) 'Developing practice, developing practitioners: toward a practice-based theory of professional education' in Darling-Hammond, L. and Sykes, G. (eds) *Teaching as the learning profession: Handbook of policy and practice*. San Francisco: Jossey-Bass, pp. 3-32.

Berliner, D. (2001) 'Learning about and learning from expert teachers', *International Journal of Educational Research* 35 pp. 463–482

Bernstein B. (1970) 'Education cannot compensate for society', *New Society* 15 (387) pp. 344-347.

Coe, R., Aloisi, C., Higgins, S. and Major, L. E. (2014) 'What makes great teaching? Review of the underpinning research', Project Report. London: Sutton Trust.

CPRE Knowledge Hub (2018) *Emerging Evidence on the Effectiveness of Coaching as a Professional Development Strategy.* Available at: www.bit. ly/3iu9SOQ

Department for Education (2016a) *Letter from Teachers' Professional Development Expert Group.* London: Stationery Office

Department for Education (2016b) *Standard for teachers' professional development.* London: Stationery Office.

Department for Education (2016c) *Standard for teachers' professional development: Implementation Guidance.* London: Stationery Office.

Fletcher-Wood, H. (2018) 'Designing Professional Development for Teacher Change', *Ambition Institute* [Online] March. Available at: www.bit.ly/30Cpw4y

Heyns, B. (1978). *Summer Learning and the Effects of Schooling.* New York: Academic.

Kraft M.A., Blazar D. and Hogan D. (2018) 'The Effect of Teacher Coaching on Instruction and Achievement: A Meta-Analysis of the Causal Evidence', *Review of Educational Research* 88 (4) pp. 547-588.

Kyriakides, L., Creemers, B. P. M. & Antoniou, P. (2009) 'Teacher behaviour and student outcomes: Suggestions for research on teacher training and professional development', *Teaching and Teacher Education* 25 (1) pp. 12-23.

Lampert, M. (2010) 'Learning teaching in, from, and for practice: What Do We mean?' *Journal of Teacher Education* 61 (1-2) pp. 21-34.

Mccrea, P. (2018) 'Expert Teaching: What is it, and how might we develop it?', *Institute for Teaching* [Online] 29 March. Available at: www.bit.ly/3lmyDhx

Muijs, D. and Reynolds, D. (2000) 'School effectiveness and teacher effectiveness. some preliminary findings from the evaluation of the mathematics enhancement programme', *School Effectiveness and School Improvement* 11 (2) pp. 323-327.

Nye, B., Konstantopoulos S. and Hedges L. V. (2004) 'How Large Are Teacher Effects?', *Educational Evaluation and Policy Analysis* 26 (3) pp. 237-257.

Rutter, M., Maughan, B., Mortimore, P., Ouston, J. and Smith, A. (1979) *Fifteen thousand hours: secondary schools and their effects on children.* London: Open Books

Teddlie, C. and Reynolds, D. (2000) *The international handbook of school effectiveness research.* London: Falmer Press.

Author bio-sketch:

Jon Hutchinson is Assistant Headteacher at Reach Academy Feltham, all through school in southwest London. Jon is also a visiting fellow at Ambition Institute, teaching on the Masters in Expert Teaching Course.

SURVIVING AND THRIVING IN UNCERTAINTY

BY MATTHEW EVANS

If there is a recent book that complements this one, then it is *Leaders with Substance* by Matthew Evans. If there is a blog that complements this book, it is his blog which regularly highlights the relationship between school leadership and complexity. I haven't had the privilege of meeting Matthew yet but he is a prolific and excellent writer. This book was well underway when I discovered his book which takes a similar perspective, and hence I asked him to write the concluding chapter.

There is no better way to end than the way this chapter does: Matthew takes us through uncertainty and complexity, drawing out some of the themes that this book has explored and applying the lens of an expert school leader to the unpredictable challenges, problems and situations we face.

'You are uncertain, to varying degrees, about everything in the future; much of the past is hidden from you and there is a lot of the present about which you do not have full information. Uncertainty is everywhere and you cannot escape from it.' – Dennis Lindley, *Understanding Uncertainty* (2006)

What have we learned so far about leading in a school?

I defy you to have read this book and conclude that leading in a school is simple. Indeed, it would not be accurate to describe the task as complicated even. A cryptic crossword is complicated. Fixing a broken-down piece of machinery is complicated. Running a school is much more than that: it is immensely complex, but the task is often underestimated. As Taleb (2012) wryly put it, complex organisations are 'closer to the cat than the washing machine, but tend to get mistaken for washing machines'.

If you are like me, you will read this book and, at times, feel overwhelmed by the sheer quantity of things you are expected to know and by the intractability of the problems you are expected to solve. Acknowledging the complexity of schools and the enormity of the task of being a leader within such a context means you pass over a threshold. It is too late to turn back but, don't worry, although life is much less certain this side of the threshold, it is much more exciting too. I appear to be talking about feelings. What place do emotions have in a book about research? It is often said that leadership is a lonely and challenging job. Understanding *why* it is so difficult helps us come to terms with the inevitable setbacks and frustrations: we can learn to accept the limits of our control, find strategies to deal with uncertainty, and be successful against the odds. Riding the wild horse of complexity can be exhilarating once you know how to tame it sufficiently to stay on its back.

In this chapter, I hope we can come to understand complexity better and in doing so make some kind of peace with it. If we are to survive and thrive as a leader, this is a necessity. I hope also to draw together the themes of this book, succinctly outlined in the first two chapters by Jen Barker and Tom Rees, namely: expertise and the persistent problems of school leadership. These themes have been given substance through the insights of the various contributors, each of whom are evidence that leadership starts with an in-depth knowledge of the domain in which you lead.

Complexity: so what?

In the opening line of the opening chapter of this book, Jen Barker and Tom Rees state that schools are 'fascinating and complex places'. I believe that it is their complexity that makes them so fascinating; they are unpredictable, surprising and constantly evolving. An understanding of complexity helps us make sense of what we see happening in our schools. Complexity manifests itself in many ways. I will highlight what I believe to be the most relevant and interesting implications in this chapter, namely how we think about:

1. Order

Order is desirable in a school, but stability and predictability are exceptions within a system which thrives on uncertainty and disorder. Out of complexity arises counterintuitive organisational behaviour, unintended consequences and random events.

2. Problems

In complex systems, problems are interconnected and embedded within bigger problems. Complex problems cannot be 'solved' in the common sense of the word – they are persistent in that they recur in new forms. There will also be multiple ways to perceive the problem and, therefore, a variety of solutions which present themselves, each with their own merits and risks. For this reason, there are no perfect solutions to complex problems, only ways forward that are 'good enough'.

3. Expertise

The expertise required by school leaders is 'mainly a matter of knowledge' (Bereiter and Scardamalia, 1993), where knowledge is defined in broad terms. Experts develop sophisticated mental models which enable them to organise and apply their knowledge to solve the problems they face. However, in complex systems, these problems emerge and re-emerge in novel ways. Expertise in such organisations therefore requires a sophisticated sense-making capability which relies heavily on contextual knowledge and an insight into how the school is evolving. Given all of this, how should we define *leadership* and what are the implications for how we lead? Perhaps our inability to agree on an exact (or even broad) definition of leadership is a clue to the fact that leadership is not fixed. Uncertainty is an inevitable feature of our schools, and so too may it be a defining quality of how we lead them.

An understanding of complexity changes how we view leadership, in particular:

1. How order is achieved

It is not possible to control a complex system, but we may seek to reduce complexity and buffer its effects to achieve order through structure, stability and simplification.

2. How leaders influence change

Leadership theories often promote a rationalist, linear view of change whereby the leader envisions a desirable future, plans to achieve this vision, sets criteria for success, then executes the plan. The assumption is that the leader can exert his willpower as if the object of his leadership is predictable and controllable. Leadership theory places the leader at the centre or the pinnacle, looking down omnisciently. An understanding of complexity enlightens how the leader is shaped in turn by his environment: a constant interplay between leader and school – an endless, evolutionary waltz.

3. The limits of a leader's influence

In ignorance of complexity, leaders can make matters worse, not better by:

- a creeping managerialism and urge to control.
- simplistic solutions which do damage to diversity.
- naïve interventions driven by a desire to be seen to take action.

Allowing leaders to persist in such ways does damage to our schools, also to the leader's own wellbeing as they are frustrated by the lack of progress and by the negative feedback they receive. Leaders are not powerless, but there are limits to their influence which must be accepted and understood.

Schools as an attempt to create order

'Complexity's emphasis on non-linearity, unpredictability and recursivity is not meant as an argument against or denial of order. It should instead be understood as a case to see order differently, not as something that can be predicted and controlled from preceding conditions but rather as something that emerges in genuinely generative ways.' (Osberg and Biesta, 2010)

Schools, as social institutions, are an attempt to create order. School buildings isolate children from their everyday lives, partitioning them into classrooms and social spaces. The school year, the timetable and curricula place learning within temporal boundaries. We put children of a similar age, ability or achievement together to simplify the task of educating them. Examinations, taken in orderly halls under controlled conditions, capture the residue of formal schooling and in doing so signal the particular outcomes which are valued and certified. Even the actions of school children are given boundaries through hierarchies of rewards and sanctions.

Seeing the school as a complex place – one that would tend towards disorder were it allowed – does not suggest that order is not possible or desirable. Instead, 'order, stability, structure and "simplicity" ... are the exception and deviation from the normal course of affairs' (Biesta, 2010). An understanding of complexity helps us understand our role as leaders in deciding how much order is required and how it might be achieved. Our efforts to create order never end as entropy is at work: a continuous undoing and tendency towards disorder. This insight helps us appreciate the nature of many of the 'persistent problems' Barker and Rees discussed early on in this book. Appreciating complexity also leads us to understand that we should not attempt to control our environment and be too certain in our leadership of it, rather our role is to reduce disorder through simplification, stability and less uncertainty. This is a subtle but important distinction. By reducing complexity, the leader limits its tendency to towards spontaneity.

In the chapter by Thompson and Sparkes on school culture, we can see numerous attempts to create order. We can choose to interpret the culture-building of the school as 'controlling' pupils, or as reducing complexity so that order might emerge. Thompson and Sparkes describe the moment at 8:03 every morning when everyone's hand is raised and the school falls silent. They justify the precision and regularity of this daily act by arguing that 'the pedantic timings prevent a drift'. The 'drift', we might assume, is towards disorder, unpredictability and delay. Is this an act of excessive, stifling authority, or an attempt to contain disorder so that leaders can fulfil their duty in creating a positive, productive environment? It is no coincidence that the schools which have gone furthest in creating tight routines and simple, consistent expectations of pupil conduct are those in the most challenging social contexts. The disorder and unpredictability of children's lives outside of school is met with simplicity, order and calm. Done poorly, leaders seek to control. Done well, complexity is reduced and more predictable, stable states emerge.

The darker side of complexity

In 2010, Professor Eileen Munro from the London School of Economics was asked to chair a review of child protection services in England following some high-profile avoidable child deaths (Munro, 2010). The key question the review sought to answer was 'what helps professionals make the best judgements they can to protect a vulnerable child?'. Munro found a system which had been shaped by four 'driving forces', including a 'commonly held belief that the complexity and associated uncertainty of child protection work can be eradicated' and 'a readiness… to focus on professional error without looking deeply enough into its causes'. Munro's criticism of previous enquiries was that they stopped at the point of identifying who was to blame, rather than continuing to question what the systemic circumstances were that led up to these mistakes.

The result of the failure to move beyond apportioning blame was that the response in each case of a child's death was to find more ways of controlling people so that they would be less likely to make such mistakes again. This control takes the form of psychological pressure (a high-stakes culture whereby individual professionals are fearful of making a mistake), more, and more detailed, procedures and rules (which would avoid the mistakes of the past if followed systematically), and an increased level of monitoring and supervision. This creeping managerialism was a rational response to mistakes identified in each case review, but over time had created a stifling and counter-productive work environment. Munro noted: 'Each addition in isolation makes sense but the cumulative effect is to create a work environment full of obstacles to keeping a clear focus on meeting the needs of children.'

Munro's answer to this inquiry error was to take what she termed a 'systems approach', where human error is treated as the starting point for investigation. 'When you go behind the label "human error", you see people and organizations trying to cope with complexity, continually adapting, evolving along with the changing nature of risk in their operations. Such coping with complexity is not easy to see when we make only brief forays into intricate worlds of practice.' The complexity of the environment within which decisions were being made is the significant insight offered by Munro. She draws upon contexts as diverse as aviation, anaesthetics and nuclear power stations to demonstrate how catastrophic events can be understood as being a consequence of misguided attempts to control complexity rather than reduce it.

Munro's analysis applies equally to education, where a blame culture has emerged in response to repeated failures to improve educational outcomes for children from the most deprived communities. The 'solution' has been a cycle of fire and hire for school leaders and continuous re-launching of schools with a new name, building and identity. 'Under new management' is the motto of this approach which has ended the careers of many devoted and resilient school leaders. The 'stuck schools' rhetoric from Ofsted and government reflects a fundamental misunderstanding of complexity, laying the blame on the school, its staff and leaders for an inability to dominate complexity – to 'manage' their way out of chaos. What is needed instead is a reduction in complexity in these communities: to make the task of the school simpler. If the school is 'stuck', it is because the context is so sticky.

Simple and simplistic solutions

'Acknowledging complexity involves in the first place an acknowledgement of our limitations.' (Cilliers, in Osberg and Biesta, 2010)

The problem with complexity is the complexity of problems. The interconnectedness of schools means that isolating a particular problem is not possible. Uncertainty is rife: what caused the present condition, how is it connected to other phenomena, how will this scenario unfold and what happens when we try to influence it? There are multiple ways of perceiving such 'swampy problems' (Beech et al, 2011), therefore there are no 'correct' solutions, merely ones that are 'good enough' (Harford, 2016). In Matthew Syed's 2019 book *Rebel Ideas*, he observes that problems which arise from complexity require diverse perspectives, what he terms 'cognitive diversity'. Leaders must calibrate their interpretations with as diverse a range of cognitive perspectives as possible. Managerial certainty often reflects a lack of cognitive challenge: paradoxically, we should become less certain but more confident in our solution as we know more about the different ways of defining the problem.

Attempts to create order in organisations can, however, stifle cognitive diversity. The hierarchy of the school can create what Syed calls a 'dominance dynamic' where the HiPPO (Highest Paid Person's Opinion) is unchallenged. Studies show that the mere presence of the boss prevents others even suggesting ideas. This is an effect which must be actively rallied against by those in senior positions in a school to avoid leaders operating in a cognitive bubble, assured of their correctness by a deficit of dissenting voices. A further trap is the allure of solutions which 'appeal to our own imagined range of actions' (Allen and White, 2019). In other words, we are likely to define a problem and favour solutions which fit the narrative of personal influence and job role. If our job title is 'data manager' then we will pay attention to the data. Problems will manifest through the prism of data analysis and solutions will be attractive if data might play a significant role. Similarly, pastoral leaders will define problems as being caused by pastoral deficits and seek to identify pastoral solutions. Interpreting our environment in biased ways gives our role meaning – it makes us powerful leaders able to deliver the improvements required by our performance management targets. The size, roles and remits of the leadership team of a school will largely determine how many problems are identified, how these are defined, and the solutions which will come forth. We should guard against a dominant leader-perspective and the lure of the 'obvious' solution.

In acknowledging complexity, we accept that there is 'no neutral or objective framework for understanding... [and that] we have to make choices which cannot be reduced to calculation alone' (Cilliers, 2005). There is, therefore, an inevitable role-played by values as a means by which we distinguish the merit of solutions. With all the talk of expertise and domain-knowledge, one may assume that there is no room for beliefs and values, but these are a form of knowledge also. In recognising that leadership expertise is enacted in conditions of complexity, we ensure that expertise is defined not as 'knowing it all', but as a nuanced understanding of how to operate when facing uncertainty and moral dilemmas.

Ultimately, leaders must make sense of complexity, be decisive and live with the consequences of their actions. Cilliers (2010) observed that when faced with 'a specific problem in the real world… we have to frame the problem in a specific way and use specific tools and methods': we cannot be diverted by 'life, the universe and everything'. There is a necessary simplification of the problem to avoid cognitive overload. However, as leaders we must be cautious of conflating simple with simplistic, or general with the generic. Generic leadership, rather than reducing the level of complexity, overlays it with 'one size fits all' systems and policies which restrict the diversity, richness and distinctiveness of the school (Evans, 2019). Genericism may be observed in the data systems and pedagogic 'non-negotiables' which do damage to disciplinary distinctiveness. Such approaches have managerial benefits – providing simple metrics and control mechanisms to help the leader cope with complexity – but achieve this at the expense of professional autonomy and decision making, therefore disrupting the rhythms and practices which make sense at the local level. In short, genericism places the needs of the manager over the child.

Naïve intervention

Nassim Taleb, in his book *Antifragile* (2012), introduced me to the word 'iatrogenic', which in medical terms means an illness caused by medical examination or treatment but more generally may be used to describe harmful unintended consequences caused as a result of trying to be helpful. The maxim 'do no harm' was adopted by the medical profession following the recognition of iatrogenic effects. School leaders would be wise to adopt this maxim and strive to better understand the negative consequences of their well-intended interventions.

Intervention whilst in denial of complexity is harmful. It is better to do nothing than to act when not in possession of sufficient knowledge. One of the reasons school leaders ignore this truth is that action is valued over inaction, and the consequences of doing something are more attributable than the outcome of choosing to do nothing. Taleb points out that we recognise people for what they *did* do, not for what they *didn't* do, or avoided. Heroism is going into battle (whether we win or lose), not choosing to avoid the conflict. What remains unseen is the wise decision to delay whilst more information is gathered, the abandoned policy which would have wrought havoc, or the prevention of contradictory initiatives which overload those subject to them. Avoiding future disorder is an invisible act of strong leadership.

A complex system, contrary to what people believe, does not require complicated systems and regulations and intricate policies. The simpler, the better. Complications lead to multiplicative chains of unintended consequences, followed by apologies about the 'unforeseen' aspect of the consequences, then to another intervention to correct secondary effects, leading to an explosive series of branding 'unforeseen' responses, each one worse than the preceding one (Taleb, 2012). Iatrogenic effects abound in schools where there is a 'just do something' management culture. There is a compulsion to act: a belief that inaction is weakness. This culture arises through the ambition of rising leaders, the pressure of accountability and an expectation of rapid improvement.

Consider for a moment why people are promoted to senior leadership positions within schools. In my experience, they are often those that have mastered the complicated, not the complex. They are 'doers': the ones that volunteer to lead staff training, create the impressive scheme of work, stay late each evening to mark every book in triplicate, monitor everything that happens in their domain and develop slick systems for filing, recording and auditing. Of course, the complicated can be mastered, its problems solved but with seniority comes greater complexity. The naïve interventions of those who are yet to grasp organisational complexity can be damaging to the school and perplexing to the inexperienced leader who cannot understand why their earnest initiatives are more often met with failure, resistance, unexpected side-effects, asymmetric impact, inconsistency and complaint. Learning the limits of our leadership is not an admission of impotence. We wield most power when we intervene selectively, knowing when to act and when to step back. To be too dominant or active as a leader risks iatrogenic effects, and may crowd out those that may know better than us. Complex organisations can arrive at their own solutions with minimal intervention: good things happen in the absence of a leader! The art of leading complexity is the wisdom to know when to be passive.

Complexity in the classroom

Perhaps one of the most complex environments in a school is the classroom, where the core business of the school happens: the invisible process of learning. Learning can only be judged retrospectively and in doing so we are reducing complexity (simplifying). How so? When we talk about learning we are

223

describing a change that has taken place in the memory of the child and one that is not a result of the normal maturation process but as a result of their engagement with their environment. In schools, we look for the changes which we value and which were intended and attribute these to the child's exposure to the curriculum through instruction. We cannot know whether any activity the child engages with will lead to a durable, valuable change in the child. For this reason, learning is not a term we can use to necessarily describe what is happening in the classroom (we simply don't know). Learning is uncertain, unpredictable and generally hard to pin down. It can only be approximated in hindsight, and this judgement is heavily values-laden (see Biesta, 2010).

In the *Hidden Lives of Learners*, Graham Nuttall (2007) paints an evidence-based picture of the complexity of the classroom environment. Nuttall illustrates the difficulties of directing pupils' attention to the curriculum, the different ways they will engage with what is taught, and the unpredictability around how knowledge will be understood and whether it will be retained. The 'hidden' nature of pupils' interactions and inner lives means teachers are grappling with a high degree of uncertainty. Successful teachers are those who recognise this complexity and seek to reduce it through simplification, order and careful instruction. The unique experiences of every child up until the point they walk into a lesson means they will interpret what they are taught in different ways. This 'unavoidable ambiguity' should be met with precision so that there is 'only one possible logical interpretation' of the concept (Needham, 2019). This argument is the basis for explicit instruction (Engelmann, 1980) – a teaching method which acknowledges and seeks to reduce uncertainty and ambiguity. Where leaders fail to recognise the inherent complexity of the classroom environment and how learning emerges from this witches' brew, naïve intervention follows. In the recent past, this has taken the form of simplistic observation judgements, meaningless data trawls and formulaic teaching 'non-negotiables'.

Intransigent minorities

Possibly one of the most counter-intuitive features of a complex system is how a small minority influence the rules to which the population must submit. Taleb (2012) estimates that this minority might be as little as 3-4%, and terms this group the 'intransigent minority'. I shall illustrate the argument with examples from a school context. It takes only one child to have an extreme reaction to peanuts (particularly where contagion can be airborne) for a whole school to become peanut-free. Even a small group who are less allergic may cause the entire population to submit to their needs. In this example, there are arguably minimal consequences for the majority who are allergy-free, but potentially serious consequences for the minority. Who would object to a peanut-free school? However, as with bacteria and other contagions that 'attack' the body, there is evidence that peanut intolerance increases when young children do not come into contact with them. The body becomes less resilient as it is not exposed to a healthy level of 'stressors' in the environment. Minority rule need not apply if it is possible to separate the minority (intransigent group) from the majority (flexible group) effectively. If we view school behaviour policies from this perspective, we might justify the need for removing pupils from lessons as a way of avoiding imposing the intransigent minority's 'preferences' on the entire population. The intransigent pupil/s may require less distraction and closer supervision than others, therefore, rather than the whole class being made to work in conditions that enable the teacher to ensure the good conduct and learning of the intransigent minority – separation enables both group's needs to be met.

Where schools implement exceptionally high expectations for conduct and rigid systems for dealing with transgressions, it may be because the intransigent group is too big to be isolated from the flexible group. So-called 'zero-tolerance' becomes necessary. Although many pupils walk between lessons without shouting, swearing and pushing, if a significant proportion cannot then conditions (such as a 'silent corridors' policy) will be imposed. It also costs little to apply tight structures everywhere, therefore schools lean towards doing so. Undesirable behaviours which are exhibited by larger groups (e.g. slight lateness to lessons or incomplete homework) also require whole-population rules, whilst minority behaviours like fighting can be dealt with without imposing conditions on the many.

Teachers form intransigent minorities too. Schools can be tempted to adopt lowest common denominator requirements for teaching lessons, for example, in response to an intransigent group of low-performing teachers. An example is the three-part lesson format which for some time in many English schools was seen as a viable strategy for increasing the quality of teaching. For those whose lessons lacked structure, any attempt to start the lesson in an orderly way, or to periodically stop and review what had been taught, the three-part lesson may have improved things. However, for the flexible majority, such policies were a straitjacket which undermined practice. Similar practices continue in the form of policy which requires 'retrieval practice' in every lesson, or knowledge organisers for every unit studied. Raising standards of teaching and learning rarely requires whole-population rules as it is possible to isolate the intransigent minority, in doing so protecting professional freedoms for the competent.

We should be wary of unnecessarily imposing conditions on the majority for the sake of the minority because it weakens the complex system. As with the human body when it is not exposed to moderate stressors, complex organisations become more fragile too. Overly controlling how teachers teach will undermine their expertise and excessive controls on behaviour may reduce pupils' ability to make good personal choices about their conduct. Some degree of disorder, inconsistency and randomness makes the school more resistant to future shocks – and the people within it more able to stand on their own two feet. By understanding the effect that intransigent minorities can have in a complex environment, school leaders may make better decisions about how and when to isolate them from the flexible majority.

In conclusion

In this chapter, we have glimpsed a largely unexplored territory of how school leadership might meet the challenges of complexity. I have argued that an appreciation of complexity is essential if we are to understand the persistent problems of leadership and the nature of the expertise which is required to tackle them. Rather than seek 'perfect solutions' to these problems, the expert leader will seek to understand the problem from multiple perspectives. Knowledge-building, where knowledge is defined in broad terms, is foundational to developing the expert mental models which lead to better decisions and policy.

We have touched upon the question of how much order is required in our schools and how this can be achieved. An understanding of complexity leads us to the subtle distinction between imposing order through control (detailed systems and rules, close monitoring and supervision, and psychological pressure), versus creating order through reducing complexity. If we are to avoid creeping managerialism, every leader must understand this distinction. They must also understand the pull of genericism, where an attempt to make sense of complexity leads to an over-simplification – a 'one-size-fits-all' approach – which suffocates diversity and distinctiveness at the local level. But the naïve interventions of leaders do not stop at managerialism and genericism. Acting when not in possession of sufficient knowledge and an appreciation of complexity leads to iatrogenic effects: unintended harm caused by well-intentioned intervention. Leadership carries with it the responsibility to know when to step back, resist innovation and delay action. Acknowledging our limitations as leaders and understanding when leadership is (and is not) required – humility and wisdom – will mitigate the tendency to be seen to do something, anything! The defining features of complexity – uncertainty, ambiguity and unpredictability – are to be found in greatest abundance in the classroom. The core business of schools is where the highest levels of complexity reside. The topics covered in this book are a testament to the complexity of the classroom: learning and memory; achieving fluency in reading; assessment; the curriculum; special educational needs, and improving teaching. Each of these aspects of schooling requires extensive domain-knowledge, considerable expertise and an ability to survive and thrive in conditions of uncertainty.

Feeling good about leadership

And so, we return to the matter of how it feels to lead a school. There is no doubt that certainty is a comfortable feeling. When we know what is going on, have the answer, understand why, and can predict what happens next, we are in control. Unfortunately, uncertainty is the reality for school leaders. Uncertainty can be stressful, particularly when it is our job to find a way through the confusion. People are looking to us to be decisive, to have a vision and a plan.

When we acknowledge the immense complexity of leading a school there is a risk that we feel impotent. How can we ever master this domain and bring it within our control? Our leadership indeed has limits, but understanding this makes us better leaders. We can learn about how uncertainty behaves, the traps that are laid for us, and how we can reduce complexity and tackle the persistent problems schools face. Our leadership need not be perfect, but 'good enough'. Our schools will not thrive unless we learn how to survive, and this begins with an understanding of complexity.

References

Allen, R. and White, B. (2019) 'Careering towards a curriculum crash?', *Becky Allen: Musings on education policy* [Online] 4 December. Retrieved from: www.bit.ly/33yZnFw

Beech, N., Kajzer-Mitchell, I., Oswick, C. and Saren, M. (2011) 'Barriers

to change and identity work in the swampy lowland', *Journal of Change Management* 11 (3) pp. 289-304.

Bereiter, C. and Scardamalia, M. (1993) *Surpassing ourselves: An inquiry into the nature and implications of expertise.* Chicago: Open Court.

Biesta, G. J. (2010) 'Why 'what works' still won't work: From evidence-based education to value-based education', *Studies in philosophy and education* 29 (5) pp. 491-503.

Cilliers, P. (2005) 'Knowledge, limits and boundaries', *Futures* 37 (7) pp. 605-613.

Cilliers, P. (2010) 'Difference, identity and complexity' in Osberg, D. and Biesta, G. (eds) *Complexity, difference and identity*. Springer, Dordrecht, pp. 3-18.

Engelmann, S. (1980) *Direct Instruction* (vol. 22). Englewood Cliffs, NJ: Educational Technology Publications.

Evans, M. (2019) *Leaders with Substance*. Woodbridge: John Catt Educational.

Harford, T. (2016) *Messy: How to be creative and resilient in a tidy-minded world*. London: Hachette.

Lindley, D. V. (2006) *Understanding Uncertainty*. Hoboken, NJ: Wiley-Blackwell.

Munro, E. (2010) *The Munro review of child protection interim report: The child's journey*. London: The Stationery Office

Needham, T. (2019) 'Teaching through examples' in Boxer, A. (ed.) *The researchED Guide to Explicit & Direct Instruction*. Woodbridge: John Catt Educational.

Nuthall, G. (2007) *The Hidden Lives of Learners*. Wellington: Nzcer Press.

Osberg, D. and Biesta, G. (2010) *Complexity Theory and the Politics of Education*. Boston, MA: Sense Publishers

Syed, M. (2019) *Rebel Ideas: The Power of Diverse Thinking*. London: Hachette.

Taleb, N. N. (2012) *Antifragile: Things that Gain from Disorder*. London: Allen Lane.

Author bio-sketch:

Matthew Evans is headteacher of a secondary comprehensive school in Gloucestershire and has been a senior leader in schools for over 15 years. He is author of *Leaders with Substance* and blogs at educontrarianblog.com.